SEVEN SHILLINGS A YEAR

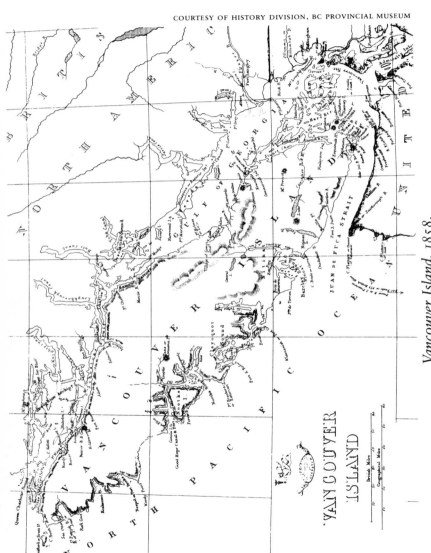

Vancouver Island, 1858.

Seven Shillings a Year

The History of Vancouver Island

Charles Lillard

Horsdal & Schubart

Copyright © 1986 by Charles Lillard

Horsdal & Schubart Publishers Ltd.
Box 1
Ganges, BC
V0S 1E0

Cover photograph courtesy of the Government of British Columbia. Design and typesetting by The Typeworks, Vancouver, BC. This book is set in Sabon. Printed and bound in Canada by Hignell Printing Limited, Winnipeg, Manitoba.

The publisher gratefully acknowledges the financial assistance of the British Columbia Heritage Trust in the publication of this book.

This book is dedicated to Steve Zablosky—companion, friend and teacher—who introduced me to his country.

Canadian Cataloguing in Publication Data

Lillard, Charles, 1944–
    Seven shillings a year

    Includes index.
    Bibliography : p.
    ISBN 0-920663-03-6

    1. Vancouver Island (B.C.) - History. I. Title.
FC3844.5.L54 1986   971.1'34   C86-091131-4
F1089.V3L54 1986

Contents

Introduction and Acknowledgements

From the very beginning of man's time on Vancouver Island, history has been shaped by the island's location and unique topography. After centuries of being pushed westward by waves of prehistoric migrants moving down the Fraser River and out across the Gulf and San Juan islands, the people now known as the Nootka found a stronghold on the western edge of the world. They were almost certainly forced west by the movement of the Kwakiutl and Salish, and for the Nootka, the isolation of the island was an advantage. After 1849, when European colonization of Vancouver Island began, isolation was a problem, not a solution. It was the terrain, not man, that controlled the Europeanization of the island. The land is so incredibly rough that, to cite but one example, the roads connecting the east and west coast towns were not completed until the 1970s.

From the outset *Seven Shillings a Year* was planned as a historical sketch—an overview for the curious. Even so, this "sketch" outgrew its original scope; from the beginning the island's story demanded a wider perspective than the one outlined by its geographical boundaries.

For all the complacent isolationism that is one of the wonders of life on any island, no island is completely independent. Great Britain, which has never been free of influences from the European mainland, is but one well-known example. Not one of the major events that shaped Vancouver Island's history grew from native soil. All were external, and while some were definitely more important than others, to ignore one is to throw the others out of kilter. As these external events created patterns that can be traced from the 1840s through to the present, the decision to conclude this book at the onset of World War II may seem highly arbitrary.

There are several reasons for the choice of 1939 as a closing date. During the war the island began to experience an economic prosperity unrivalled by any previous period. Politically, a new and extremely complex era began when the Social Credit party won the provincial election in June 1952. The arrival of post-war immigrants from Europe, eastern Canada, and the British Commonwealth created the foundations of an independent culture, after more than a hundred years of imitating British culture, and its growth has been parallelled by a rebirth of, and a steadily increasing interest in, the island's indigenous culture. As the world changed after 1939, so did Vancouver Island, and this date is a solid line between the past and the present.

This book is a continuation of my personal search into the history of the Northwest Coast, but it could not have gained its present shape without the assistance of various individuals. If it were not for the knowledge and assistance of Robert D. Turner, many of the photographs in this book would still be gathering dust. David Parker and Robert Griffin led me to a number of photographs, unpublished documents, and long-out-of-print brochures. Dr. Daniel T. Gallacher, Curator of Modern History at the British Columbia Provincial Museum, gave me permission to use photographs from his division's collection. The staff of the University of Victoria's Special Collections Library assisted me throughout the final stages of this book's growth. Gregory Evans allowed me to use numerous details his own research has unearthed. Maralyn Horsdal, my editor, contributed her knowledge freely to every page of this book. My special thanks to my wife, Rhonda, for without her patience and love this book would still be a vague project.

Charles Lillard

CHAPTER ONE

The West-Coast People

Vancouver Island history begins with its first explorers and settlers, the Nootka people. Next came the Kwakiutl and Salish, and between them, these people controlled the island until the arrival of the Hudson's Bay Company in the early 1840s.

The Nootka believed that time began on the west coast of Vancouver Island, and their view of the world was of a disc mounted on a pole. Their picture of the immediate world around them was not unlike what is found on maritime charts today. This west-coast world reached north from Port Renfrew on the southwest coast to Cape Cook on the Brooks Peninsula, some 225 miles as a crow might fly, but the actual shoreline is many times this distance. The major strongholds were located in Nootka, Clayoquot and Barkley sounds, but the people fished and hunted all along the outside coast during the summer months, and every inlet, bay, and creek on the coast belonged to one or another of the chiefs. Every landmark had a name, and each had its own history.

The Makah at Neah Bay and other villages on the outermost shores of the Olympic Peninsula were closely related to the Nootka, and the groups maintained steady contact. Between the people on the west coast and the Kwakiutl and Salish there was a certain amount of contact, some of it maritime and probably unintentional, such as when fishing and hunting groups encountered each other during the summer months. More important, and intentional, were the meetings when one group or another crossed the island on any of the three overland trading routes. One led from the head of Alberni Inlet to Qualicum Beach, another from Kyuquot Sound to Nimpkish Lake, and a third from Quatsino Sound to the present site of Port Hardy, and these trails are so ancient they may suggest the original routes of the Nootka as they migrated to the outside coast of Vancouver Island. Farther afield, the Nootka supposedly made coasting voyages for trading purposes south to the Columbia River. Despite these various contacts, the Nootka knew very little, and cared even less, about the world beyond their coast.

One reason for this was the typical Amerindian fear, or at least distrust, of anything beyond their well-established boundaries. In the case of the Nootka people, they also needed nothing from outside their hunting and fishing grounds. They lived with their backs to the mountains and their faces to the sea, and this relatively narrow seaboard was incredibly abundant with fish and mammals, berries and herbs; out on the open ocean or within the entrance to the Strait of Juan de Fuca the Nootka hunted a variety of whales successfully.

It was a harsh environment. One of the earliest of European west-coast residents saw: "On the ocean coast outside, between the entrances to the great inlets the line of the shore there is broken by low headlands which project from the seaboard, and appear, with their shapeless, outlying rocks, not unlike the shattered angles of a fortified work; between these capes are narrow beaches, backed by a curtain of rock, over which hill upon hill appears, woody and ragged. As the coast lies exposed to the uninterrupted western swell of the North Pacific, the waves are generally large, and even in calm weather they break with a noise on the shore and roar among the caverns."[1]

Inside these sounds the coast is quite different. Calmer and darker, the stillness rises from the water itself. Cedar, hemlock and spruce covered the rugged sidehills that sometimes rise almost perpendicularly from tidemark, and elsewhere may rise gradually from the many river deltas. Deer come down to this open country at dawn and dusk to find salt and the luxuriant graze. Throughout the summer months the migrating salmon attract bear, sea gulls, crows, ravens, eagles, porpoises and seals, and many small nocturnal creatures. Lovely as it is, this inland country is difficult; the rain and wind, the countless miles of steep coast, and the rocks that rise just high enough from the sea bottom to break the keel of the unwary traveller's vessel combine in endlessly fascinating and dangerous variations.

COURTESY OF HISTORY DIVISION, BC PROVINCIAL MUSEUM

Interior of Nootka Sound. Early etching showing British hydrographic surveyors.

The Nootka had little use for the forests and mountains beyond the seaboard. First of all they were full of the most malignant spirits imaginable. Even though some were not particularly dangerous to man, such as the Thunderbird (a huge man until he donned his bird costume to hunt whales) and the Wolf People who lived in a large house under the mountains, the average person thought it better to avoid the deep forests. More to the point, the Nootka required nothing from the interior ranges. A few followed the elk and deer into the mountains, but this was done mostly by the people at the head of Alberni Inlet, people other Nootka considered to be hillbillies.

The entire coast is wet, averaging from 100 to 140 inches of rain yearly. At the head of many of the sounds the average is in excess of 140 inches. It is a temperate area and this combination of rain and warmth created the best-known forest on Vancouver Island—the rain forest. This forest is characterized by trees growing to average heights of 200 feet, such as those in Cathedral Grove near Parksville. One of the largest and oldest trees in any rain forest is the western red cedar (*Thuya plicata*). Commonly called red cedar, this tree is also known as the giant cedar, an accurate term, for it often reaches heights of 175 feet and a basal diameter of well over ten feet. It grows everywhere on Vancouver Island except on the highest slopes, and fringes the entire coast well into Southeastern Alaska. It is impossible to understand Nootka culture without knowing something of its basis, the red cedar.

Cedar is light, aromatic, and extremely rot-resistant. From a cedar log clear of knots (and many are for the first 60 to 80 feet from the ground upwards) it is possible to split long and wide planks with a stone, bone, or wooden wedge. For the Indians with their stone or bone tools, and later for the Europeans whose iron tools were often no better, the cedar was indeed a gift. Out of cedar logs the Nootka constructed canoes, houseposts and beams, and some totems, but only rarely, for they were not totem-carvers to the extent of the northern tribes. From similar logs they split house planks and boards to be used

Forest on the west coast of Vancouver Island.

for a variety of purposes. From the finest and thinnest boards the craftsmen made storage boxes, while shelving, drums, spirit boards, and siding were devised from the heavier boards.

Cedar bark was used in basketry and other forms of weaving, in matting, clothing and cordage, and the soft shredded bark served as diapers, towelling, and padding for cradles. Other uses were medicinal, and some strictly utilitarian—the shredded bark burns slowly, which made it possible to transport fire. The withes or small branches were used for lashing. Such withes have been tested for their strength and found to be equal in strength to the cordage used by American and European sailors well into the 20th century.

Everyone who has seen a Nootka canoe remarks on its sleek grace. Many of these canoes were larger than the Spanish vessels that reached Nootka Sound from San Blas and Monterey.

Galiano and Valdés circumnavigated Vancouver Island in two ships that were barely 50 feet in length; cedar logs were transformed into magnificent canoes that might be 60 feet long, and far more seaworthy than many of the Spanish ships. Such canoes have given rise to nonsense concerning ocean voyages. There is little evidence that the Nootka, or any other of the northwest peoples, travelled to any extent. Except for the Nootka and Makah whaling expeditions, there was no seagoing travel.

Travel was limited to island-hopping, from the known to the visible. While there is positive evidence suggesting the Nootka travelled to the Columbia River, even this was a coasting voyage. The sailors chose their weather and at the hint of a storm they headed for shore, where they camped waiting for the weather to clear. Nootka voyagers may have been blown to sea by storms, or towed by whales out of the sight of land, and some of these men probably returned with strange and fascinating stories that grew in the telling, but such tales are the common property of sailors the world over.

Red cedar made canoes possible. There is no other Pacific Northwest tree from which such canoes as the Nootka used can be built. In turn these canoes made the highly complex material culture of the west-coast people possible. This culture was based on a yearly hunting and gathering cycle that took the people from their winter villages deep inside the sounds and inlets to summer camps or villages on the outer shores. From these spots they moved north and south along the coast and, as travel by foot is impossible in these areas, canoes made the difference between abundance and starvation.

The economic year began some time in February with the arrival of the herring. It was a happy event, for the winter stores were nearly exhausted, and people needed fresh fish and oil. As the herring arrived in massive schools they were easily caught in dipnets or with herring rakes. Captain James Cook wrote that these rakes resembled oars; they were approximately 20 feet long and four or five inches wide, with teeth set along two thirds of their length and the upper third serving as a handle. The fishermen struck the schools of herring, catching the fish with the teeth. Once caught, most were eaten immediately, either raw, broiled on sticks over a fire, or boiled in wooden boxes. In this latter instance, boxes were filled with water and brought to a boil by dropping hot rocks into the water. After the initial herring feasts were over, hundreds of pounds were smoked or sun-dried by each family and stored in wooden boxes.

Herring spawn was a much-loved delicacy. The spawn was taken on herring fences (boughs or small trees anchored in various coves), and when the fences were covered with spawn they were taken out, the spawn stripped from the branches, cut into manageable sizes and dried. Properly stored herring eggs might last for months. As these fences were set in coves belonging to the aristocracy, commoners required permission to use the property, and a part of their catch was paid as rent.

The herring season rarely lasted more than a week or ten days. However, the yearly round of seeking food began days prior to the herring fishery. Scouts returned to the winter villages from the outer coast with word of the arrival of the herring. Shortly thereafter the chief's family and slaves began taking his house apart and loading the canoes with his belongings. This was the sign for the village to begin the preparations to move to various locations near the inlet mouths and outside coast. In the case of the Mowachaht, one of the 24 Nootka groups on Vancouver Island and the one controlling Nootka Sound, the people usually left Tahsis and the nearby village of Kopti for Yuquot (also known as Friendly Cove and Nootka), at the mouth of Nootka Sound. Some families stayed at Yuquot for the summer while others moved to camps at various points along the coast.

When moving in the spring, the people first stripped their houses of the lighter planks and timbers. These were placed across two canoes to make rafts or catamarans. Atop the deck the Nootka placed their belongings. Some of the larger planks were placed on edge to act as sails, but this was a post-contact arrangement, for the Nootka were unaware of sails and how to use them until the arrival of the Spanish and British vessels. Such rafts were suitable for use only in inside waters; lashed together and loaded, they were too clumsy to handle in ocean currents and swells.

Sometimes the Mowachaht fished for herring from Yuquot, but more often it was the arrival of the spring salmon (the largest of all Pacific salmon) that was the first attraction. Fishermen trolled for these fish with a baited but barbless hook. These salmon had to be cooked immediately, a process that took about two hours, and eaten. Ritual forbade the keeping of spring salmon overnight.

In April, a time known as "Flying Flocks" by the people at Yuquot, duck and goose hunting began. Ducks were caught in nets, or hunted with spears; the more skilled hunters, when fresh meat was not such a necessity and required in large quan-

COURTESY OF HISTORY DIVISION, BC PROVINCIAL MUSEUM

Drying halibut at an Indian village in Quatsino Sound, ca *1900.*

tities, used bows and arrows. It was also the period for halibut fishermen to begin fishing on the banks, and whaling crews to begin readying themselves. The halibut grounds belonged to the aristocracy, and permission and payment were required to fish there. These men used methods still common today. Octopus was a favourite bait and, from all accounts, it often required more skill and time to catch the bait than it did the halibut.

Every aspect of fishing had its privileges and taboos. The Herring People and the Salmon People must be treated with respect. If not, they would not return from their ocean villages to feed the Nootka. Yet nothing seems quite as complicated as the preparations and considerations, the traditions and procedures before, during, and after a whaling voyage.

Whaling was the climax of the Nootka maritime culture. Except for the Makah, they were the only group to hunt whales continually and successfully. Whaling was a fine art in their hands, an art reserved for the aristocracy. The season began at the time of the "Flying Flocks" and lasted through early summer. "The career of the whaler, with its difficulties and dangers, was believed to require the help of a particularly strong tumanos (guiding, protecting spirit) and the securing of such a tumanos was the whaler's first task. In order to obtain the tumanos he prayed, bathed in a prescribed manner, and subjected himself to severe discipline and hardship."[2] Even after obtaining this spirit, he continued the harsh routine to the point where later observers commented that these men appeared to have lacerated themselves with briars.

These rituals continued up to the time the whaling expedition set out. The crew also had rituals to perform. Once aboard, the whaler and his men (usually eight) were controlled by other traditions and rituals. Failure to conform might lead to no whale being taken; worse, it could mean death by sea or storm.

The whaling canoe was approximately 35 feet long and beamy, as much as five feet wide or more. Traditionally, two types of whales were hunted: the Spring Whale (named for the season they arrived on the coast), and the Winter Whale. The first was said to scoop clams and mussels off the rocks, thus making its flesh red. This was the California grey whale that migrates north along the west coast each spring. The Winter Whale had a thick layer of white fat over its red flesh; this may be the humpback whale that winters along the BC coast. The killer whale was not hunted, except by young men testing their strength and abilities. Both the California grey and the humpback may grow to lengths of 45 feet and weigh more than 30 tons.

Each crewman on a whaling expedition, and there might be four or five canoes travelling together, had his task and knew it well. When the whale was approached, the harpooner, standing in the bow, either threw or thrust his harpoon. The killing of the whale seems to have been exceptionally difficult, sometimes taking the crews of several canoes all day. The death blow was struck by the harpooner, who jumped on the whale's back to deliver the ritual death stroke. Sometimes he went down with the whale as it dove one final time, but the man generally came up again—alive. Another reason for jumping on the animal was to cut a hole in its back to let cold water in. It was said that if this was not done, the meat might spoil on the voyage home.

Some of the voyages were long and arduous. A large whale might tow a canoe to sea for several days. Often when the death blow was delivered the expedition was out of sight of land, and it took all the endurance and strength of the crew, and all their navigational knowledge, to bring the whale to the village beach. One Nootka towing song records the respect these men had for the dead whale: "Ah, Queen, go straight to my home beach, where the water is sweet."

Once ashore the harpooner had certain rituals to observe, and then the butchering began. The harpooner got the best piece, the saddle of the whale's back, and the rest of the meat and blubber was distributed in order of rank to the rest of the villagers. For the next four days the harpooner and his wife followed certain ritual procedures; afterwards, there was a feast to which all the men in the village were invited.

All other west-coast sea mammals were hunted. Porpoises were prized as food and sea lions and seals were also hunted for food. Fur seals and sea otter were hunted for food and clothing; their fine fur made highly valued clothing for the aristocracy. Although all of these animals could be hunted year-round, the best season for the Nootka was late spring. There were several reasons for this: each animal provided much-needed fat, and after a winter of dried food the people craved oil; the pelts were thickest at this time of the year; and the men were restless, and spring hunting was valued as good sport and exercise.

Gathering began in the spring. Berries, roots, clams, mussels, spruce gum, camas, and a variety of other items from the seashore and forest were harvested, almost entirely by women. The tools required for this work were basic—a wooden stick or digging tool and a basket. As Captain Cook observed, the Nootka were almost totally reliant on the ocean for food, but they did use an almost infinite number of plants, trees (particularly the young shoots), seaweeds, roots, and bulbs in their economy. Some were used for food, such as the much-valued camas, and others for medicinal purposes, while still others had ritualistic value. All of these played a minor role, yet as the British Columbia coast had the densest population of any area in pre-contact Canada (the population may have reached 50,000), the use of everything available was significant.

Learning the uses of all this native flora must have required a lifetime's study. Elderly women would have carried an immense amount of knowledge about in their heads. Gathering was drudgery for the most part, yet much of it was communal work. With the men away fishing, the women would sit around the campfires in the good places usually reserved for the men and visit; no one had to be waited on hand and foot, and the time, hard as the work may have been, passed in a leisurely manner. No wonder many older women at the turn of the century remembered summer camps of the past fondly.

As the weather began turning stormy in late August and early September, the Mowachaht in the camps along the outer beaches began returning to Yuquot. This move corresponded with the dog salmon run. Although the Nootka harvested all the various types of salmon, the dog was the most important. They entered the streams by the countless thousands, and the time of the year was perfect for utilizing them as winter subsistence stock; as the dog is not a fat fish, it is better than any other salmon for drying. So important were these fish that if they did not return to the streams yearly, the Nootka would starve. Consequently, the rituals and taboos surrounding them were strictly observed during the four-to-six week run.

The salmon did return and in numbers unimaginable today. Europeans arriving on the scene after 1900 claimed it was possible to walk across streams on the backs of these fish and not wet more than the soles of one's shoes. For weeks the salmon ran upstream, the fishermen caught them in every way known to man, and the women cleaned and dried them. When the season finally came to its close, the time had come to return to the winter villages.

Most of these were on sandy, gently sloping beaches deep in the sounds. There, protected from the worst of the winter storms and enjoying a slightly warmer climate than that of the outside coast, the people could hunt and fish if necessary. More important, they were protected from their enemies (generally other Nootka groups, for intertribal wars were incessant), to some extent by distance, and to a greater degree by the outside weather, which made travelling a near impossibility. A gentle beach was a necessity, for the canoes were fragile; the grain and texture that make cedar so easy to split and carve also make it crack and break under the slightest strain. A fresh-water stream was a second requirement. Above the beach the people built their huge rectangular houses, broadside to the shore.

John R. Jewitt's 1803 description of Yuquot, which was sometimes used as a winter village, cannot be easily improved upon. "The village of Nootka [Yuquot] is situated at the bottom of Friendly Cove, on the west or north-west side. It consists of about twenty houses or huts, on a small hill, which rises with

Village at Nootka/Yuquot, date unknown.

a gentle ascent from the shore. The eastern and western shores of this harbour are steep and in many parts rocky, the trees growing quite to the water's edge, but the bottom to the north and north-west is a fine sandy beach of half a mile or more in extent."[3]

"The houses," Jewitt continues, "are above twenty in number, built nearly in a line. These are of different sizes, according to the rank or quality of the *Tyee,* or chief, who lives in them, each having one, of which he is considered as the lord. They vary not much in width, being usually from thirty-six to forty feet wide, but are of very different lengths, that of the king, which is much the longest, being about one hundred and fifty feet, while the smallest, which contain only two families, do not exceed forty feet in length; the house of the king is also distinguished from the others by being higher."[4] It is important to note here that the construction of such houses predates the European contact period by at least a thousand years.

The houses were constructed with huge uprights and beams, planked with cedar boards. The larger timbers were permanent and the boards, as previously noted, were taken down and moved, along with the contents of the house, to the summer camps and villages. The roofs were made of similar planks, overlapping so as to make a water-tight ceiling, and weighed down with stones. Much has been made of the drafts coming through the wall planking, but this was a necessity. Many of these houses were the homes of three or more families, and each family had its own fire which required a draft to lead the smoke to the smoke-hole in the roof.

Captain Cook's lively account of the appearance and atmosphere of the interior of a house at Yuquot is one of the best. "Their houses, on the inside, may be compared to a long English stable with a double range of stalls, and a broad passage in the middle; for the different families are separated only by a piece of plank. Close to the sides is a bench of boards, raised five or six feet higher than the rest of the floor, and covered with mats, whereon the family sit and sleep. In the middle of the floor, between them, is the fire-place, which has neither hearth nor chimney. This part appeared common to all. The nastiness and stench of their houses are at least equal to the confusion within; for, as they dry their fish within doors, they also gut them there, which, with their bones and fragments, thrown down at meals, and the addition of other sorts of filth, lie everywhere in heaps, and are, it should seem, never carried away. Their furniture consists chiefly of chests and boxes of various sizes, piled upon each other, at the sides or end of each house, wherein they deposit all their valuables, such as skins, garments, masks, &c. To complete the scene of confusion, in different parts of their habitation are hung up implements of fishing, and other articles."[5]

Too often, complaints about the house interiors have been taken seriously as a sign of the "primitivity" of the Nootka and other Northwest Coast peoples. Yet only 400 years earlier, English living conditions were equally "primitive". Few houses had glass in their windows. People lived in dank houses with most of their farm animals and the accompanying vermin, rats and mice. The floors were covered with straw that was almost never thrown out; it was merely covered with fresh straw periodically. The inhabitants had no room to be alone; most slept several to a bed—even the king's servants slept two to a bed; and light and fresh air were unknown. In 19th-century London conditions had improved little among the poor. Curiously, the English did not think themselves savages, nor their ancestors primitive; yet an Indian longhouse that was lived in only a few months each winter, that had fresh air and light moving through it continually, and that was perfectly conditioned to the coastal climate, was considered primitive and filthy.

It was in these houses and closely knit villages, with winter stores laid in and two to three months of enforced solitude and leisure, that the Northwest Culture, which was unlike anything elsewhere in North America, developed. It was also a time for falling cedar, for carving artistic and utilitarian items and, depending on the weather, for a limited amount of hunting and fishing. Although canoe-construction began during this time, it was finished in the late spring, again according to ritual.

Leisure and abundance allow man the full play of his imagination, and create a period when class structures and their obligations are most obvious. The Nootka social structure and their concept of wealth, though common to the Northwest Coast, were unique in North America.

Nootka society was divided into three classes: aristocrats, commoners and slaves. Wealth and inherited position were the two benchmarks for prestige among the leisure class or aristocracy. A wealthy man, no matter the amount of his wealth, could not command the highest official standing without inherited position. On the other hand, a man of the highest standing could do little without wealth. In the 1860s Gilbert Malcolm Sproat noted: "The high consideration in which rank or actual authority is held by these savages is extraordinary. After deciding whether a stranger is a friend or enemy, the first question is as to rank,—whether he is a chief or common man. If several travellers are together, the natives are not satisfied till they know who is the leader, and who is next in command."[6]

The leading chief's position was inherited from his uncle, and owing to the value put on the true line, no commoner could aspire to the position. To these men belonged everything within their territory: beaches, coves, streams, and fishing and hunting rights. Also, through inheritance or marriage, they owned certain songs, stories, and ceremonies. The authority of these men was nominal, as they consulted the village elders on all important matters. Actions such as war required the consent of the entire village.

A chief's sisters held a high social position; thus the early English term "princess" for such women was not entirely inaccurate. Chiefs, and there were at least three ranks or levels in this social position, married women of equivalent positions from outside their group, just as the chiefs' sisters married men of equal standing in other family groups. A bridegroom might become suddenly rich, materially and spiritually, because of the inherited rights his bride brought to him as dowry.

One estimate claims that in a Nootka group of 200 men, about 50 could be considered aristocrats. Fully half of these 200 were considered commoners or "independent members, less rich as body than the men of rank, but the difference of position being noticeable only on public occasions."[7] The remainder were slaves.

Slaves were a sign of strength. The more slaves one owned, the more successful one had been in war. Slaves were also an indication of wealth and prestige. They were the winner's gain in war, and could be sold or killed, depending on their owner. The lucky slaves might be bought back by their relatives, for it was a disgrace to have family members held in slavery. Except for living at their owners' whims, and the lack of consideration for slaves in time of famine, when they were allowed to starve and die, the slaves' lot was not all that different from their owners'. All lived in the same house, and hunted and fished together;

though slaves always did the hardest jobs, often the women's lives were equally hard. Aristocratic men did nothing, and were expected to do nothing, but hunt and fish. Slaves could mate only with slaves, and their children were born into slavery. Because of their closer links to the village, these children were not usually sold to anyone outside their home town.

More interesting than the Nootka social institutions was their concept of wealth. The gift-giving ceremony known as the potlatch was not only unknown outside the Pacific Northwest, it is an important illustration of the close-knit economic ties in and between Nootka villages.

Potlatches were held for a variety of reasons, but the basic purpose behind them was increasing the family's social status. "Blankets are usually given to men; beads, trinkets, and paint for the face, to women. Not more than two blankets are usually given to any person at one time. Sometimes a new musket is divided, and given to three different persons. The destruction of certain kinds of property serves the same purpose as its distribution. Canoes, for instance, are rarely given away. The practice is to make a hole in them, and allow them to sink. The distributor shows by this act his total indifference to his property; he gives it away, he destroys it; his heart is very strong."[8]

Although there was a great deal more to the potlatch than this, this is what many Europeans saw in the latter half of the 19th century. There were many reasons for potlatching. A child was to be given a new name, a girl reached maturity, debts had to be paid or compensation for injuries rendered — all were reasons, and there were cases when the potlatcher gave away everything he owned but his house. Poor though the man now was, he held himself in great esteem; his reputation soared far and wide, and when those he had given gifts to potlatched, as they had to do for their own self-esteem and reputations, he was paid back with interest. Suddenly poor, yes, but he was potentially a rich man.

Basically these were the reasons for a potlatch before the arrival of the first explorers and maritime traders. Up to that time they were modest affairs, limited to the aristocracy. Later, when trading or fishing, and work in the canneries and sawmills made it possible for anyone to accumulate wealth, the pot-latches got out of hand. Thousands of dollars worth of goods might be given away with only one purpose—prestige. Another reason behind these later shows was that since so many people had died from diseases, commoners with only tenuous links to the leisure class could potlatch their way into the highest ranks. This was the system that the Canadian government, prodded by missionaries and local government officials, outlawed.

Man cannot live without religious institutions and the Nootka were no exception. Religion, shamanism, and the winter ceremonies dominated Nootka life, yet much of this could only be clearly observed during the enforced leisure periods in the heart of winter. As most of the earliest European observers and writers were summer visitors to the outside coast of Vancouver Island, little is known about Nootka religion, and shamanism, potentially the most interesting of these institu-tions, is largely a blank. The ceremonies about which so much has been written were not dissimilar to modern Mardi Gras celebrations.

Captain Cook remarked that nothing he saw gave him any idea of the Nootka religion. The figures called *Klumma* he thought might be idols, but as the word *acweek* was frequently used when referring to the *Klumma,* Cook decided they were the images of ancestors, whose memories they worshipped. These *Klumma* were house posts, the carved uprights that sup-ported the immense house beams—large tree trunks, four to five feet high and set up singly or in pairs at either end of the house. The interior surfaces were carved to represent figures that Cook thought horrifying. A few years later, a Spanish visitor with more curiosity or perception than Cook identified the chief Nootka deity as Qua-utz, and said that when the chiefs made sacrifices to him they threw whale oil on the fire and feathers into the wind. Jewitt wrote: "They believe in the exist-ence of a Supreme Being, whom they call *Quahootze,* and who, to use Maquina's expression, was one great *Tyee* in the sky, who gave them their fish, and could take them from them, and was the greatest of all kings. Their usual place of worship appeared to be the water, for whenever they bathed, they addressed some words in form of prayer to God above, entreating that he would preserve them in health, give them good success in fishing, etc."[9]

A 20th-century observer maintains the Nootka had no supreme god, but believed in four who were Above Chief, Horizon Chief, Land Chief, and Undersea Chief. As these were noted only after the Nootka had endured almost two centuries of acculturation, the observer may have confused a subtle blend of the original Nootka religion and Christianity for the prehistoric religion. In the 1870s Father Brabant, the first Catholic missionary to live and work among the Nootka people, watched them "pray to a queen, Wakouix—in, above or beyond the seas. They ascribe to her the heaving or swelling of the waves. They shout out to her asking her to cause the waves to calm down."[10] In all probability this Wakouix was a creation of the Nootka after they watched the Spanish sailors pray to the Virgin Mary. Sailors are among the most religious and superstitious of men, and as daily services were held on Spanish vessels, their rites and prayers may have made a profound impression on the watching Nootka.

According to a creation myth, only the bird and animal people—the Kyaimimit—existed in the earliest days of time, but everyone knew that one day the Transformers would descend from the sky country and change the Kyaimimit into real animals and people. On hearing that these magicians had arrived, the Son of Deer said, "I will kill them." He picked up sea shells and sharpened them, and as he tested the edges against his tongue the dust dribbled down his chin. Looking up he saw two people approaching him, and too late he realized they were the Transformers. They struck Son of Deer's forehead with his sea shells and these became antlers. Next the magicians smeared his backside with the spittle from his chin. After this Son of Deer bounded off into the forest, now a whitetailed deer. At the first village they came to, the Transformers changed the Kyaimimit into real animals and birds. Because Land-Otter had a long spear and Beaver a broad sword, Otter was given a long tail and Beaver a short broad one. Men and women were created next, two to a village, and each village spoke a different language, and some towns were powerful, others weak. Finally the villagers were taught to pray to the sky, and this is why the chiefs pray to Kaotse to make them rich, for he lives in the sky and this is what the Transformers taught them to do.

Certain individuals among all of the American Indian groups were credited with powers beyond the knowledge or grasp of the average man. Elsewhere these people have been called "witch-doctors" or "medicine men" or "conjurers"; on the Northwest Coast they have come to be known as "shamen". The source of their supernatural powers is beings who take possession of the shaman and speak through him—or her. A surprisingly large number of Nootka shamen were women, and some were credited with awesome powers. Shamen could cure the ill, foretell where a whale might be beached, steal the souls of enemies, and change the salmon runs, among other feats. The missionaries laughed at the shamen, calling them charlatans, yet everywhere on Vancouver Island it would seem that this was the one group or profession to fight the European inroads into indigenous island culture. It is worth noting, too, that as a profession, shamanism was the only way in the earliest years of bettering one's social position substantially.

The months of December and January, known as "No Food Getting for a Long Time" to the Mowachaht at Tahsis, were the quietest time in the Nootka year. It was the period of the winter ceremonies, of which the best known was the Wolf Dance. This was a quasi-religious ritual invoking and honouring the spirits of the animal world. Such a dance lasted for a week or more, involving both the actors and the audience and was, from all descriptions, extremely complicated. During its performance there was a holiday period in the village; the usual songs were forbidden, family disputes were avoided, and behaviour was lax. The dance has been summed up as "the spiritual initiation in West Coast life, a major means of transmitting ceremonial rights, and the greatest public entertainment."[11]

As dozens, if not scores, of people might attend winter potlatches and ceremonies, the village larders were depleted when these events came to a close in January. Tired of feasting and indoor entertainment, the villagers longed for exercise and the open air. One such year, some time in February, the scouts returned to Tahsis and reported to Maquinna that the herring were shoaling near Yuquot. Soon afterwards his family began dismantling the house, and thus began another yearly cycle. This year would be different, but even had they known this, no one, not even the shamen, could have foreseen how drastic this difference would be.

Nothing about the year was untoward until the time known to the villagers as "Spring Salmon" arrived. It was a month known to the Spanish as *"Augusto,"* which the English call "August". The exact day is known, the 8th, and the year 1774. These are exact coordinates pinpointing the arrival of European time at Yuquot in the form of Juan Pérez and his crew aboard the frigate *Santiago,* anchoring off the mouth of Nootka Sound.

CHAPTER TWO

Closing the Pacific

By rare good fortune, the diary Friar Tomás de la Peña kept during the voyage of the *Santiago* in the spring and summer of 1774 was not lost. *"A las 11 divisamos tierra por la proa que es al N.E. Bendito sea Dios alabado de todas las criaturas"* — "At 11 land was descried on the bow, in the N.E. Blessed be God and let Him be praised by all creatures."[1] It was July 18 and the land was Graham Island, the northernmost of the Queen Charlotte Islands.

The *Santiago*, sometimes known as the *Nueva Galicia*, had sailed from San Blas, Mexico, on January 25. She was the largest vessel on the west coast, some 62 feet long, with a 20-foot beam, and only two years old. Her commander was Ensign Juan Josef Pérez, the best and most experienced pilot on the coast and, regrettably for Spanish interests, far too cautious as later events would prove. Pérez was a graduate pilot, and had served on the Manila galleon route (Acapulco to Manila) which, despite its name, was the Spanish trading link with China. In 1769, Pérez had commanded the *Principe*, the ship that carried some of the first settlers to Monterey and San Diego. Born in Mallorca, probably in 1725, Pérez was about 49 when he led the first Spanish expedition to sail, willingly, far into North Pacific waters.

On June 14, after inexplicably wasting two months at anchor, the *Santiago* sailed north from San Diego. On that day Pérez opened the sealed orders, now almost half a year old. They informed him that he could sail north as far as he wished, as long as he reached 60° north before turning south. Pérez was to follow the shore as closely as possible, and wherever there was a site for a possible settlement he must go ashore and take possession "using the standard form attached to his instructions, and erect a large wooden cross supported by a cairn of stones hiding a glass bottle, stoppered with pitch, containing a copy of the act of possession signed by the commander, chaplain, and two pilots, 'so that in future times this document will be kept and will serve as an authentic testimony.' "[2] These instructions further dictated how Pérez and his crew were to deal with the Indians—peacefully and honestly; in the eventuality that he met foreigners his actions and conduct were strictly outlined.

Foreigners—they are the key to the reasoning behind the *Santiago*'s voyage. Since the publication of a papal bull in the 15th century, the Spanish considered themselves the sole proprietors of the Pacific Ocean. Except for the British, Dutch and French pirates ravaging the coast periodically in the 16th and 17th centuries, this claim had not been tested. By the 1760s, as far as the west coast of North America was concerned, south of Monterey was secure, but to the north, the Russian empire was expanding east and south. No one in Spain or the New World knew just where the Russians were trading or, far worse, establishing settlements.

Where did Asia end and America begin? This was a haunting question to geographers and politicians during the early years of the 18th century. The Spanish were well known for their secrecy: charts and reports were sent directly to Spain or Mexico City and no copies were made; each commander sailed into the unknown, even though the area might already have been charted thoroughly. The Russians were equally tight-mouthed, and compounding their secrecy were a magnificently inept bureaucracy, and tremendous distances—it is 4,500 miles from Kamchatka to St. Petersburg, and information often took years to reach the tzar. By 1700 the Russians considered Siberia conquered, yet Peter the Great did not know how far his empire extended eastward. As curious as he was irrational, Peter sent two men east to determine whether or not Asia and America were one land mass. Returning in 1723, the men made a verbal report to the tzar, reportedly so lacking in facts that it satisfied no one.

Peter the Great died in 1725, none the wiser. The question did not fade away, and in 1728, Vitus Bering, a Dane in the service of Catherine the Great, sailed in search of an answer. Unbeknownst to everyone involved, the question had already been answered, not once but twice. Semyon Ivanovich Deshnev had solved the riddle in 1655, and in 1713 Henrich Busch had sailed to present-day Alaska and back in six days. Both men filed reports which were not forwarded to St. Petersburg.

On his first expedition Bering discovered the strait that now bears his name. In 1741 he set sail on a second expedition in command of the *St. Peter,* with Captain Alexei Chirikov in charge of the *St. Paul.* The vessels lost sight of each other on June 20; Bering sighted Mount St. Elias at the very northern tip of the Alaska Panhandle on July 16, then turned east and sailed the length of the Aleutian Islands before the *St. Peter* broke up on one of the Komandorskie Islands on November 28. There Bering died; his men built another vessel from the wreckage of the *St. Peter* and sailed home early in 1742.

By late June 1741, Chirikov in the *St. Paul* had sailed south far enough that it can be said he was off the mouth of the Columbia River, though so far off shore it made no difference to history. Not until the morning of July 15 did he sight land, the west coast of Prince of Wales Island. During the next ten days he coasted north, losing both of his ship's boats and 15 crewmen, presumably to Indian attack, near the north end of Chichagof Island. Turning east Chirikov next made a landfall on the Kenai Peninsula. Like Bering he sailed along the Aleutians, but his luck (and that is all it can be attributed to) was better and he reached port without incident in late October 1741.

Thirty-three years later, while trading with the Haida off Graham Island, Pérez noticed that the Indians had several small pieces of iron, half a sword and half a bayonet, and speculated these came from the men lost by the *St. Paul*. Secretive as the Russians were about their explorations, the news had reached western Europe. Pérez traded with the Haida for a few days but he failed to go ashore, as instructed, due to a combination of foul weather, fear of treachery, and concern for the *Santiago*. Continuing north Pérez reached 55° 30', where he named Cape Muzon *"Punta Santa Magdalena"* and Forrester Island *"Santa Christina"*. Again, he did not go ashore, nor did he attempt to, before turning south, unaware that he had nearly reached the area where Chirikov had made his landfall.

On August 8, Pérez sighted land and at six in the evening the *Santiago*'s anchor was dropped in a C-shaped cove on what is now called Vancouver Island. According to Friar Tomás, Pérez named this cove *"la Rada de San Lorenzo"*; since then others have claimed he named it *"Surgidero de San Lorenzo"*; either way it means "the Roadstead of San Lorenzo". Even though fog shrouded the coast when they awoke the next morning, Pérez ordered that the launch be put into the water as soon as it was light enough to work. This activity was interrupted by the arrival of 15 canoes, carrying some hundred men and women, who were encouraged to come alongside. They soon did so and thus began the first recorded trading session on Vancouver Island, with the Spaniards trading knives, shells (abalone shells the men had gathered on the California beaches) and cloth for conical hats and fur cloaks. At about six that morning as the men again turned their attention to the launch, the wind came up so suddenly that the anchor cable had to be cut to allow the

Santiago to put to sea and safety.

Juan Pérez sailed south, not once having stepped ashore on the Northwest Coast. A number of his contemporaries criticized him harshly for not following orders, but Pérez was old for the time, ill, and cautious. His discovery of various Alaskan islands, the Queen Charlotte Islands and Vancouver Island far outweigh his supposed failings. Contention still surrounds his *San Lorenzo*; was it the mouth of Nootka Sound as the Spanish were to claim? It would make a great deal of difference within a few years.

Between them, in two brief voyages, Chirikov and Pérez had sailed all but a few miles of the entire length of what is today the Northwest Coast. The future locations of Sitka and Nootka Sound, both of which were to play major roles in coastal economics and politics within a few decades, were on the charts. That these charts were often wildly inaccurate and not well known is immaterial; Chirikov, Pérez, and Vitus Bering to a lesser extent, had closed the ocean that Ferdinand Magellan had opened in December 1520.

Although the European history of Vancouver Island begins the day the *Santiago* dropped anchor, it has been argued, not always unconvincingly, that the island's contact period began centuries earlier. Of the many voyages labelled apocryphal, only the story that Juan de Fuca reported to Michael Lok in 1596 still grips the imagination. History now concedes he did exist; his name was Apostolos Valerianos, but he was widely known as Juan de Fuca, and he was probably born on Cephalonia (a Greek island) some time around 1536. De Fuca was a pilot in the service of the Spanish American government, as he told Lok, and he was certainly in Mexico during the late 1580s and early 1590s.

According to de Fuca, he sailed through a "broad Inlet of Sea" between 47° and 48° north in 1592. He cruised in these waters for more than 20 days, and found a "very much broader Sea" than that at the entrance, many islands, people wearing fur and skin clothing, and gold, silver, and pearls. At the mouth of this inlet de Fuca described a headland "with an exceeding high Pinacle, or spired Rocke, like a piller."[3] The riches can be discounted immediately as a typical embellishment to a sailor's yarn, but everything else is substantially correct. What is now known as the Strait of Juan de Fuca lies approximately where de Fuca claimed he found a "broad Inlet"; the "broader Sea" could be the Strait of Georgia that separates Vancouver Island from the mainland, and the "high Pinacle" is today known as Fuca's Pillar, 157 feet high, standing solitary and dark, leaning to the northwest, a little south of the westernmost point of Cape Flattery.

If the possibility of the Greek's voyage is admitted, it is the first step into the mysterious history of Vancouver Island. One 1768 map of western North America places the island of Fou Sang at 50° north, but so far east that its westernmost tip is located at present-day Kelowna, British Columbia. "Fou Sang" or "Fusang" is the result of a story recorded by the Chinese some thousand years before Columbus sailed west. A Buddhist monk, Hui Shen, reported in the year 499 that he had only recently returned from a land called Fusang some 20,000 li (7,200 miles) to the east, where he and four other priests had sailed in the year 458. Most of the story is a fable, or badly garbled, but the distance recorded would have placed the monk on the North American continent, and one detail is of interest. According to Hui Shen the natives of Fusang possessed ditches filled with water-silver. At one time, the coastal peoples filled pits with eulachon, and as this fish ferments, the scales, which are bright silver in colour, float to the surface. These pits of rotting fish may have been the ditches of Fusang. Noteworthy, too, is one historian's opinion that the various accounts of Fusang, and the scholarly interpretations of them in the 17th and 18th centuries were among the reasons Peter the Great sent the Bering expedition eastward from Kamchatka.

Japan adds more facts to this mist-shrouded coast. It is recorded that a Japanese junk was at Acapulco in 1617, and other Japanese or Chinese junks were reported off Monterey at about

this time. During the next 250 years numerous junks are reported to have been wrecked at various locations in the North
Pacific. There were, for instance, three wrecks near Nootka
Sound, at least one in the Queen Charlotte Islands, and who can
guess the number that washed ashore only to be pounded to unidentifiable splinters?

The frequency of these shipwrecks had less to do with the
skills of Japanese sailors than with deliberate policy decisions in
Japan. Around 1639, the fiercely isolationist Tokugawa rulers
of Japan forbade the building of ocean-going ships. The authorized design guaranteed that any vessel blown off the coast
in a storm would soon lose its rudder and go adrift, with little
or no hope of returning. This was to prevent sailors who may
have met foreigners from returning home, just as a decree in
1636 forbade any Japanese who left the islands to return. A few
archaeologists are beginning to claim that the Japanese may
have reached the New World at almost unbelievably early
times, and so many Northwest Coast Indian myths record visits
of men from the sea that one is forced to believe they may have
a basis in fact.[4]

One Haida myth records the visit of a European sailor. As it
certainly predates Pérez's voyage, one must look elsewhere for
hints to this mariner's possible identity. It has been argued that
Sir Francis Drake was off Vancouver Island on June 10, 1579.
As his own log-book was handed directly to Queen Elizabeth I
on his return, and never seen again, it may never be known how
far north Drake sailed the *Golden Hinde*. That he was at
Drake's Bay near San Francisco is no longer disputed, but it is
improbable that he reached the Queen Charlottes.

Beyond reasonable doubt some European ships were on the
Northwest Coast before Pérez and Chirikov. More than two
dozen European pirate vessels were harrying the Manila gal-
leons during the 16th century. It has been proved that at least
one galleon went ashore at Nehalem at the mouth of the Columbia River during this time. There is also substantial proof of
a naval encounter between the Spanish and the French or Brit-

ish in this same area in the 16th century. During these years one English pirate sailed north from Baja California and was not seen again.

Whether fact or fiction, none of these voyages and encounters are important in themselves; their value lies further afield. It has long been the tradition to date Vancouver Island's history from the arrival of Captain James Cook at Nootka Sound in 1778, but such a conception is too simplistic. It is known that the Pacific was being explored by Asians when future Europeans still lived in caves, and these apocryphal voyages illustrate an important point: Vancouver Island's story does not begin at any one particular time. The island's history does not belong solely to a few brief centuries of European expansion, but to the history of the Pacific rim and all the mystery that involves.

The Northwest Coast was still mysterious to the Spanish after Pérez's voyage of 1774. In 1775 a second expedition sailed north, commanded by Bruno de Hezeta in the *Santiago* with Pérez aboard as pilot, and accompanied by Juan Francisco de la Bodega y Quadra in the tiny, 36-foot schooner *Sonora*. On July 30 a storm separated the two vessels, and Hezeta sailed north far enough to sight land near Nootka Sound. Here he turned his bows homeward eagerly for he had been sailing north reluctantly since early May.

Aboard the *Sonora* there was nothing but enthusiasm, despite the fact there were 14 men aboard her, and there was no room below decks to stand upright. Quadra was a creole career naval officer from Peru and with him was Francisco Mourelle, an experienced hydrographic surveyor; the two were determined to survey as much of the coast as weather and the inevitable scurvy would allow. The *Sonora,* which along with her inadequate size was slow and difficult to manage, fought her way to 59° north, near Mount Fairweather, landed in two locations and took possession formally as demanded by Spanish law, and then headed home on September 1. This voyage proved there were no Russians south of the Gulf of

Alaska, and it established the foundation for the Spanish claim to the coast from that gulf south to Monterey. But, as one writer claims: "The results of these [the voyages of Pérez and Quadra] most important expeditions were not published as they should have been, by the Spanish. By this mistaken policy the Spanish discoverers lost much of the honor due them".[5]

About the time the *Sonora* crept back to Monterey and the waiting *Santiago*, the world-famous Captain James Cook accepted the post of Captain at the Greenwich Hospital (soon to be known as the Royal Naval College) in London. Officially he had retired from the sea, but as his life *was* the sea it is not surprising to find him volunteering to lead a British expedition in search of the elusive Northwest Passage. Since he was the best navigator and mariner of his day, the government happily gave him command. An added inducement for Cook was the £20,000 reward offered by an Act of Parliament to the man who discovered the Northwest Passage.

Cook was 50, an old man by the standards of the day, when he sailed from Plymouth in July 1776 in command of the *Resolution* and *Discovery*. Sailing by way of the Cape of Good Hope, New Zealand and the Hawaiian Islands, which he discovered, Cook raised the Oregon coast on March 7, 1778. The weather was terrible, as it almost always is at this time of the year, and after naming Cape Foulweather and various other landmarks, he was forced off shore by storms. On March 22 Cook sighted and named Cape Flattery, and commented in his journal: "It is in the very latitude we were now in where geographers have placed the pretended *Strait of Juan de Fuca*, but we saw nothing like it, nor is there the least probability that iver any such thing exhisted."[6]

Again the weather drove Cook off the coast; it was not until the morning of March 29 that he again sighted land. "The Country had a very different appearance to what we had before seen, it was full of high Mountains whose summits were covered with snow; but the Vallies between them and the land on the sea Coast, high as well as low, was cloathed with wood."[7]

The *Resolution* anchored inside Zuciarte Channel, Nootka Sound, that evening; the *Discovery,* having lost her wind, anchored near the channel's mouth. Even while the ships were searching for anchorage, canoes began approaching and the people aboard showed no fear or distrust of the strange vessels: "at one time thirty two Canoes filled with people about us, and a groupe of ten or a dozen remained along side the Resolution most part of the night. They seemed to be a mild inoffensive people, shewed great readiness to part with any thing they had and took whatever was offered them in exchange, but were more desireous of iron than any thing else, the use of which they very well knew and had several tools and instruments that were made of it."[8]

On March 31, the ships were moved to Resolution Cove, on Bligh Island, and moored. When the crews went ashore it was not to take possession, as demanded of Spanish officers by their government; instead they set up an observatory, cut wood, brewed spruce beer (a specific against scurvy), and began repairing their vessels. They fell a tree at this time to replace a mast, which may to some constitute the first "logging" on Vancouver Island. Here they stayed, trading and visiting with the Nootka, and exploring and charting the area, until late April when the ships set sail for the north. Almost immediately a storm, with strong squalls and rain so heavy the men could not see the length of the ships, forced them far out into the open Pacific.

Cook spent exactly 31 days at Nootka, which he originally named "King George's Sound", and then renamed "Nootka" under the mistaken impression this was the Indian name for the sound. It was not; Nootka *(nu·tka·)* is a verb meaning to "go around," as in *nu·tka· icim* — "go around the harbour". Only four years earlier this was Pérez's Roadstead of San Lorenzo, a name even the Spanish did not retain.[9] A great deal has been written about the significance of Cook's visit; while the charts and observations are justly famous, as are the drawings made by John Webber, the various diaries and journals are not of great historical significance.

Only one line in Cook's comments on Nootka catches and holds the imagination. "Here I must observe that I have no where met with Indians who had such high notions of every thing the Country produced being their exclusive property"—what an ominous portent of future events.[10]

Cook filled in one tiny blank on the Vancouver Island coast. Far more important than his surveys was the trading his men did for sea otter pelts. The prices paid for these at Canton were so high that Captain John Gore (Cook was killed in the Hawaiian Islands in 1779) faced a near-mutiny when the crews of the *Resolution* and *Discovery* demanded the ships return to the Northwest Coast. When Cook's *Voyages* was published in 1784, it opened the North Pacific to world commerce, some maintain. Again, this is only partially true; the Russians already knew the value of the sea otter pelts, but they quite wisely saw no reason to inform the rest of the world about the riches in what they considered to be their private hunting grounds. By the 1780s several books on the Russian and Spanish explorations were in print in western Europe and Britain. The lasting value of Cook's account was that it supplied a virtual ground-plan for a maritime fur trade.

The first trading vessel to reach Nootka Sound was the *Harmon*, commanded by James Hanna. She sailed from Macao, China, in April 1785 and reached Vancouver Island that August. Due either to a practical joke on the part of Hanna and his crew (setting off a charge of gun powder under Chief Maquinna's chair) or to the theft of a chisel by one of the Indians, a battle between the *Harmon* and the Nootka ensued. Twenty commoners and chiefs were killed before peace was re-established. While trading at Nootka, Hanna managed to collect 560 sea otter pelts, which he sold in China that December for $20,600.

It is ironic that Maquinna emerges from the shadows of the past side by side with James Hanna. Maquinna was one of the greatest of all the chiefs of the west-coast people; he probably

A *later Chief Maquinna,* ca 1900.

led the trading with Pérez's crew, and was almost certainly the unnamed chief who was of so much assistance to Cook. Yet no one bothered to record his name until Hanna encountered him, and today more is known of Maquinna than of Hanna, whose life prior to 1785 is an absolute mystery.

During Hanna's second trip, now aboard the *Sea Otter,* in 1786, he explored the area to some extent, and decided that the north end of Vancouver Island was a separate island, which he named "Cox Island". This mistake was probably due to his incomplete explorations of Quatsino Sound, which almost bisects the northern part of the island. On this voyage Hanna only managed to collect 100 pelts, due to James Strange's arrival a month earlier with the *Captain Cook* and the *Experiment;* still, the pelts sold for $8,000 in China.

At least eight ships were on the Northwest Coast in 1786, and there may have been more. The following year six ships reached the coast, and they carried some of the first truly colourful characters known to the earliest days of the maritime fur trade. As well, this was the year the first Englishwoman arrived on the coast.

The *Imperial Eagle,* Captain Charles William Barkley commanding, arrived at Nootka Sound in June 1787. She arrived under Austrian colours, because Barkley lacked a trading licence from the East India Company as stipulated by British law. Barkley was 23 and Frances, his bride of less than a year, only 17. The log of the *Imperial Eagle* was lost so the following is taken from work of Captain Walbran, who read Mrs. Barkley's diary before it was in turn lost. "Shortly after the ship had moored in Friendly cove a Canoe was paddled alongside and a man in every respect like an Indian and a very dirty one at that, clothed in a greasy sea-otter skin, came on board, and to the utter astonishment of Capt. and Mrs Barkley introduced himself as Dr John Mackey late surgeon of the trading brig, Captain Cook. This visitor informed them that he had been living at Nootka amongst the Indians for the previous twelve months, during which time he had completely conformed himself to their habits and customs, which Mrs Barkley in her diary emphatically states were disgusting. Dr Mackey had learned the language and also had made himself acquainted more or less, with the surrounding country."[11]

John Mackey (or Mackay), the assistant ship's surgeon aboard the *Experiment,* was an Irishman; no one knew where he had picked up his medical knowledge but he was intelligent, and through his use of medicines became a favourite of Maquinna, according to some. At least one contemporary saw him in a different light, but this was after Mackey's demoralizing year with the Nootka. Although Strange left him with supplies, books, and a gun, Mackey soon broke a taboo by stepping over

Maquinna's daughter's cradle. After this he was banished and virtually ignored for the rest of his stay. Worse, he lost parts of his gun and his supplies were stolen. Strange's idea, of course, had been to leave Mackey there so that by the next season he would have the "jump" on the competition, but the *Captain Cook* did not return. Despite Mackey's winter-long banishment, he did learn enough of the language to assist Barkley in collecting 700 pelts. Mackey also suggested to Barkley that Nootka Sound was part of a large island.

After trading in Nootka Sound the *Imperial Eagle* turned south, as Barkley hoped to continue his business, which had thus far been highly profitable, in previously untouched areas. " 'A day or two after sailing from King George's sound [Nootka Sound]'," wrote Frances Barkley," 'we visited a large sound which Captain Barkley named Wickaninnish's sound, the name given it being that of a chief who seemed to be quite as powerful a potentate as Maquilla [Maquinna]. Wickaninnish has great authority and this part of the coast proved a rich harvest of furs for us. Likewise close to the southward of this sound, we came to another very large sound, to which Captain Barkley gave his own name. Several coves and bays and also islands in this sound we named. There was Frances Island, after myself; Hornby peak, also after myself; Cape Beale after our purser' ".[12]

Of these names only Cape Beale and Barkley Sound survive. "Wickaninnish's sound" is today's Clayoquot Sound. Today, the Nootka chief Wickinanish is not as well remembered as is Maquinna, though evidence suggests he was far richer and thus a more powerful chief than Maquinna. Because his villages were within Clayoquot Sound, an area not often visited by the early traders, Wickinanish was not involved with the British and Spanish, and later the Americans, to the extent his northern rival was. Peter Puget, second lieutenant on the *Discovery*, Captain George Vancouver's ship, thought Wickinanish was the emperor of the west coast from the Strait of Juan de Fuca to the Queen Charlotte Islands. Wickinanish appears to have flourished between 1788 and 1818, during which time his name is often mentioned by traders. Whether or not this was the same Wickinanish is arguable, as at one point the original chief gave his name to his son while he took the new name of *Hiyoua* meaning "Ten Whales on the Rocks".

Leaving the sound he had named in his own honour, Barkley continued southeastward and, writes Walbran, "to the great astonishment of Capt. Barkley and his officers, a large opening presented itself, extending miles to the eastward with no land in sight in that direction."[13] Immediately realizing this was the entrance to the Strait of Juan de Fuca, whose existence Cook had scorned, Barkley renamed the waterway in de Fuca's honour.

The *King George* and *Queen Charlotte,* companion vessels owned by the King George's Sound Company of London, were on the coast in 1786 and, after wintering in the Hawaiian Islands, returned the next season. Nathanial Portlock was commander of the *King George* and of the expedition, George Dixon was captain of the *Queen Charlotte*. Both men were aboard the *Discovery* during her northward trip in 1778, and thus were shipmates of William Bligh's—Bligh of *Bounty* fame, whose name is remembered locally by Bligh Island, in Nootka Sound. Dixon Entrance commemorates Dixon's travels on the coast where he rediscovered the Queen Charlotte Islands and named them after his ship.

More important by far than Dixon or Portlock was the man they encountered at Prince William Sound, Alaska, on their return from the Hawaiian Islands in the spring of 1787. John Meares, of the *Nootka,* had decided to winter in Alaska with disastrous results, losing 23 of his men to scurvy. The *Nootka* traded on the coast that summer, then disappeared, but Meares reappeared in 1788 leading an expedition of two vessels: the *Felice Adventurer* which he commanded, and the *Iphigenia Nubiana,* under William Douglas. Meares and his associates owned both ships and to circumvent the restrictions placed on British ships by the East India Company, Meares's vessels flew the Portuguese flag.

This year Meares sailed directly for Nootka where, after buying land from Maquinna "for eight or ten sheets of copper and some trifling articles," he built the first European-style building on Vancouver Island.[14] It was a fairly large building with a mess hall, separate quarters for officers and men, space beneath for the workmen in stormy weather, and an attached shed housing the blacksmith's quarters. The whole affair was surrounded by a defensive breastwork. The reason for an establishment of this size was that Meares intended to construct a

COURTESY OF HISTORY DIVISION, BC PROVINCIAL MUSEUM

John Meares.

sloop with the assistance of Chinese labourers he had brought
along for this purpose. These were the first Orientals known to
work on Vancouver Island, though certainly not the last, and
they built the boat through the summer while Meares and
Douglas traded with the Indians elsewhere. After Meares
returned, the 40-ton sloop, the *North West America,* was
launched with much fanfare on September 20, 1788.

This late summer was a busy time at Friendly Cove. A few
days before the first ship built on the Northwest Coast was
launched, the *Lady Washington* arrived, commanded by Captain Robert Gray. In all probability she was the first American
ship to arrive on the coast, and she was soon joined by the
Columbia, under Captain John Kendrick, both ships having
sailed from Boston. Her appearance on the coast was of little
importance, but Gray would soon secure a place for himself in
American history by sailing on from Nootka (now command-

COURTESY OF HISTORY DIVISION, BC PROVINCIAL MUSEUM

The launching of the schooner North West America *in Nootka
Sound. From an early painting.*

ing the *Columbia*) to Canton and home to Boston, thus becoming the first American vessel to circumnavigate the world. More consequential to Vancouver Island's history was Gray's return to the coast in the *Columbia* in 1792. During this voyage he discovered the Great River of the West, which he named in honour of his ship. Gray's discovery—or act of sailing into the river—established the American claim to a portion of the coast.

However, at Nootka Sound in 1788, Gray's discovery was four years in the future, and the only future to concern the crews of the Boston vessels was the immediate preparation of their ships for winter quarters. There they remained until the following spring and, in the lovely language of Robert Haswell, "Fue incidents marked the time. The natives visated us allmost every day with fish and deer and oil and a fue skins. Our chief amusements were fouling and hunting. In both we had tolerable sucess. The weather was general rainey and very disagreable."[15]

The *Lady Washington* left Nootka on a trading voyage northward in March. It was on this trip, somewhere near Cloak Bay, in the Queen Charlotte Islands, that Gray made one of the few still-legendary barters in the maritime fur trade's history. During a very few moments, according to Haswell, Gray obtained 200 sea otter pelts for the same number of iron chisels. On the sloop's return to Nootka Sound the men discovered, to their amazement, a fort standing on San Miguel Island, barely more than a stone's throw from Yuquot. Two Spanish vessels, the *Princesa* and *San Carlos,* were lying at anchor close at hand.

Because of the number of British vessels trading on the coast, the British effectively controlled the area, but the Spanish had forgotten neither the coast nor their claims to it. It seems that the Spanish were either unaware of, or unconcerned by, the British presence on the coast. Curiously, it was again the Russian "menace" from the north that was behind the third and fourth Spanish expeditions to the Northwest Coast. The Spanish were not particularly interested in the maritime fur trade, but they were determined to retain control of the coast, so when they learned of the growing Russian strength, ships were ordered north. The *Princesa,* commanded by Ensign Estaban José Martínez, and her consort, the *San Carlos,* with Gonzalez López de Haro as master, sailed from San Blas on March 8, 1788. At Unalaska in the Aleutian Islands Martínez met Russians who told him that they were expecting two frigates from Siberia in 1789. With these, the Russians bragged, they planned to establish a trading settlement at Nootka Sound. Martínez also learned of the presence on the coast of Captains Meares and Douglas from these Russians; and when they took their eyes off him, he took formal possession of Unalaska.

Martínez was back at San Blas by December. After a hurried refitting he and his ships were sent north again, this time to occupy and fortify Nootka Sound. Only on paper was Martínez a good choice for this mission; hot-headed (especially when drinking), dreaming of a northern empire that would include the Hawaiian Islands, and a conceited braggart as well, Martínez was a spark looking for a fire to start. At Nootka he found no Russians. Instead, he found the Americans, Kendrick and Gray, whom he decided posed no immediate threat to Spanish sovereignty, but also the *Iphigenia Nubiana* which, like almost everyone else who encountered her, he immediately recognized for what she was—a British vessel flying Portuguese colours. By July 3, 1789, the Spanish finished the construction of Fortress San Miguel on the island of the same name, and at this point the *Argonaut,* a British ship sailing from China, commanded by James Colnett, arrived at Nootka Sound.

When Martínez learned of Colnett's plans to fortify Nootka Sound, he immediately arrested ship, captain, and crew. Earlier, the Spanish commander had seized the *Iphigenia,* but almost as quickly released her; Colnett, who compounded his problems by insulting Martínez as thoroughly as he was able, was not given his freedom. Several days later the *Princess Royal,* Thomas Hudson master, arrived and she too was captured. As these ships were owned by John Meares and his associates, the captures led Meares to present a memorial to the British Crown.

The Nootka Incident or Nootka Sound Controversy was a "tempest in a teapot", despite its results, which would not have occurred had it not been for Meares's memorial. This document has been described as nothing but war propaganda; it was not a statement of facts. Meares and the truth were not boon companions, as every trader dealing with him on the coast unhappily learned. Almost immediately after his presentation to the Crown, the British inexplicably began preparations for war. According to the terms of their Triple Alliance, they asked Holland and Prussia for assistance, and the former quickly offered ten men-of-war, while the latter prepared to fulfill her obligations should war occur. Spain appealed to France, but King Louis XVI, soon to take the short walk to the guillotine, was too busy with his own problems to assist Spain.

The Nootka Controversy at this point was a battle of politics and nerves played out in the courts of Europe. Nootka itself was not at stake; it was Spain's belief that because she had discovered the Pacific, all the lands on the Pacific rim were hers. This claim had been made legal by a papal bull of 1493, which gave to Spain all the lands bordering the Pacific Ocean. On the other hand the British did not believe that discovery granted ownership; only occupation and development did that, so Meares, having bought land from Maquinna and developed that land, made Nootka Sound British.

With a British-Dutch fleet prepared to sail against her, and with no ready assistance from her friends, Spain was bullied into signing a treaty that to the world "was the first external evidence of the ebb of the tide—the beginning of the collapse of the Spanish colonial system."[16] In his memorial, Meares claimed immense damages and the treaty—known as the Nootka Sound Convention—acknowledged Martínez's error in seizing Meares's ships and property and awarded him $210,000 in damages. This was less than a third of Meares's claim, but still outrageous. Other than this, the only immediate result of the Convention was the opening of another era in Vancouver Island history.

CHAPTER THREE

Years of Expansion

The Nootka Convention of 1790 did nothing to resolve the sovereignty issue on the Northwest Coast. What it did was break Spain's exclusive grip on the Pacific. Now Britain, or any other country, could navigate, conduct business, and fish in the coastal areas controlled by Russia and Spain. Essentially this was the coast of what is now Oregon, Washington, British Columbia, and Southeastern Alaska. While the generally inhospitable coast of Oregon and Washington was relatively well known, very little was known officially of the northern coast.

The sea otter, a large marine mammal measuring up to five feet in total length and weighing as much as 80 pounds, with a soft and extremely dense coat that can only be described as "silky", was the basis of the maritime fur trade. At one time the animal was found everywhere from the Aleutian Islands to the coast of California. Like the gold of later decades, these sea-going mammals were the key to instant wealth, and the Nootka Controversy did not affect the fur trade. Six ships traded off the Vancouver Island coast in 1790, and in 1791 the number doubled. Most of these vessels were British and American, but the British *Mercury* flew the Swedish flag in 1790 and was known as the *Gustavus II,* and *La Solide,* the first French trading vessel to reach the Northwest Coast, began business in 1791.

No Russians traded off the coast during these years, but they were well aware of Nootka and its strategic importance. Since 1741 they had been on the move, and by the 1780s the Spanish had granted them trading rights to Prince William Sound, bordering the northern tip of the Alaska Panhandle. They did not trade on the basis of summer voyages, as did the Americans and British; the Russians established trading posts and manned them year-round. Until 1790 their ventures were badly planned and poorly executed—then came the energetic Alexander Baranof. By 1800 he had completed posts on Kodiak Island, Cook Inlet, and Prince William Sound, established a colony at Yakutat, and re-organized the trading to such an extent that he changed the entire face of Russian Alaska. In 1804, Baranof established New Archangel (now Sitka), which is today the oldest European settlement in the Pacific Northwest. He has been called "the Lord of Alaska," for good reason, but his reach extended far beyond that area. In 1812, he established Fort Ross (a site later sold to Captain John Sutter on whose property the California gold rush began in 1848), and opened up a lucrative trade with the Spanish, the Hudson's Bay Company, and the Chinese.

Along with the British and Americans and Russians, there were the Spanish. The Nootka Controversy and their weak position did not quell their interest in the northern coast. Even before the Convention could be signed, the Viceroy of New Spain, Revilla Gigedo, met with Captain Bodega y Quadra to plan the re-occupation of Nootka. Although they encountered problems with ships and men, these were typical problems faced by every expedition sailing from San Blas, and the next expedition sailed on February 3, 1790, for Nootka Sound. Francisco de Eliza was named commander and sailed aboard the recently built frigate *Concepción;* Ensign Manuel Quimper was master of the *Princesa Real* and Salvador Fidalgo commanded the *San Carlos,* a San Blas packet. Ironically, the *Princesa Real* was the captured British vessel *Princess Royal,* and when she sailed, her captain, Thomas Hudson, and James Colnett, captain of the *Argonaut* (which the Spanish agreed not to send north on this voyage), were still under detention in Mexico.

The expedition reached Nootka Sound in April 1790. After formally taking possession of the area, Eliza sent Fidalgo north along the coast towards Alaska, and Quimper and Gonzalez López de Haro, pilot aboard the *Princesa Real,* to the Strait of Juan de Fuca. After wasting a good deal of time in Clayoquot Sound, Quimper sailed into the strait. On the Vancouver Island side he explored the coast from Port San Juan, which still bears the name he gave it, southward to what is now the greater Victoria region. Most of the names he gave to various landmarks are gone, regrettably, but it was common practice in later years for the British and Canadians to change what could have been honoured names. Thus *Punta de San Eusebio* has become Sheringham Point, *San Antonio* is now Otter Point, and the lovely *ensenada* or bay between Sheringham and Otter points was named *Orbea* —a name that was never changed but only rarely remembered.

While Fidalgo and Quimper were exploring the coast, Eliza was busy at Nootka. With the help of Maquinna and his men, the Spaniards built eight houses, including a small hospital and a shelter for the Indian labourers; the *Santa Saturnina* was constructed, and six 24-calibre cannon were prepared and placed in position. Eliza, who would remain commandant at Nootka until 1792, began his own explorations of the Strait of Juan de Fuca in May 1791.

Between May and August this expedition explored portions of Clayoquot and Barkley sounds, entered the mouth of the Strait of Juan de Fuca, sighted the entrance to Puget Sound (but did not enter it), discovered what is now known as the Strait of

The Strait of Juan de Fuca. From an early painting.

Georgia, and, due to the fresh water they encountered on the mainland shore, guessed that there was a large river debouching nearby. One day the river would be known as the Fraser, but it would be years before a ship actually sailed into its current. From here Eliza sailed north far enough to discover Texada Island and Cape Lazo; by this point he had realized that Nootka was on the west coast of an island. Why he did not continue sailing north is unknown; equally mysterious is his rush to return to Nootka. So keen was he to get back that he did not bother to continue his explorations at the mouth of that magnificent inland sea soon to be discovered and surveyed by Peter Puget.

The best known of all the expeditions to reach Nootka Sound and Fortress San Miguel at this time was the around-the-world Spanish cruise of the *Atrevida* and *Descubierta,* commanded by Alejandro Malaspina. This expedition was designed to overshadow the voyages of Captain Cook and the French explorer Rear Admiral Jean-Francois Galaup, Comte de La

Pérouse, and it might well have done so had Malaspina not fallen into disgrace on his return to Spain. Consequently, his valuable journals were not published until 1885. The expedition reached Nootka in August 1791, where it spent two weeks collecting artifacts and surveying the region, while Tomás de Suría, one of the artists on the voyage, painted the scenery and a number of the Nootka people.

It is noteworthy that Malaspina's was the only Spanish expedition to reach Vancouver Island decently outfitted for its task. His were also the largest Spanish vessels to anchor off Fortress San Miguel; each was 120 feet long with a 31-foot, six-inch beam. These were large vessels by the standards of the day, half again as large as most of the ships to leave San Blas northbound. Malaspina's scientific observations at Nootka, plus the work of earlier Spanish explorers, gave their country a well-defined understanding of the northwest coast. Certainly the charts made during this period prove that, while lacking details in many areas, the west and southeast coasts of Vancouver Island were well known. Only the northeast coast, between the Strait of Georgia and Queen Charlotte Strait, remained a question.

The last of the important Spanish expeditions to concern Vancouver Island was that of Dionisio Galiano and Cayetano Valdés who, in the *Sutil* and *Mexicana,* circumnavigated Vancouver Island in the summer of 1792. The two schooners were sister ships; both were just over 50 feet in length, awkward to handle and slow. They did not reach Nootka until mid-May, after a difficult passage from San Blas, and in June both set out for *Nunez Gaona* (Neah Bay, Washington), where Salvador Fidalgo was establishing a fort. From there they sailed to *Puerto de Cordova* (Esquimalt Harbour) with Chief Tetacui (Tatoosh) aboard the *Mexicana.*

He obviously impressed Galiano and Valdés, for they wrote that he "caused us to draw very different inferences about these Indians from what up to the present time voyagers have said about them. What they called ferocious treachery only seemed to us to be bold manliness."[1] Tatoosh, after whom Tatoosh Island is named, was the Makah equal of Maquinna; he was chief of a village at Neah Bay and another at Esquimalt Harbour.

By June 12, Galiano and Valdés were exploring and surveying the *Gran Canal de Nuestra Senora del Rosario la Marinera* (Strait of Georgia) when they sighted two vessels whose sails made them European. At seven the next morning they met the *Chatham,* commanded by Lieutenant-Commander William Broughton. She was the armed tender to Captain George Vancouver's *Discovery.* From this time on, much of the work of Galiano and Valdés along the east coast of Vancouver Island plays a subordinate role to Vancouver's, yet more than one authority has claimed that these two Spaniards first circumnavigated Vancouver Island, and that their charts of the inlets indenting the mainland of BC have more details than the British ones, even though Vancouver would claim that he charted these areas carefully.

Captain George Vancouver sailed from Falmouth, England, early in 1791, outbound for the Northwest Coast. That spring he was not quite 34; his early years had been spent sailing with Captain Cook, and he then spent nine years aboard warships in the Caribbean and elsewhere before the Admiralty chose him to command an expedition to the west coast of America. He was to sail as directly as possible to the Hawaiian Islands, where he was to winter. From the islands he was either to "proceed, in the first instance to Nootka, or elsewhere, in order to receive, from the Spanish officers, such lands or buildings as are to be restored to the British subjects" or to explore the coast between 30° and 60° north.[2] There were further instructions: he was to search out and explore any body of water that might constitute a northwest passage, and he was to ascertain "with as much precision as possible, the number, extent, and situation of any settlements which have been made within the limits above mentioned, by any European nation, and the time when such settlement was first made."[3]

The *Chatham* and *Discovery* reached the coast some hundred miles north of San Francisco Bay on April 17, 1792, and late that month they reached the mouth of the Strait of Juan de Fuca. Between April 29 and August 28, Vancouver and his crews (particularly the men, who rowed the longboats hundreds of miles that spring and summer) explored the Strait of Juan de Fuca, Puget Sound, the Strait of Georgia, Johnstone and Queen Charlotte straits, and the mouth and surrounding area of Queen Charlotte Sound.

To solve the question of the Northwest Passage once and forever, as well as to chart the intricate coast, Vancouver decided to follow the continental shore mile by mile, curve by twist. By any standard the job was a brutal task, and it was done as well as time and weather allowed. Curiously, in the light of the British argument during the Nootka Controversy, one of Vancouver's actions during the summer of 1792 was to go ashore (on Whidbey Island, Puget Sound) and take possession of the coast, roughly between San Francisco Bay and Campbell River. It was a rather meaningless gesture, but it was June 4—King George III's birthday.

On August 28, Vancouver finally decided it was time to make for Nootka Sound. "On reaching its entrance," he wrote in his journal, "we were visited by a Spanish officer, who brought a pilot to conduct the vessel to anchorage in Friendly cove, where we found riding his Catholic Majesty's brig the *Active,* bearing the broad pendant of Senor Don Juan Francisco de la Bodega y Quadra, commandant of the marine establishment of St. Blas and California."[4]

Quadra was now 49, a frigate captain, sometime commandant of the Naval Department of San Blas and, as well, a Knight of the Order of Santiago. By west-coast standards his career had been meteoric since 1776, the year he first sailed north as captain of the *Sonora.* This year Quadra sailed from San Blas in the huge frigate *Santa Gertrudis,* but he seems to have moved aboard the *Active* at Nootka Sound. His sole reason for going to Nootka was to act as the Spanish commissioner in the wary negotiations that would fulfill the terms of the Nootka Convention. As he had been waiting for Vancouver, his British counterpart, since late April, and knew of Vancouver's presence on the east coast of the island throughout this period, Quadra's patience should have been wearing thin.

Such was not the case. Quadra's amiability is noted everywhere in Vancouver's journal of this period. The two men discussed the transfer of property, visited each other socially, together called on Maquinna at Tahsis, and exchanged charts of the coast. Ultimately, they could not reach an agreement concerning their commission. Vancouver's position was based strictly on the Nootka Convention. Quadra, disliking the terms of that agreement, which were vague at best, and having learned during his summer at Friendly Cove what a liar Meares was, believed that only a small portion of the disputed land could be handed over to Vancouver. The two representatives finally agreed that their governments should settle the question. Late in September, Quadra sailed for Monterey, followed two weeks later by Vancouver.

One can only wonder how much of the friendship between Vancouver and Quadra was due to their inability to speak each other's language. There can be no possible doubt that Vancouver was deeply affected by the time he spent with Quadra, and that the Spaniard was amiable, but he was also a diplomat who chose to take a genial approach to the problems of negotiating with Vancouver. The relationship between Quadra and Maquinna was longer and, in some respects, had greater results. By 1792, Maquinna more than likely spoke a good deal of Spanish; his table manners (observable daily as he dined with Quadra) were near-perfect, and he was well aware of the acculturational and political situation in which he and his people were involved. Joseph Ingraham observed that "Most of the chiefs of any consequence were quite polish'd by the Spanish gentlemen, if the Spaniards had the tuition of these people but a few years longer they would be quite civiliz'd."[5] This remarkable situation, so in contrast to the relationship between the Nootka and the majority of British and American visitors and

traders, strengthened the Spanish grip on the west coast im-
measurably—had anyone in Spain cared enough to put this to a
test.

All that two subsequent Nootka Conventions (1793 and
1794) led to was the agreement to leave Vancouver Island (then
known as Quadra and Vancouver Island) uncolonized. The
great period of maritime discovery was over. Spanish, British,
and American sailors had put Vancouver Island on the map
once and forever. It is fascinating to observe that, after all the
exploration, all the planning and work, and all the political
posturing, the island was once again as isolated as it had been
prior to 1774. Moreover, despite all the exploring and charting,
not a thing was known of the island beyond its foreshore.

While the hunting and trading of sea otter skins continued at
an uneven pace until 1820, during which time some 340 ships
reached the coast, the features of the trade changed significantly
after 1792. Violence replaced honesty and friendship. Cook and
Vancouver, and the Spanish and Russian explorers were all under orders to treat the indigenous people they met fairly, and by
all accounts the Indians generally reciprocated. With few exceptions the earliest maritime traders appear as gentlemen in the
written records, at heart if not by birth, and usually they treated
the Nootka and other peoples decently. The second wave of
traders, largely Americans, belonged to a new generation. It
was at this time the notion that "the only good Indian is a dead
one" began gaining momentum. The Americans, afraid that
they would be barred from the coastal trade no matter who
won out in the Nootka Conventions, sought a quick profit before the inevitable restrictions, and when they began selling rum
and firearms to the Nootka, it was the beginning of the end.

Tangential to the maritime fur trade, but indirectly of far
greater importance to the island in the 19th century, was the
westward movement of American and British fur traders. The
first date of immediate importance to Vancouver Island is
1778. That winter Peter Pond was in charge of the Old Establishment on the Athabasca River, and his understudy and sec-

ond in command was Alexander Mackenzie. Pond believed that a great river in the north flowed from Great Slave Lake to the Gulf of Alaska, and Mackenzie inherited this dream.

Mackenzie's first major trip in search of this northern river led him to a great river (now known as the Mackenzie) and the Arctic Ocean in 1789. On a second trip he crossed British Columbia and reached tidewater at Bella Coola on July 20, 1793. This trip made Mackenzie the first man to cross the North American continent by land, and suggested the feasibility of opening up a land-based trade with the west coast.

Mackenzie's route was too difficult for the large trading canoes of the day, so the idea rested until 1808. On May 22 of that year Simon Fraser and 23 others set out from Fort George in central British Columbia bound for the Pacific. He followed the Grand River (now the Fraser) southward, and after a hellish trip through the Fraser River Canyon, reached the still-extant Indian village of Musqueam on July 2. The next day Fraser recorded two disappointments: he had not seen the Pacific Ocean, and the river he and his men had followed was not the Columbia. Another disappointment, though he did not note it in his journal, was the realization that this river was of little value to the fur trade; the great canyon could not be navigated by canoe.

For reasons unknown Fraser did not name the river now bearing his name; this was done by his fellow North West Company partner David Thompson, who discovered the only navigable waterway to the Pacific. Accompanied by seven others he started down the Columbia from Kettle Falls, Washington, on July 3, 1811. Twelve days later he reached the recently erected establishment of the Pacific Fur Company, owned jointly by John Jacob Astor and a group of Canadians. The fort was known as Astoria, and the surrounding area was firmly in American control.

The downriver trip was not one simply of exploration. A year earlier Thompson had been dispatched to the mouth of the Columbia to erect a fort before the arrival of Astor's men. Only bad luck slowed him down and foiled his plans, so he played

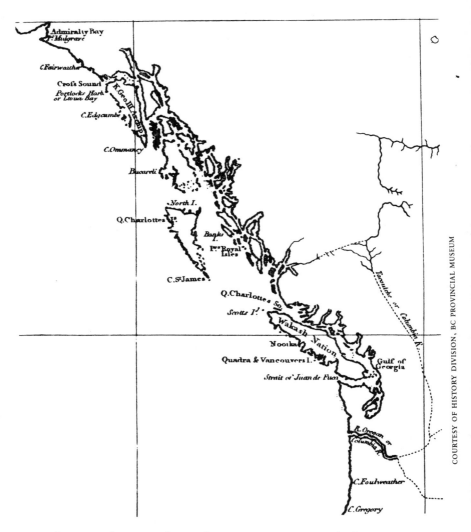

What was known about the west coast around 1800.

another card. He was authorized by the North West Company
to make an agreement with the Pacific Fur Company, Thompson said: if they would not interfere with his company's trade
east of the Rockies, his would not interrupt their trade on the

western slope. If they did not agree to this, the company would occupy the west with as many traders as it could rally, and make the district forever British.

This offer made little difference, for the War of 1812 broke out, and in 1813 the Astorians learned from the North West Company that a British naval force was on its way to seize or destroy the American holdings on the coast. After relaying this information the officers of the company offered to purchase Fort Astoria and its holdings. Reasoning that it was better to salvage what he could from the forthcoming destruction, the factor agreed to sell. The agreement signed on October 16, 1813, gave all of Astor's furs and merchandise, and Astoria, to the North West Company for less than two-thirds of the original value. This episode was one of the issues involved in the Oregon Question, which would lead directly to the settlement of Vancouver Island.

The North West Company held Astoria, which they renamed "Fort George", until 1818, when it was returned to the Americans; at this time the English and Americans agreed to a joint occupation of the Oregon Territory for a ten-year period. Treaties with Spain and Russia left Britain and the United States in joint control of the whole area between what is now the southern boundary of Oregon and the southern tip of the Alaska Panhandle. Who would control and own this area was of vital concern to both powers, a question not easily answered after 1821 when, after a merger with the North West Company, the Hudson's Bay Company gained control of the area. This company now controlled the fur trade from the east coast of Canada to the Pacific coast of the Oregon Territory.

At this time the Oregon Territory included what is today the province of British Columbia, the states of Oregon, Washington, Idaho and northwestern Montana. Roughly 1300 miles long and 650 wide, it was a territory of some 845,000 square miles. Drake named the coast "New Albion", a name which was in general usage until the 19th century. In 1808 Simon Fraser named the interior and central area of British Columbia

"New Caledonia". By the 1830s "Oregon Country" or "Oregon Territory" was the common term for the area west of the Rocky Mountains. The Hudson's Bay Company knew most of this area officially as the Columbia District or Department.

In 1824 Governor George Simpson, of the HBC, personally appointed Chief Factor John McLoughlin General Superintendent of this westernmost district. McLoughlin was born and grew up in eastern Canada before studying medicine in Scotland; returning to Canada, he joined the North West Company in 1803. At 40, when he took charge in the west, Dr. McLoughlin was described as more than six feet tall, blue-eyed and pink-cheeked, with white hair worn long. For the next 20 years he was the single most powerful man on the Northwest Coast. He built Fort Vancouver on the Columbia, extended the HBC interests to San Francisco Bay and the Hawaiian Islands, and leased Southeastern Alaska from the Russians in 1839. With the help of the *Beaver,* the first steam vessel to appear on the coast, and a number of earlier vessels, McLoughlin managed to maintain British-HBC control of the coast. The Indians knew him as "the White-Eagle Chief", and due to their respect for him there were no Indian wars in the Oregon Territory as long as McLoughlin was in command.

Initially, the location of Fort Vancouver on the north bank of the Columbia was ideal for the fur trade, but as centres were established along the Fraser and at the mouths of the Nass and Stikine rivers, it became increasingly obvious to George Simpson that the HBC's headquarters should be moved north. He thought of establishing this post at the mouth of the Fraser until he saw the canyon upriver. Simpson also believed that the proposed establishment should be at some distance from the international boundary. At this time, late in the 1820s, Simpson and McLoughlin assumed the boundary would be the Columbia River.

An HBC supply ship went aground and was wrecked on the Columbia bar (constantly shifting sand banks in the river's mouth that made navigation hazardous) in 1829, and a year later, a smallpox epidemic broke out among the Indians and lasted for two years. These incidents, and Fort Vancouver's distance from the ocean, formed the core of a letter Simpson wrote to his superiors in London in 1834, suggesting a depot or fort be built inside Puget Sound. Nothing was found on those shores suitable for a depot, but in 1837 Captain W. H. McNeill, master of the *Beaver*, explored the southern coast of Vancouver Island. The harbours that are now Sooke, Victoria, and Esquimalt impressed McNeill, but McLoughlin, totally opposed to a northern centre, all but ignored his findings.

McLoughlin loved Fort Vancouver, and fought everything that suggested harm to the fort. Worse, in the eyes of Simpson and the HBC, was McLoughlin's relationship with the Americans. During the 1830s, in direct opposition to HBC policy, he made Fort Vancouver a refuge for American immigrants; not only that, he helped them locate, and extended them credit. This encouraged immigration and by 1843, the first large

The Beaver *in Victoria Harbour, 1862.*

wagon train crossed the mountains via the Oregon Trail. Consequently, McLoughlin is known today as the "Father of Oregon" to Americans, while Canadians believe he paved the way to the Oregon Treaty of 1846, one which was extremely advantageous for the United States.

Four conferences were held between the US and Britain to deal with the Oregon Question. The first three succeeded in agreeing to nothing but extending the right for both countries to occupy the disputed territory. Finally, after a great deal of rambunctious politicking in the US Congress, the British and Americans signed a treaty setting the international boundary at the 49th parallel, but when this line reached the shores of the Strait of Georgia it made a sharp dip and then more or less split the length of the Strait of Juan de Fuca.

This treaty was signed on June 7, 1846, but the news did not reach Fort Vancouver until March 1847. When it did there was a sigh of unhappy resignation. Still, most of the HBC officers were pleased to learn Vancouver Island remained British, and that the fur trade west of the Rockies was not a total write-off. What was not known by these men was the official position in London: no one among the cooler heads in England thought the area worth another squabble with the United States.

Five years before the treaty's ratification, Simpson made a trip to Sitka with Chief Factor James Douglas, who was at that time in charge of Fort Vancouver in McLoughlin's absence. During this voyage Simpson decided, much to McLoughlin's disgust, that the northern forts should be closed, the trading done by the *Beaver* expanded, and a new fort established on the southern tip of Vancouver Island. This must have been partially on Douglas's recommendation; he had travelled the coast in 1840 and written to McLoughlin that a post should be built at the north end of the island. McLoughlin ignored Douglas's suggestions, and he fought hard against Simpson's. Interestingly, he had personally sailed into Camosun (Victoria Harbour) and admitted it was a fine place, but thought it unsuitable for HBC purposes.

Simpson paid no attention to McLoughlin. It was now Simpson's belief that, because of the American necessity for a harbour on their Northwest Coast, the final Oregon treaty would certainly give them Puget Sound. Thus a fort on the southern tip of Vancouver Island would be important, politically and strategically. Surprisingly, in the light of their interest in Vancouver Island, the HBC knew almost nothing about the island and its people.

One reason for this was the immediate concerns at Fort Vancouver. Expansion elsewhere also took up an inordinate amount of time and energy. In 1824, descending the Columbia River on the way to Astoria, George Simpson stressed the need for an establishment on the Fraser River. Ten days after reaching Astoria, James McMillan, who had just crossed Canada from York Factory on Hudson Bay in record time with Simpson, turned the bow of his newly constructed boat north. Among the men accompanying McMillan were Jean Ba'tiste Proveau, who had travelled with Fraser in 1808, and John Work, later to be a chief factor on the British Columbia coast and a member of the BC Legislative Assembly.

The men left Astoria on November 18 and on December 13, after dragging their boats across one of the worst swamps in British Columbia, reached the Fraser, more commonly known as the Cowichan at this time. The Coast Salish Indians inhabiting the lower valley of the Fraser, as well as Salish tribes from Vancouver Island, were then known as the Cowichan; early explorers such as McMillan and Work gave the river their name. The men quickly explored what they could of the river, reached the waters of the Strait of Georgia on December 20, 1824, and almost immediately headed home, sick of the ghastly weather.

Writing in a report in February 1826, that the HBC wished a fort on the Fraser River to be established the following summer if possible, with McMillan in charge, George Simpson (living up to his nickname of "the Little Emperor") again set history in motion. On June 22, 1827, the HBC's brigantine *Cadboro*, under Captain Aemilius Simpson, entered the Fraser River (the first European vessel to do so) with Chief Factor James McMillan and his men aboard. In November, after much unrelenting labour and a great deal of excitement caused by local Indians and groups from as far away as Vancouver Island, the flag was raised over Fort Langley, named in honour of Thomas Langley, an HBC director.

Within a few years following the establishment of Fort Langley, the HBC built numerous other forts on the Northwest Coast. Among them were Fort McLoughlin, built in 1833 on Milbanke Sound (the site is now Bella Bella); Fort Salmon River, a small post at the head of Burke Channel (probably across the river from the present site of Bella Coola); Port Essington, which stood briefly near the mouth of the Skeena River, and Fort Simpson (later Port Simpson), built near the mouth of the Nass River in 1831, and moved to the Tsimshean Peninsula three years later. With the establishment of these forts, and several along the Alaskan coast still under lease from the Russians, the HBC was, it is often maintained, in complete control of the Northwest Coast by the early 1840s.

As Vancouver Island was so close to a number of their establishments, the HBC could claim control of it, but only nominally. All of their northward expansion was based on the mainland, usually at the mouths of rivers. It would appear that the HBC's interest in westward expansion stopped at the Strait of Georgia and then turned northward. They attempted no trading with the Nootka people, with whom the American traders based in the Hawaiian Islands still did a lucrative business well into the 1820s, and their trading with the east-coast peoples was done largely at the mainland forts. Even their exploration of the island was limited to brief stops in various coves and bays along the east coast, none of which had any positive result so far as can be told.

Not until American expansionism, and the foresight of Sir George Simpson, forced John McLoughlin's hand was something done regarding Vancouver Island. Reluctantly, and bowing to orders from Simpson, McLoughlin dispatched James

Douglas and six others to the island early in 1842, to locate a site for a future fort. The men joined the *Cadboro* at Fort Nisqually in Puget Sound and sailed for the southwest shores of the island. In his final report of July 12, 1842, Douglas wrote: "I made choice of a site for the proposed new Establishment in the Port of Camosack which appears to me decidedly the most advantageous situation, for the purpose, within the Straits of De Fuca."[6]

"As a harbour," Douglas continued, "it is equally safe and accessible, and abundance of timber grows near it for home consumption and exportation." Although there were no powerful streams flowing into the harbour, "the canal of Camosack, at a point where the channel is contracted to a breadth of 47 feet through which the tide rushes out and in with a degree of force and velocity capable of driving the most powerful machinery" would do the work of many fresh-water streams. And, as if anticipating the decades of critics who would see Esquimalt as the better harbour, Douglas wrote: "At Camosack there is a range of plains nearly six miles square, containing a great extent of valuable tillage and pasture land" whereas the other harbours (Sooke and Esquimalt) were "surrounded by rocks and forests, which it will require ages to level and adapt extensively to the purposes of agriculture."[7]

"Camosack" is now spelled Camosun, Douglas's "Port of Camosack" is Victoria Harbour, and the "canal of Camosack" is The Gorge, that beautiful and well-known channel. Pleased as Douglas seems to have been with the site, he was not blind to certain problems. "The situation," he wrote in conclusion, "is not faultless, or so completely suited to our Purposes as it might be; but I dispair of any better being found on this Coast, as I am confident that there is no other Seaport North of the Columbia where so many Advantages will be found combined."[8]

Even as Douglas was writing this report at Fort Vancouver, the HBC passed several important resolutions. McLoughlin was ordered to close down the existing coastal forts by 1844, and to fit out the *Beaver* to take up the slack caused by these closures. It was also resolved that a suitable location should be found on Vancouver Island, and that the fort should be constructed as quickly as men and supplies could be transported to the island.

CHAPTER FOUR

Fort Victoria

Chief Factor James Douglas, accompanied by 15 men, boarded the *Beaver* at Fort Nisqually on March 13, 1843. After a brief stop near Dungeness Spit for fresh fish, the ship steamed across the Strait of Juan de Fuca and late in the afternoon, anchored off Shoal Point, Victoria Harbour. According to a story later told by the Douglas family, James Douglas landed at Clover Point the next morning, and named it in honour of the red clover growing everywhere in the vicinity. He and his men then walked along the shore to Beacon Hill before crossing to the Inner Harbour, where they would soon begin building the fort.

Noteworthy is the fact that Douglas only rarely mentions the local inhabitants during these earliest days at "Camosack" or Victoria Harbour. One important comment was noted in his pocket diary on March 16: "Spoke to the Samose [Songhee] to-day and informed them of our intention of building in this place which appeared to please them very much and they immediately offered their services in procuring pickets for the establishment, an offer which I gladly accepted and promised to them a Blanket for every forty pickets of 22 feet by 36 inches which they bring."[1] Luckily, J. B. Z. Bolduc, a Catholic missionary attached to the Columbia Mission at Fort Vancouver, accompanied Douglas and later wrote of the Songhee-British contact in some detail.

"It was about four o'clock in the afternoon," wrote Bolduc, "when we arrived there. At first we saw only two canoes; but, having discharged two cannon shot, the aborigines left their retreats and surrounded the steamboat." The next day the people were even less hesitant for canoes came from every point in the harbour. Several days later, convinced the people were friendly, Bolduc visited their main village at Cadboro Bay, which he thought a charming body of water. There the people lived in a fort some 150 feet square. These forts or stockades were apparently a common feature along the inner shores of the Strait of Juan de Fuca, and were built for protection against the Euclataw, a Kwakiutl group with a bad reputation. It was their practice to raid southern villages at night, kill the men, and enslave the women and children. Inside this fort Bolduc observed "many human heads sculptured and painted in red or black, and occasionally both colours together" on top of posts.[2]

The bay was later named in honour of the HBC's brigantine *Cadboro*, perhaps the first vessel to enter the interior of Victoria Harbour. The Songhee knew the bay as *Sungayka* and their fort was apparently located where the Royal Victoria Yacht Club is now situated. Six different groups made this area home, and it seems this was the principal village on the southern end of the island prior to the building of Fort Victoria. On one of the slopes leading up from the beach was located the Mystic Spring; a curious legend surrounding this spring has entertained generations of Victorians.[3]

Bolduc counted 525 individuals in the village at Cadboro Bay, and suspected many people were absent. This comment, and the later note that 1200 people assembled for his Sunday morning service a few days later are of more than passing interest. The Camosack vicinity was not uninhabited; in fact it was a well-known gathering spot. Furthermore, it was a location known to the Kwakiutl, Haida and Tlingit. That the fort was being constructed in a region with a large population would be beneficial to trading in the days to come; that the northern tribes knew it too would cause more trouble than anyone could possibly foresee in 1843.

Since the Songhee moved to the Inner Harbour soon after the fort's construction, this location has often been assumed to be one of the original village sites, and the Songhee one group. To confuse the issue further, "smallpox" (a term including most contagious European diseases) began sweeping the coast early in the 19th century and this, along with the introduction of firearms that caused warfare to be far more deadly than previously possible, decimated the Songhee. A census taken by Douglas in 1850 listed the entire population at 700. Yet once their numerous winter villages could be found in various sheltered bays and harbours from Sooke to Cordova Bay, and they owned summer villages and fishing sites on several of the San Juan Islands.

The Songhee were a loose confederation of family groups, surrounded by other Salish groups, who spoke a number of different dialects, and their own name for themselves was *Lekwungen.* Songhee is derived from *Stsanges,* the name of a subgroup living on the east shore of Albert Head, Metchosin. A series of treaties made by Douglas with the Songhee and surrounding Vancouver Island people between 1850 and 1852 indicates something of the original geopolitical landscape of the Victoria region.

The *Soke* or Sooke owned the land roughly from Point No Point to the southeast shore of the entrance to Sooke Harbour. Two Clallam groups, having migrated to the island from the Olympic Peninsula, controlled the coast from the Sooke boundary to the eastern shore of Albert Head. Six Songhee groups—the *Teechamitsa, Whyomilth, Kosampsom, Swengwhung, Chilcowitch,* and *Chekonein*—owned the area from Albert Head to

Gordon Head. The Saanich Peninsula was sold to Douglas by groups listed simply as "South Saanich" and "North Saanich". What Douglas paid the Indians for all of this land is not known, as he failed to list the amount of one payment. The largest payment was £79, so it can be assumed Douglas bought the southernmost reaches of Vancouver Island for not more than £564.

Ridiculously low as this sum is, the actual treaties were far more humane than many made during this period in North America. "The condition of, or understanding of this Sale, is this, that our Village Sites and Enclosed Fields are to be kept for our own use, for the use of our Children, and for those who may follow after us. It is also understood that we are at liberty to hunt over the unoccupied lands, and to carry on our fisheries as formerly."[4] That this passage in the treaties was largely ignored in the years following Douglas's retirement was typical of the time.

The Songhee names for several Victoria locations are of interest socially and economically. A meadow in Beacon Hill Park was called *"Meeqan,"* "warmed by the sun," and was a favourite spot for sunbathing. Where the Empress Hotel now stands was *Whosaykum,* "the muddy place," and the Songhee camped above the mud flats there while gathering camas in the area surrounding *Meeqan.* Laurel Point was a burial site, as was Halkett Island (once known as "Deadman's" Island) in Selkirk Water at the mouth of The Gorge. The only name of importance in the immediate vicinity of Victoria to be retained by Douglas and the HBC is Esquimalt, around which there is some confusion. Esquimalt is supposedly derived from *Is-whoy-malth*—"a place gradually shoaling". However *Is-whoy-malth* is clearly James Douglas's original spelling of *Whyomilth,* the name of the Songhee group living at the time in Esquimalt Harbour. Their name for the harbour was *Kalla,* "spring water gushing down the beach".

One reason for Douglas's initial lack of interest in the Songhee may have been their similarity to groups he already knew. Certainly another reason was business. He did not remain to supervise the clearing of land and early stages of the fort's construction, but departed aboard the *Beaver* to dismantle several of the northern forts, and redistribute their personnel. Returning to Camosack on June 1, 1843, Douglas found "A large number of the natives then encamped around us, all armed, without any of their wives or children, which looked suspicious".[5] Since the combined HBC forces now at Camosack numbered 50 men and officers, all well armed, the Indians were relatively harmless, though their petty thievery did annoy the men.

Shortly after returning from the north, Douglas again departed, this time for Fort Vancouver. Charles Ross, formerly Chief Trader at Fort McLoughlin, was left in charge of the new establishment. Roderick Finlayson, only 25 but already a veteran of Fort Vancouver and several northern posts, was second in command. So little had been done toward constructing the fort in Douglas's absence that, years later, Roderick Finlayson claimed he was the pioneer builder on Vancouver Island. From this time until 1848, James Douglas, now a travelling agent for the HBC, made only infrequent visits to the new fort on Vancouver Island.

Even though he departed early in the season of 1843, a letter from Douglas to Simpson contains one of the best descriptions of the fort as it stood that September: "In planning the Fort, I had in view the probability of its being converted into a Depot for the coasting trade and consequently began on a respectable scale, as to size. It is in form a quadrangle of 330 x 300 feet intended to contain 8 buildings of 60 feet each, disposed in the following order say 2 in the rear facing the harbour and 3 on each side standing at right angles with the former leaving the front entirely open. The outhouses and workshops, are to be thrown in the rear of the main buildings and in the unoccupied angles, so as not to disturb the symmetry of the principal square".[6] When finished, the fort was surrounded by an 18-foot stockade, and contained six 60- by 30-foot buildings, and two of 60 by 40 feet, all with pavillion roofs. In addition to this an

COURTESY OF HISTORY DIVISION, BC PROVINCIAL MUSEUM

Bastion at Fort Victoria, ca *1860.*

octagonal bastion was built in the southwest corner of the
stockade. Four years later the fort was enlarged to 465 by 300
feet and the extended stockade enclosed 13 buildings.

Writing in 1842, Douglas referred to the "Port of
Camosack", and "Camosack," contrary to various claims, is
obviously derived from *Camossung,* the Songhee name for The
Gorge. Since the first Europeans saw this narrow channel,
which connects Selkirk Water and Portage Inlet, it has been
something of a tourist attraction, but for the Songhee The
Gorge was a holy place. When seeking the water's spirit, the
men would plunge into The Gorge and dive to the bottom holding onto rocks, until Camossung gave the swimmers the powers
they requested. Camossung was the name not only of The
Gorge, but of the spirit of the place. Local historians have
claimed the earliest names for the fort were "Fort Camosun"
and "Fort Albert". There is no evidence that the first name was
ever used, except perhaps among the men building it, and while

"Fort Albert" does appear in the log of the *Cadboro* on August 6, 1843, the new fort had already been officially named "Fort Victoria" by an HBC council at Fort Garry on June 10, 1843.

Life at Fort Victoria during the winter of 1843–44 consisted of hard work and little else. In Douglas's letter to Simpson that November, he commented that the summer returns had been 300 beaver and otter and thought the trade would improve when the Makah and Nootka began their trading at the fort. Writing the following January Ross added a hundred beaver and land otter to Douglas's tally, and described the farming, begun almost as early as the construction, as having barely started. There were only about five acres then planted, and another five were cleared and ready to be ploughed.

If life was dull at Fort Victoria, it was not so farther south. Early in 1843, the American settlers in the Willamette River valley, almost all of whom had been assisted in settling by McLoughlin, petitioned the United States government for annexation. The handwriting on the wall was obvious to James Douglas, if not to Dr. McLoughlin, at nearby Fort Vancouver. Worse was to come—at the beginning of 1843 probably fewer than 300 Americans lived in the area, but by that December more than 900, some say more than 1,000, Americans had reached the Oregon Territory.

At Fort Victoria, Charles Ross died on June 27, 1844. Little is known of the man Simpson described as "A good classical Scholar and a man of very correct conduct but so nervous at times that it is quite painful to see him."[7] Apparently he was ill even as he took charge of Fort Victoria, and his death came as no surprise. Ross Bay, just east of Clover Point, was named in his honour; the legend that his "farm" overlooked Ross Bay is now part of Victoria's folklore.

Roderick Finlayson replaced Ross, and Ross's son, John, became Finlayson's assistant. It was probably this son, and his brothers, Alexander and William (both of whom are buried in the Ross Bay Cemetery), who purchased the land at Ross Bay and later developed the Ross estate. The difference between

Ross and Finlayson is remarkable. Ross was about 50 when he took command of the fort, Finlayson 26; two years later Douglas wrote of him: "Finlayson has managed the affairs of Fort Victoria, remarkably well, since his accession to the charge of the Post, and I assure you it will not be an easy matter to find a better man for the place. He is not a man of display, but there is a degree of energy, perseverance, method and sound judgement in all his arrangements, which from what I had seen of him in a subordinate situation, I was not prepared to expect. He is besides a young man of great probity and high moral worth."[8]

For good reason some consider Finlayson "the Founder of Victoria"; except for Ross's brief tenure, he was in control of Fort Victoria until 1849, when James Douglas assumed command. Finlayson was a Member of the Legislative Council for Vancouver Island and its Dependencies from 1851 to 1863, retired to Victoria in 1872 after a ten-year period as chief factor

Roderick Finlayson.

COURTESY OF HISTORY DIVISION, BC PROVINCIAL MUSEUM

in the BC interior, and in 1878 served as mayor of the city. When he died in Victoria in 1892, Finlayson was one of the last survivors of the HBC period in Vancouver Island history.

By 1844 the Songhee were living near the fort on the shores of the Inner Harbour. The fort stood between what are now View and Broughton streets below Government Street, and the village was erected along the edge of a wood growing along the banks of a gorge where Johnson Street is today. The HBC realized that sooner or later, there would be trouble with these people and, sure enough, it came shortly after Ross's death.

"In 1844 matters went on for some time smoothly enough," Finlayson wrote in his unpublished autobiography, "when it was found that the natives killed some of our oxen feeding in the open spaces." When Finlayson demanded payment from a Songhee chief, the man "went away in a rage, assembled some Cowichan Indians to his village and the next move I found on their part was a shower of bullets fired at the fort, with a great noise and demonstration on the part of the crowd assembled, threatening death and devastation to all the whites."[9]

After a parley, and a ruse to ensure the vacancy of one of the Indian lodges, Finlayson fired a nine-pounder loaded with grapeshot into the lodge which, being built of poles and cedar boards, "flew into the air in splinters like a bombshell, after this there was such howling that I thought a number were killed, and was quite relieved when the interpreter came round and told me none were killed but much frightened, not knowing we had such destructive arms."[10]

Shortly afterwards, a talk with Finlayson convinced the Songhee chief that the HBC would level the village and drive them out of the harbour, if they did not pay for the slaughtered oxen immediately. He did so the next day amid much handshaking. Thus ended the first and last popular uprising at Fort Victoria.

This "argument" was the highlight of life at Fort Victoria in 1844. In 1845, the British lieutenants Henry J. Warre, Aide-decamp to the Commander of the Forces in Canada, and Mervin

Vavasour of the Royal Engineers, arrived on what has been called a "secret mission" and a "military reconnaissance" of the Oregon Territory. Their final report described the fort's farm as being a few hundred acres in extent, on which the HBC raised wheat and potatoes and the fort as a distribution centre for provisions, supplies and men for the various posts to the north. Warre and Vavasour were among the first to comment on the problems apparent in Victoria Harbour; it was neither a good harbour for shipping nor worthwhile as a military position. They did find some fine harbours, one of them, "about three miles distant, and nearly connected by a small inlet, is the Sqimal Harbour, which is very commodious, and accessible at all times, offering a much better position, and having also the advantage of a supply of water in the vicinity".[11]

Nor were they impressed with Fort Victoria. At that time they found 35 men living behind the stockade, and counted seven horses, 23 cattle, and one hog. Warre, a talented amateur artist, sketched the fort and "The H.B.C. Settlement and Fort Victoria", has a reality lacking in the many later and relatively romantic sketches and paintings. Trees are growing inside and outside the stockade; the ground now lying between View and Johnson streets still remains uncleared, and Indian houses stand close to the stockade. All of this suggests Finlayson was not worried by any "Indian menace," or surely he would have cleared the trees and forced the Indians to build at some distance. Only a short time later a brush fire, which the HBC had some difficulty in bringing under control, led Finlayson to persuade the Indians to move across the harbour.

Another of Warre's sketches shows "My partner at a Ball given at Fort Victoria, October 6, 1845". Actually there are two sketches; one is a frontal view of a squat woman dressed in what seem to be a European dress and leggings, and Warre did nothing to idealize his "partner". The second sketch is smaller and shows her head in profile. If it were not for her deformed head, she would be pixieish. Twenty years later the Reverend Thomas Crosby was to observe that "Many of the southern

Indian girl, showing deformed skull. Ca 1860.

tribes of British Columbia Coast were in the habit of deforming the heads of their children. This custom resembles that of foot-binding among the Chinese," and like that custom a flattened forehead was considered a mark of beauty.[12] As it has been suggested that Warre's dancing partner's head displays a sugar-loaf deformation, this would imply (according to Crosby) she was a Kwakiutl visitor from the northern end of Vancouver Island.

Another visitor during the summer of 1845 was the HMS *America*, her master Captain the Honourable John Gordon. Her exact purpose on this coast, to which she was detailed, remains unclear, though Sir George Seymour, Commander-in-Chief, Pacific, believed she would prove to the British colonists in the Oregon Territory that the home government was willing to protect them. If this was the case, 1845 was late in the game for such a show of strength. As the *America* drew too much water to enter the Columbia, and Gordon was disinclined to be-lieve Finlayson's description of Esquimalt Harbour (because the harbour was not on Gordon's chart), the *America* took up her station at the mouth of Puget Sound.

Finlayson took Captain Gordon deer hunting, and when the deer they were following disappeared into a thicket, where neither man nor horse could follow, Gordon was disappointed. Finlayson later remembered that on their return they were "riding through an open, fine country, with the native grass up to the horses' knees," when he "happened to remark, 'What a fine country this is,' to which he [Gordon] replied that he 'would not give one of the barren hills of Scotland for all he saw around him.' " Gordon's disgust was even greater when he learned the migrating salmon would not rise to a fly; he thought trolling an "awful manner" to catch such mighty fish.[13]

Humorous as these anecdotes are now, they may have played a less-than-funny part in the subsequent report Gordon filed. One of his charges on this coast was "to examine and give a report of the country," according to Finlayson, which he was to then pass on to his brother, the Earl of Aberdeen—at the time Prime Minister of Great Britain. The report was so misleading and negative that it changed the course of the Oregon Territory negotiations, much to the surprise and delight of the Americans.

Rather than obey Simpson's order to cease assisting American immigrants, McLoughlin resigned his position with the HBC in 1846. He was replaced by the capable and pro-British James Douglas as chief factor, but it was too late for Douglas to do anything other than wait for the inevitable. Judging from Finlayson's memoirs, none of this affected Fort Victoria. It was now the main supply depot from which goods arriving from England by ship were distributed to the Columbia District. Fort Victoria was also the supply depot from which goods, and British and local-grown produce were shipped to Sitka, the headquarters of the Russian American Company. Since this trade with the Russians was guaranteed by the HBC as part of the legal obligations in the lease of Southeastern Alaska, it was one of Finlayson's major concerns.

"With this in view," wrote Finlayson, "a force of men and Indians were employed here [Fort Victoria] to clear land and cultivate it"; subsequently cattle were imported from HBC farms in Puget Sound, and three dairies opened. These were at Church Hill, where the Law Courts now stand; Gonzales (later to be known as Pemberton's) in Fairfield, and North Dairy Farm in the Cedar Hill area—"each with seventy milch cows, in charge of dairymen, which produced seventy kegs of butter each in season."[14] Various other farms produced oats and barley, peas and potatoes, all of which were exported, as was the wheat that grew 40 bushels to the acre.

During 1846, six line-of-battle vessels anchored in Esquimalt Harbour at various times. One of these was the HMS *Constance,* commanded by Captain George William Courtenay. At Finlayson's request Courtenay landed a number of marines, "who performed various evolutions, such as is customary on parade ground". Afterwards, the captain asked a local chief what he thought of the marines, and the chief replied, "Is that the way the whites fight, killing each other in the open? We fight behind the trees and rocks and kill our enemies in this way."[15] For some reason this response did not please Captain Courtenay.

Coal, one day to be the island's economic backbone, was first mined in 1846. It was found on the north end of the island at a place Douglas referred to as "Chislakus," undoubtedly in the vicinity of Port Hardy. Only 60 tons were mined and this amount, once loaded aboard the *Cormorant,* the first naval steamer in these waters, was used by her engineers for welding and forge work.

Work on the fort continued under Finlayson's command. He added two 100- by 40-foot buildings to those already inside the stockade. Outside on the nearby meadows, a "cowhouse" and dairy were built. Douglas reported 63 calves had been reared that year, and a substantial increase was expected in the spring of 1847. According to him the Fort Victoria milk was richer in colour than that of Fort Vancouver, a result of better pastures.

Finlayson and his men were also planting a six-acre orchard.

In his autobiography Finlayson never speaks of enjoying any of his tasks, yet one pleasant duty during the early months of 1846 must have been his trip to San Juan Island, for the island is lovely and serene except during the worst storms; there Finlayson drove in "British Possessions" markers at various locations where they were sure to be seen by wandering Americans. Certainly this was more enjoyable than dancing "attendance on maritime *magnificos*" from the warships anchored at Esquimalt for whom, among other things, Finlayson ordered beef cattle driven up for the officers to shoot, "and wild horses for them to break."[16]

Visiting Fort Victoria at this time, Berthold Seeman, the naturalist aboard the HMS *Herald*, thought the area from Ogden Point to Fort Victoria "a natural park; noble oaks and ferns are seen in the greatest luxuriance, thickets of the hazel and the willow, shrubberies of the poplar and the alder, are dotted about. One could hardly believe that this was not a work of art; more particularly when finding signs of cultivation in every direction," but he had to ruin his reverie on an all-too-typical note of the day: "Civilization had encroached upon the beautiful domain, and the savage could no longer exist in the filth and indolence of mere animal life."[17]

Only months later a man arrived at the fort whose sole purpose there was to study and paint the Indians, and he seems to have been singularly unimpressed by the merits of civilization. Judging from Douglas's annual report of 1847, and what little other information survives from that year, one highlight of the year was the arrival of Paul Kane. Relatively unknown in his own day, Kane has since become internationally famous for his sketches and paintings, the results of his trips into the American and Canadian west in the 1840s, and his *Wanderings of an Artist* remains a fascinating collection of ethnological information.

Kane reached Fort Victoria from Fort Nisqually by canoe on April 9, 1847, and remained on the coast until early June. Two of his observations are worth quoting at length. "The men," Kane wrote, "wear no clothing in summer, and nothing but a blanket in winter, made either of dog's hair alone, or dog's hair and goosedown mixed, frayed cedar-bark or wildgoose skin like the Chinooks [a Columbia River group]. They have a peculiar breed of small dogs with long hair of a brownish black and a clear white. These dogs are bred for clothing purposes."[18] This breed has long been extinct, yet once it was known from the Columbia to the northern islands and mainland of Southeastern Alaska. Captain Vancouver, seeing the dogs in Puget Sound villages in 1792, thought they resembled large Pomeranians. According to Vancouver "They were all shorn as close to the skin as sheep are in England; and so compact were their fleeces that large portions could be lifted up by a corner without causing any separation."[19]

That civilization left at least one Songhee untouched is suggested by an unpleasant story related by Kane. "One morning while I was sketching, I saw upon the rocks the dead body of a young woman, thrown out to the vultures and crows, whom I had seen a few days previously walking about in perfect health. Mr. Finlayson, the gentleman in charge of Fort Victoria, accompanied me to the lodge she belonged to, where we found an Indian woman, her mistress, who made light of her death, and was doubtless the cause of it. She told us that a slave had no right to burial, and became perfectly furious when Mr. Finlayson told her that the slave was far better than herself. 'I,' she exclaimed, 'the daughter of a chief, no better than a dead slave!' and bridling up with all the dignity she could assume, she stalked out, and next morning she had up her lodge and was gone."[20]

The *Vancouver*, an HBC barque, had been the first supply ship to reach Fort Victoria from England in 1845. Three years later the first fur brigade from the interior came directly to Fort Victoria, via a new trail from Kamloops to Fort Hope, instead of going to Fort Vancouver. Now the five-year-old fort truly was the HBC's centre west of the Rocky Mountains and, Finlayson wrote, this contributed to the growing proportions of the dairies and farms. In 1848, a sawmill, the first on Vancouver Island, and a flour or grist mill were built near the head of Esquimalt Harbour—thus one of Esquimalt's larger creeks is still known as Mill Stream. Even with this creek, water remained a problem. There was sufficient water power to operate both mills in the winter months, but at the height of summer so little water existed that only one mill managed to function.

Fort Victoria was humming. Due to the HBC's agreement with the Russians in Alaska, the *Columbia, Vancouver,* and *Cowlitz,* three company vessels, and now and again other ships, sailed continually between Fort Victoria, England and Alaska, with British manufactured goods, and cargoes of grain, beef, and other agricultural items from the Columbia River and Fort Victoria bound for Sitka.

Among the facts and figures in Douglas's yearly report appear two items of interest. Douglas remitted $73,402.55 to London as the gross income of Fort Victoria in 1848. Of a great deal more interest than this total, for it hints of the future, is the 189 ounces of California gold dust included in the remittance. Finlayson explained how this gold reached the fort. "In the Spring of 1849 a vessel appeared in the harbor, the crew of which wore red flannel shirts, and when they landed we took them to be pirates. I ordered the men to the guns, manned the bastions [by this time a second had been added] and made ready for defence. I then interviewed the men, from the gate, who told me they were peaceable traders, come from San Francisco, with gold, to trade for goods, as this was the only station on the northern coast where they could get the goods they wanted."[21] Not having handled gold previously, Finlayson was hesitant, but after referring to his book on minerals and having his blacksmith hammer a nugget out flat to prove it was malleable, he offered the Californians $11 an ounce. In his letter Douglas commented that the gold was a new export from Fort Victoria, a remark that must have haunted him more than once in the near future.

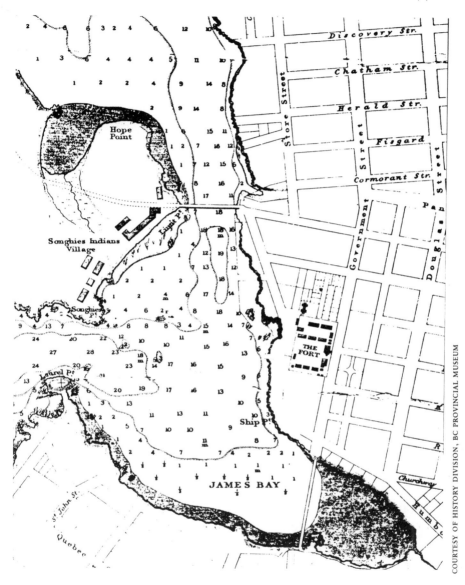

*Victoria town and harbour, from surveys done in 1859–60 by
J. D. Pemberton, Surveyor General, and Captain G. H.
Richards, of the* Plumper.

The second item communicated to London in Douglas's letter was his plan to establish a post in the vicinity of the north-island coal fields, to be manned by the staff of the soon-to-be-abandoned Fort Stikine. The important point here is not that this was the first mention of the soon-to-be-established Fort Rupert, but how drastically Douglas was changing the features of the HBC interests on the coast. In the two years since stepping into McLoughlin's place, he had widened the HBC's vision to include large farms and dairies, a sawmill and grist mill, and a sheep ranch and salmon fishery on San Juan Island, expanded the trade with the Russian American Company, continued the trade with the Hawaiian Islands and Californian ports, and by the fall of 1848 was planning a post which, as he already knew, would be the headquarters for a coal mine.

Obviously, by the winter of 1848 Fort Victoria was no longer the isolated trading post so often pictured. Yet the fort still lacked a hospital and doctor, schools and teachers; there were no white women at the fort and none had yet visited, and while Father Modeste Demers was consecrated Bishop of Vancouver Island at Oregon City in 1847, he had not visited the island. There were no ministers or priests, nor any house of worship at Fort Victoria. By European standards the fort was a primitive outpost of the empire and, in many eyes, not even of the British empire, but of the Hudson's Bay Company.

The many sketches and paintings dating from the 1840s, and the numerous reports and descriptions, published and unpublished, left by visitors and residents, make it possible to imagine "Fort Victoria as it was" in some detail. It requires a greater effort to visualize Vancouver Island during the same period.

The appearance of the Arrowsmith map, dated April 11, 1849, is quite an eye-opener. In 1846 the survey vessels, *Fisgard* and *Pandora,* commanded by Captain John Alexander Duntze and Lieutenant-Commander James Wood respectively, charted Victoria and Esquimalt harbours. At the same time Captain Henry Kellett, commanding the *Herald,* surveyed Sooke Harbour and nearby waters. All this is obvious on Arrowsmith's map; it is also obvious that no one had added substantially to the general knowledge of the remainder of Vancouver Island since the circumnavigation of the island by Vancouver, Galiano and Valdés.

Fort Victoria was clinging to the very toe of a largely unknown island. Substantial as the fort's grip may seem, it amounted to an establishment of a few hundred acres of farm land, and two mills, already outdated, as the events of the next year or two would prove. In 1848, after five years of occupancy, building and land clearing, business and expansion, Fort Victoria was, all things considered, little more important or substantial to the world at large than the Spanish holdings at Nootka in 1792.

CHAPTER FIVE

Company Men

Few years in the history of the Northwest Coast have proved to be as crucial as 1849. In California the gold rush began; in Oregon the first territorial government took office; the HBC headquarters were moved from Fort Vancouver to Fort Victoria; and Vancouver Island was ceded to the Hudson's Bay Company at a yearly rent of seven shillings, by a Royal Grant. The *Charter of Grant of Vancouver's Island* is dated January 13, 1849 and one would assume this action, with its long-range potential, was the notable event of 1849. Such was the case at the time, yet in the long term it was the gold rush that would change the shape of the island's history.

The story behind the grant, which stipulated in no uncertain terms that the HBC must establish a settlement or settlements of colonists on the island within five years or lose their rights, is curious. It was not the first plan to colonize the island, only the first to be approved by the British government. As early as the 1790s there were suggestions that it be made a prison colony. Throughout the early years of the 19th century, various religious groups discussed sending missions to the island. In the 1840s the Mormons in Utah exchanged letters with Her Majesty's government concerning their settling Vancouver Island. James Edward Fitzgerald, later prime minister of New Zealand, submitted a proposal to the Colonial Office for a colony in June 1847. This was no daydream on Fitzgerald's part; at the same time he published a prospectus seeking capital to fund this colony, and within the next three years he wrote two articles and a book opposing the HBC's grant. He felt the island was too important to be entrusted to the honourable company.

Due to the events in Oregon, the British government realized the value of colonizing Vancouver Island as an effective bulwark against further American immigration. However, the government was not interested in involving itself in such a scheme. The cost was one reason for its negative attitude. The HBC could afford the project, and was willing to undertake it, but as the company's motive was purely financial, would it allow people not attached to its control to settle on the island? English politicians directly involved with the matter at this point leaned towards the HBC, but they were aware that public opinion sided with a statement made by Fitzgerald: "The Hudson's Bay Company want to get the island into their own hands in order that they may *prevent* any colony there, except of their servants and dependants."[1]

Facing the politicians of the late 1840s was another problem: in their view, the lack of substantial knowledge about Vancouver Island was worse than the public outcry against the HBC being given a grant. Its coast was more or less charted, there was a fort on its southern shore, but what else was there? Reasonable men and women do not invest their past and future in a blank outline on the map. The failure of Fitzgerald's prospectus proved that the public's interest in colonizing the island was vocal, not financial or physical. What the average Englishman of the 1840s knew about the island was derived largely from the work of Cook and Vancouver. While these narratives might set young men to dreaming, nothing in them could provoke sensible members of the landed gentry into selling their holdings for a rocky coast inhabited by a savage people.

More than anything else, this lack of interest and information turned the government to the HBC. It was established on Vancouver Island; it had the wherewithal, publicity outlets and ships and, doubtless, the energy to succeed. The Royal Grant, which had been under discussion for several years, is a long-winded document that, for the yearly seven shillings and the legal obligation to establish a colony, gave the HBC total control of the island, as well as the right to all monies gained from the sale of the land and minerals. The colonists were to come from Great Britain, Ireland, and the Dominions; the HBC agreed to reserve land that might be required for naval establishments (but these would be sold, not given, to Great Britain), and for public purposes; as well, they agreed to apply the profits (after a deduction of not more than 10%) of land and mineral sales towards colonization and improvements on the island.

The concerns of the indigenous peoples of Vancouver Island are not mentioned in this grant. However, it is known that the British government made it clear to the HBC that the Royal Grant was subject to the rights of the people already on the land. In short, the HBC was to act as the government itself would have done, had it established the colony. British law and imperial policy recognized the Indians' claims to the soil. This right could be extinguished by military force, treaty, or purchase. The Fort Victoria Treaties of 1850 and 1852 extinguished Indian title to the lands on the southern coast between Sooke and Saanich. This was done by Douglas, not only because it was honourable, but because existing British law obliged him to do so. Douglas did not continue buying up parcels of land for two reasons: he ran out of money, and neither the HBC nor, later, the Council of Vancouver Island would provide him with further funding.

Colonization of Vancouver's Island was printed and circulated in Great Britain in 1849. This small pamphlet had no effect on the public, and for good reason: immigration and colonization were not high on anyone's list of priorities. Writing in 1860, J. Despard Pemberton, then Surveyor-General of Vancouver Island, contrasted the "principal inducements held out to immigrants" to the "obstacles having hitherto prevented the successful development" of Vancouver Island as they existed in 1849. Briefly, the six "inducements" were these: 1) no grant should contain less than 20 acres; 2) the price of land was one pound per acre; 3)colonists could provide their own passage or be provided with passage at reasonable rates; 4) "purchasers of larger quantities of land should pay the same price per acre and should take out with them five single men, or three married couples, for every hundred acres"; 5) all minerals discovered would belong to the HBC, "but the owner should have the privilege of working for his own benefit any coal mine that might be on his land, on payment of royalty of half a crown per ton" and 6) "every freeholder should enjoy the right of fishing and that all the ports and harbours should be open and free to them".

As if these "inducements" did not provide enough headaches for potential colonists, Pemberton lists five "obstacles": 1) "the attraction of the gold region in California"; 2) the almost prohibitive level of wages; 3) "the great distance from Great Britain, involving either a tedious voyage of five months and 17,000 miles, or the expense of the overland route by Panama or the plains"; 5) the price of land (when compared to the prices south of the 49th parallel in the Oregon Territory) and 5) "Duties averaging 24 per cent", on British and Canadian goods entering neighbouring American ports.[2]

The Colony of Vancouver Island was a dismal failure until 1858. Whether or not the reasons listed by Pemberton lay behind this failure are debatable, but one point in his long and involved argument does stand out. By 1850 the population of the Oregon Territory was 13,294, and there were 2,374 dwellings and 1,164 farms. The population of Vancouver Island in 1853, according to the earliest statistics available, only amounted to about 450 people—men, women, and children— and of these, 300 were at Victoria, and the area extending westward to Sooke. There were 125 people at Nanaimo and the Fort Rupert area accounted for the rest.

Pemberton described the situation on Vancouver Island (and British Columbia, for he was writing two years after its establishment as a colony) with bitter but clear-headed precision: "In neither have we, as yet, any farming population worth mentioning. America feeds us; America carries our letters to us; we reach them by American steamers, or we travel by American routes; the bulk of the merchandise we consume comes from American ports. In Vancouver Island, the rich valleys of Cowichan, Puntledge, and Barclay [Barkley] Sound are unconnected and by land unapproachable. Even between Esquimalt Harbour and Victoria the capital, three miles, the road is execrable, and while a small expenditure would render Victoria Harbour one of the most commodious on the coast for whalers or merchant vessels, it remains unlighted and unfrequented. The island is unimproved, progress being entirely limited to Victoria district and Victoria Town".[3]

Affairs were no happier on the political level. Initially, James Douglas, "a man of property, a Chief Factor of the Hudson's Bay Company, and a member of the board [of the HBC] at Fort Vancouver," was to have been appointed governor of the new colony until such time as the colony could afford to pay a governor independent of the HBC.[4] Doubts soon arose as to Douglas's suitability as governor. These were obviously due to Douglas's lifelong and intimate relationship with the HBC, and these doubts were considered well-founded, for Richard Blanshard was appointed governor on July 9, 1849.

Quite apart from the political pressure pushing Douglas's name to and fro, Earl Grey, Secretary of State for the Colonies, had no intention of appointing Douglas governor. Furthermore, there is little to suggest Douglas wanted the position. If Douglas was not to be appointed governor, everyone with even a whiff of good sense realized the position would be filled with a figurehead. The reasons for this were basic: no one with the necessary experience and qualifications, the political savvy and strength to fight Douglas and the HBC, and a private income (for it was well known to most that the colony could not afford to pay a governor) wanted the job. No one knows why Blanshard accepted the appointment; he may have had dreams, or perhaps his family pressured him into accepting. The HBC gave him the nod for he proved he was the man they were seeking by being naive enough to apply for the position.

Richard Blanshard was 31 when he accepted the appointment. As a barrister with some administrative experience, the man could not have been the fool he seems, though accepting the governorship of a colony without colonists suggests otherwise. Blanshard sailed from Southampton aboard the HMS *Driver* in September 1849—almost three months after Chief Factor Douglas arrived at Fort Victoria with his wife and family.

As expected, Blanshard's tenure as Governor of the Colony of Vancouver Island was brief. Nothing was quite what he expected. Since there was no official residence ready for him, and no room in the fort, Blanshard lived aboard the *Driver,* and the government went wherever the ship went for nearly a month. Although he did land shortly after his arrival on March 9, 1850, for Sunday services within the stockade, his only official trip ashore was to read his commission in the mess hall of Fort Victoria. The captains and officers of the HMS *Driver* and HMS *Cormorant* were there in response to Blanshard's pleading, and the HBC officers and men assembled to listen as they had no choice. This was, one historian has cynically but honestly noted, the pinnacle of Blanshard's career on Vancouver Island.

The trip from England to Fort Victoria had lasted almost six months, the weather at the fort was foul, and no one was interested in Blanshard's presence. The HBC was building a house for him (at what is now the southeast corner of Government and Yates streets), but it was not completed and no one

Fort Victoria.

knew when it would be. The 1,000 acres of land promised to
him before he left England proved to be for the office, not the
man. There was nothing for him to do. Bitterly disappointed,
Blanshard made no effort to cultivate the fort's limited potential. In an otherwise lengthy letter to the Secretary of the HBC,
Douglas spent four lines discussing His Excellency Governor
Blanshard's arrival in the most impersonal of terms. A few days
later, in a more personal letter, all Douglas could say was: "I
have not had time to become much acquainted, but I may say
that his quiet, gentlemanly, manner is prepossessing."[5]

In his first official dispatch, dated April 8, 1850, Blanshard is
reticent—and for good reason. It was obvious even to him that
without a colony to administer, and lacking a judiciary and
legislature, his position was just what Earl Grey and the HBC
had intended it to be—a figurehead. His second dispatch re-

ported that Douglas had reserved a ten-square-mile area in the vicinity of Fort Victoria for the HBC, as was his right; another of the same size was reserved for the Puget's Sound Agricultural Company, another name for the Hudson's Bay Company, according to Blanshard. He also worried that should the rumours concerning the gold discoveries on the Spokane River prove true, the subsequent rush would attract the HBC employees at Fort Victoria and Fort Rupert—in other words, the entire population of Vancouver Island.

A third dispatch was no happier. George Blenkinsop, the young clerk in charge at Fort Rupert, had locked up two miners, and Blanchard appointed Dr. John Sebastian Helmcken provisional magistrate to unravel the difficulties. Helmcken was the HBC's medical officer, and had arrived at Fort Victoria aboard the *Norman Morrison* from England just days after Blanshard's own arrival. The governor had "great confidence" in Helmcken's "impartiality, his situation too as Surgeon renders him more free from the influence which might be exercised over another servant of that Company."[6] The governor's faith in Helmcken was not misplaced, but without assistance he was unable to accomplish much, and was on the eve of mailing his resignation when he heard that deserters from the HBC's *Norman Morrison* were aboard the *England,* anchored near Fort Rupert. Shortly after this, on July 8, Helmcken learned that three deserters from the HBC vessel had been killed by Indians.

Communications between Blanshard and Helmcken were slow and misleading. It is safe to say that, unused to civil authority, the HBC men and officers were not particularly willing to assist Helmcken who, to compound the problem, lacked the experience to deal with the problems directly. By the time Blanshard reached the area in the HMS *Daedalus* early in October, nothing had been resolved but the civil problem with the miners, which had since sputtered out for lack of interest on everyone's part. The murderers of the deserters were still loose, and Blanshard did not capture them; after burning the camp or village where they had been hiding, the *Daedalus* sailed for San Francisco on October 14.

There was nothing inept in Governor Blanshard's handling of these problems at Fort Rupert—of which more will be said later—but the interrelated episodes do point out that the time was not ready for civil law. It was too slow and cumbersome, thus seeming ineffectual to the Indians. These people were not Salish, but the strong and hot-headed Kwakiutl, who were relatively undebauched by the Europeans. How the HBC might have handled this situation is speculation, but Helmcken, writing years later, thought Douglas might have stormed Newitty and taken the culprits by force. That was HBC policy: immediate and direct action at whatever cost. The country may not have been ready for the white man's civil law, but it understood the HBC's concepts of right and wrong.

Shortly after these incidents Blanshard tendered his resignation as governor, but ten months passed before he received the letter accepting his resignation. None of the surviving letters from London to Governor Blanshard show any sign of sympathy for, or understanding of, Blanshard's awkward position. He was also ill but this gained him little sympathy for Peter Skene Ogden joked that the colony could "boast of a Governor six months in the year in his bed and ten Colonists."[7] The governor's last official act, and perhaps the only one of lasting value, was the appointment of his first and last Legislative Council. It consisted of James Douglas (senior member), John Tod, and James Cooper; together they were to administer the government until a new governor was appointed.

Even though there were now some colonists on the island, all of them worked for the HBC. This, and the selection of men who made up the first council, was the handwriting on the wall for those hoping for a free colony. Douglas was a chief factor; John Tod, living in retirement on his estate at Oak Bay, had only recently retired from the HBC as a chief factor; and James Cooper, though often considered one of Vancouver Island's first independent settlers, was a former HBC ship's officer.

Little did Douglas know, that August, how complete his control was, for the letter appointing him governor reached him after the first council meeting.

Now, Douglas was not only the single most powerful man in the HBC's Columbia District, and the chief factor in control of the company's western headquarters, he was also governor and vice-admiral of Vancouver Island and its Dependencies. These positions gave Douglas powers never again to be manipulated by one man in the Pacific Northwest. Previous to this only Alexander Baranof had wielded such complete control and, to many eyes, Baranof was the logical end result of such powers — a despot. That Douglas did not become such a ruler is due to many factors.

Baranof's despotism grew slowly. Distance, a rarely functional communication system, serfs rather than paid labourers, and subordinates upon whom no reliance could be placed — these problems made Baranof "the Lord of Alaska," a position he controlled all too often with steaming kettles of punch and an ability to out-drink anyone he encountered. Douglas was, despite all his positions, merely a cog in a business empire, well organized and controlled from London. He has been described as "A man of iron nerve and physical prowess, great force of character, keen intelligence, and unusual resourcefulness" and as a "practical man, but yet a visionary" and a "humanitarian". Douglas "treated individuals, including Negro slaves and Indians, with a respect that few of his contemporaries showed."[8]

In part this "respect" can be attributed to Douglas's birth. Too often childhood, and the formative years, are blamed as the cause of flaws in a person's adult character. In Douglas's case his early years appear to have made the man. Douglas was one of three children produced by his father's liaison with a West Indian creole woman, an affair that seems to have continued for some time after the father married a Scottish woman in 1809. Born in 1803 in British Guiana (now Guyana), Douglas was soon taken from his mother's home and placed in a boarding school in Scotland where, he was later to tell his own son, he fought his way through school and made his way by sheer force. Schools of that day were famous for "making or breaking" their boys. Douglas managed well and left with a sound education. Also during this period, or shortly afterwards, he gained a remarkable command of French—a tongue he may have begun learning from his mother.

Early in 1819, Douglas was apprenticed to the North West Company as a clerk. What he had learned in school—attention to details, hard work, and punctuality,—plus his devotion to business and the company, and his continuing pursuit of education, guaranteed Douglas a bright future with the company. After less than ten years of service, no less an official than Governor Simpson wrote that Douglas would be a good man on the council board in time. The essence of his philosophy is found in a letter Douglas wrote a colleague: "obedience is the very first and most important of our duties, like the A.B.C. in literature, the groundwork of all our acquisitions and in fact the great principle which all persons entering this service should be taught to revere."[9]

A duel at Ile-à-la-Crosse with one Pat Cunningham, in which no blood flowed, and at least one official reprimand (for foolhardy actions within gunshot range of an HBC post) did nothing to harm Douglas's career. At 18 he was placed in charge of his first post, and from then on he was a man to watch. In 1839 he was placed in charge of Fort Vancouver in McLoughlin's absence, and during the same period he reached the rank of chief factor. Always a good politician, and noted for his ability to negotiate with the Indians (except the Carriers in north-central British Columbia, who did their level best to murder him), Douglas now proved to be an adaptable negotiator with the Spanish in California and with the Russians at Sitka.

In 1828, Douglas married Amelia Connolly, the half-Indian daughter of Chief Factor William Connolly. This marriage was "according to the custom of the country," but it was later solemnized by a Church of England ceremony at Fort Vancouver in 1837. Douglas's sensitivity to the problems of the blacks and Indians may be a result of the racial background of his own family.

Considering Douglas's philosophical and lifelong devotion to the HBC, and his position in the company, it comes as no surprise to find the first meeting of the Council of Vancouver Island discussing nothing, and the second meeting, April 28, 1852, largely given over to HBC affairs. In fact, most of the meetings up to June 9, 1856, (of which there were only 18) revolved around HBC considerations.

The Colony of Vancouver Island was not a democracy. During this time it was ruled by Douglas for the HBC and, as

COURTESY OF HISTORY DIVISION, BC PROVINCIAL MUSEUM

Sir James Douglas.

pointed out, his fellow council members had direct and long-time connections with the company. Douglas's many hats did not bother him unduly until he found himself also acting as sheriff and judge, which even Douglas realized was too much power for one man. He also may have been tiring of the HBC and Vancouver Island. In 1827 he had come close to retiring, and in September 1850, he wrote that he was tired of the island. At one point Douglas appointed four magistrates, but finding them "ignorant and unreliable," he looked about for competent men.[10] No suitable candidate appeared until David Cameron arrived from Demerara. Though Cameron was a man without any knowledge of the law, Douglas appointed him Judge of the Supreme Court of Civil Justice on December 2, 1853. Ignorant of the law as Cameron was, his credentials were otherwise impressive: he was an HBC employee and Douglas's brother-in-law.

Despite the Colonial Office's confirmation of this appointment, the choice of Cameron did not sit well with the growing anti-Douglas movement at Fort Victoria. This faction, sometimes thought of as independent colonists, consisted of the Reverend Robert John Staines, James Yates, and Captain James Cooper. Two of these men, Yates and Cooper, were former HBC employees, and both were engaged in the liquor traffic Douglas was planning to tax heavily; Staines was the HBC chaplain at the fort. A petition to the British government circulated by these men was to have been presented to the Colonial Office in London by Staines, but unluckily, his ship sank and he drowned. The colony's first chief justice remained in office until 1858 and retired from the bench in 1865.

Judge Cameron's salary was £100 a year. His appointment caused another crisis—how was the colonial government to pay this salary, as the Colonial Office had stressed to ex-governor Blanshard that no salaries were to be paid public officials from the proceeds of the sale of land? This would soon change under Governor Douglas; however, in 1853, the only other legitimate source of revenue was taxes and duties. This "source" was found, and it was doing a land-office business, and it was directly under Douglas's thumb. "Let justice be supported by the emoluments of vice, and let the noble institutions of Europe be planted in America with empty rum-barrels for their foundation," so, very quickly, the men engaged in the liquor traffic found themselves liable for a yearly licence of £120.[11] This paid Cameron's wages.

Between 1853 and 1855 the licences from the liquor dealers amounted to £1,020, and this was the only revenue at the government's disposal. The income from land sales and timber duties was remitted directly to the Colonial Office.

The council and governor met on June 4, 1856, to discuss "certain instructions lately received by him [Douglas] from the Secretary for the Colonies instructing him to call general assemblies of the people, for the purpose of carrying Her Majestys instructions fully into effect and for other objects."[12] This assembly was authorized and commanded by Henry Labouchère, Secretary of State for the Colonies, and Douglas unhappily followed Labouchère's instructions. In Douglas's view "people do not naturally take much interest in affairs of Government as long as affairs go on well and prosperously, and are content to leave questions of state to their ruling class."[13] In making this statement, which is in its own way quite valid, Douglas was wearing his political coat, and theorizing was more convenient than truth at the moment. Affairs were not well and prosperous; the ruling class was the HBC, and the HBC's employees (men of Douglas's background) did not belong, no matter their personal qualifications, to the "class" ruling Britain 6,000 miles away. Douglas was the bastard and creole son of a Glasgow merchant; Finlayson had been born and raised on a sheepman's property in Scotland, and John Tod, the other major HBC figure at Fort Victoria at this time, was the son of a Scottish clerk. Their marriages and their wives' backgrounds were suspect by many, for newcomers, such as Reverend Staines and his wife, were not prepared to accept the long-established standards of western North America.

On June 9, 1856, the council met and decided the qualifications of the voters and the future members of the general assembly. To be a member one had to own £300 of freehold property or immovable estate, absent members were to be permitted to vote through agents or attorneys, and a voter had to own 20 acres of freehold land or more. At the same time four electoral districts were created: Victoria, Esquimalt, Sooke, and Nanaimo.

In Victoria there were five candidates, but in the remaining districts the voting population was so small that their "election" was a nomination process. Seven members were elected at various times and places in July and August to the new House of Assembly and of these, six were directly or indirectly connected to the HBC. E. E. Langford, now the leader of the opposition in the colony, was one of the three members elected in Victoria, but as he failed to meet the property qualifications, his election was declared null and void. At the opening of the new legislative body on August 12, 1856, Douglas gave a short and optimistic speech. Reading it might easily convince one that Douglas had changed his political suit: "I feel assured that as public men holding a solemn and momentous trust you will, as a governing principle, strive with one accord to promote the true and substantial interests of the country, and that our legislative labours will be distinguished alike by prudence, temperance, and justice to all classes."[14] The "classes" were important to Douglas; he had written to the Colonial Secretary a few days after the election that "The affair passed off quietly and did not appear to excite much interest among the lower orders."[15]

At least one member of Douglas's "class" was more realistic. John Work, a retired chief factor, and one of the men who had crossed the Rocky Mountains with McLoughlin, Simpson and Douglas in 1824, wrote to a friend shortly after the election: "Our colony is not increasing in population. The home government leaves us to ourselves to get on as best we may. We have had an election lately of Members of a house of Assembly. It is to consist of 7 members chosen by about 40 voters. I have always considered such a colony & such a government where there are so few people to govern as little better than a farce and this last scene of a house of representatives the most absurd of the whole."[16]

The old chief factor said a great deal else to his friend, none of it very positive, and there were good reasons for his bitter laughter: the assembly had no money for postal services or roads, and its only accessible revenue was from liquor sales, a great deal of which may have been illegal sales to the Indians. The Speaker of the House was Dr. Helmcken, the HBC surgeon, and now Douglas's son-in-law. The truth is that no one on the island had voiced the desire to be self-governing. The creation of an elected assembly was pushed onto the colony by the home government, long before such a thing was required or demanded.

Less than 40 years later, it was claimed that the government, and all of its officials, with the exception of Governor Douglas—who could have managed just as well had he remained a chief factor—was a joke. This statement is substantiated by the *Minutes of the House of Assembly.* As there was no money to build roads, the assembly discussed marking the existing roads, a discussion that leads one to conclude the "roads" were vague trails wandering between the trees without yet the benefit of blazes. Later, a bill was brought forward to define their width. Understandably the licensing acts during this period were of particular moment, especially because this revenue paid the government's bills.

Politically, search as one will, no other events in the public arena appear to be important. Throughout this period the HBC continued to develop its affairs on Vancouver Island, just as it continued to be the "power behind the throne" within the colony. The day J. D. Pemberton notified the assembly, that he would soon table "A Bill on the subject of Castration of Cattle crossing the Plains," marks the low point of the assembly.

Happily for all concerned, American miners were already arriving at Fort Victoria. The gold rush to the lower Fraser, not to be confused with the later Cariboo gold rush, was on. The arrival of the Americans was so sudden, and their numbers so large, the assembly woke up one morning to find reasons for its existence. How welcome this change was to Douglas, with his ability and ambition, is unknown, but all of the HBC officers at Fort Victoria undoubtedly looked back from the end of the next decade, and realized those dry-as-dust days of the mid-1850s were the final hours of the old order.

CHAPTER SIX

Hardrock and Soft

Coal was "discovered" on the east coast of Vancouver Island in 1835. William Fraser Tolmie, an HBC trader and physician stationed at Fort McLoughlin, would later claim the credit for finding this coal. If he did so, he failed to mention it in his diary. Accordingly, an earlier version of the discovery is probably closer to the truth. Kwakiutl Indians on a trading voyage to Fort McLoughlin are said to have wandered into the blacksmith's shop where they remained for some time, apparently fascinated by the forge and the smith's work. On being told the coal for the forge was from the other side of the "great salt sea," a place so distant that it sometimes travelled for half a year or longer before reaching the fort, the Indians laughed at the blacksmith and his story. "White men are very wise! The great spirit tells them everything. The red man knows nothing; he is poor, yet he is not such a fool as to bring soft black stone so great a distance when it may be had at his very door."[1]

Tolmie did write, much later, that "having for two years incited the natives to search for that mineral, he [Tolmie] had the good fortune in 1835 to ascertain the existence on the north-east shore of Vancouver Island of good bituminous coal, which was tested less than a year after on board the company's new steamer, *Beaver*, just out from London."[2] There is a certain amount of double-talk here; he does not mention urging the Indians to look for coal in his diaries, and "ascertain" implies someone told him of the location of the mineral. All of this would be unimportant if it were not for the HBC's latter-day hints that, contrary to the facts, they actually did a fair amount of leg-work on the island. While the coal was used aboard the *Beaver*, the quality was not up to the expected standards. Because of this, it was not until 1849 that the HBC began developing the deposits.

The HBC's quite sudden interest in the island coal was an indirect result of the Oregon Treaty of 1846. Once the American-British ownership question was resolved, William Henry Aspinwall obtained the mail contract between Panama and the Oregon Territory. Transporting coal from Wales was costly, so in 1848 Aspinwall began negotiating with the HBC for Vancouver Island coal. The company men were as anxious to sell the coal as they were to keep the matter of its quality a secret, or perhaps they were hoping the quality would improve once they began to mine beneath the surface. From England the HBC sent out an oversman and six miners to Fort Victoria to prospect the coal fields, and at the same time Sir George Simpson ordered the construction of Fort Rupert, named after Prince Rupert, the HBC's first governor. This fort would serve a dual purpose. It would replace the now-closed Fort McLoughlin and guarantee the safety of the miners.

On May 10, 1849, the officers and men from the abandoned fort at the mouth of the Stikine River reached Beaver Harbour aboard the *Constantine*, a brig chartered from the Russian American Company and towed to Vancouver Island by the *Beaver*. Immediately on their arrival they began clearing land and building Fort Rupert. Surveying the coal deposits at the time, Chief Factor Work reported the coal fields as extensive as thought, and Douglas commented in a later report that the mining operations might someday be transferred to the head of Quatsino Sound, a port more suitable for ocean-going vessels.

The first group of miners arrived at Fort Victoria aboard the *Harpooner,* on June 1, 1849. John Muir was the oversman, and the others were all members of his family. All of the miners, except John Muir, immediately lodged a complaint with James Douglas. They had been given inferior beef on board the *Harpooner,* they said, and the officers, though not the captain, had spoken to them roughly and without reason. The complaint was a warning of things to come: less than a year later these same men held the island's first strike.

Captain William Henry McNeill was in charge of Fort Rupert and his son-in-law, George Blenkinsop, a young clerk, was second in command. John Muir, his sons, and other relatives, arrived there on September 24, 1849, only to discover the fort unfinished and proper tools unavailable. The men were a proud lot; they knew their own worth, and they owed no loyalty to the HBC, in this case Captain McNeill, who considered them common labourers. The coal fields, so impressive to Tolmie and Work, turned out to be worthless, and this, along with what Andrew Muir and others considered as the company's failure to meet its obligations, plus poor food and Indian problems, led to a series of confrontations with the HBC. Blenkinsop, in charge of Fort Rupert in McNeill's absence, foolishly brought matters to a head, by arresting Andrew Muir and his cousin, John McGregor, for sedition—at least Muir was overheard to proclaim the revolution was on its way. Shortly afterwards four other men were forced to join Muir and McGregor. After being released from their irons early in May, all six were held behind pickets until June 15. Once free, two of these men shook the Vancouver Island mist from their hair and took off for California.

The young miners would have, no doubt, come to terms with the HBC's local policy had it not been for the living conditions at the fort. It is not known what they were told in Great Britain regarding what to expect, but the truth came as a cold shock, just as it did to Governor Blanshard. The Muirs were not even settled in before 16 war canoes, fresh from a successful strike against an unknown southern tribe, landed and set up 16 poles on the beach. Atop each pole the Indians placed a human head—trophies of war—as was their custom. These warriors were in a good mood, and certainly there was nothing small about them, for they offered Mrs. Muir her choice of any two heads. Whether or not the good lady understood that this offer was made honourably is not recorded.

Dr. Helmcken thought Fort Rupert looked like a small version of Victoria, with its rectangular shape, pickets, and bastions with cannon standing ready. A house was set on either side of the entrance, and this formed an alley, with gates at either end, which was used for trading. Unlike the practice at Fort Victoria, Indians were not allowed in the open yard of the fort. All well and good, but the rations were something else. Except for the staples, the food supply was purchased from the local Indians; not everyone enjoys or has the stomach for fresh venison and duck and grouse daily. There was no domestic meat or fowl available, not fresh at any rate. Mail service was non-existent; nor was there any money circulating at the fort, the currency being trading goods. Helmcken enjoyed all the fresh air, and his cabin without windows or stove, but the doctor did not spend his days labouring in a coal pit.

Hamilton Moffatt, an HBC surveyor later to take charge of Fort Rupert, described the fort in 1856 as having two bastions and four cannon; a garden outside the stockade was large and well tended. Not all the events at Fort Rupert during this period were negative, for in 1852 Moffatt left the east coast for Nootka Sound via the unknown interior. Moffatt was 20 that summer and a relative newcomer, having arrived from England in 1850. The reason for his overland crossing of Vancouver Island is not known. Presumably he was following James Douglas's instructions, and the vague generalities in his "Remarks" at the conclusion of his journal of the trip suggest he was a poor choice. No matter: to Moffatt goes the honour of being the first European known to cross the island.

Leaving Fort Rupert on July 1, 1852, Moffatt camped the first night at the mouth of the Nimpkish River, and the next morning began his ascent of that river with six Indians. After travelling the length of Nimpkish Lake, then known as T'sllelth Lake, and entering the Nimpkish River, which he called River Oakseey, Moffatt and his men camped. The night of July 2 was "a most unpleasant night, on account of the rain which poured down in torrents the whole time," and the next morning, happy to be moving and warmer, the men continued upriver to Waakash. This camp or village was the halfway house to the second lake. While walking to Lake Kanus, now Vernon Lake, Moffatt "was informed of a tribe of Indians living inland, having no canoes or connection with the sea-coast whatever. I have since learned that these people sometimes descend some of the rivers for the purpose of trade with the Indians south of Nootka, and they offered to guide me to the place at any time I should wish; the name of the tribe is Säa Käalituck; they number about fifty or sixty men, and were only discovered a few years back, by one of the Nimpkish chiefs while on a trapping expedition."[3]

This inland tribe would haunt Vancouver Island writers until Robert Brown, making the first major exploration of the island's interior in the mid-1860s, put the matter to rest. The "Säa Käalituck" proved to be Nootka or Salish (depending on where they were sighted) hunting parties. The proof Brown offered was either ignored or soon forgotten by the credulous; an unknown interior race was a good story and it continued to be told and elaborated on until the turn of the century.

Late on July 5, Moffatt and his men reached Tlupana Inlet, which they descended the next day, reaching Friendly Cove at four P.M. The Indians were friendly and Moffatt enjoyed himself, eating and gossiping in the long houses of the chiefs, all of whom, he thought, were the best of friends.

As the coal mines at Fort Rupert were a bust, it is not unreasonable to guess that Douglas sent Moffatt across the island in the hopes he would discover new coal fields. But Moffatt was not a geologist, as his comments show: "The various kinds of rock along the bed of the river, as far as I could see, were granite, sandstone, conglomerate, and hard dark boulders."[4]

Douglas was desperate for lucrative coal fields. The colony, if it were to survive, needed revenue. £25,000 had been wasted in the attempt to make the Fort Rupert fields profitable, and all he had to show for his efforts and expenditures was the now-lucrative trading post of Fort Rupert with annual profits of £4,100 or more. This trading income was not colony revenue but the HBC's. Elsewhere, the customers complained of the quality of Vancouver Island coal, as well as the company's inability to supply it reliably. By the early 1850s another nearby market opened up as California boomed, the population growing from 15,000 in 1848 to 250,000 in 1852. The demand for coal was enormous, and filling the demands would solve the colony's financial problems, if a high-quality field could be located.

There are large deposits of coal on Vancouver Island. Most of it is either practically inaccessible because of the rough west coast, or of poor quality such as the fields at Fort Rupert, but there are several major deposits that could be mined easily. As luck would have it for Douglas and the colony, an Indian brought one to the attention of the company in 1849. As the story of the way the Indian came to tell of the existence of this coal is practically identical to what happened at Fort McLoughlin 14 years earlier, it can be discounted. At the time no one paid much attention to the Indian, but this changed in 1850 when he appeared with a canoe-load of the mineral. His efforts were rewarded with a bottle of whisky and the nickname "Coal Tyee" ("the coal chief").

Joseph William McKay, then a trader with the HBC at Fort Victoria, and later to be one of the members of the first House of Assembly of the Colony of Vancouver Island in 1856, returned to the source with "Coal Tyee" and discovered the

Douglas Vein, which was still being worked 28 years later. After McKay's return to Fort Victoria, he made a brief but favourable report, yet for some reason, and this was probably the still-continuing exploration of the coal beds at Fort Rupert, miners did not begin to work the Douglas Vein until 1852.

The vein was on the shores of what was known locally as "Wentuhuysen Inlet" or "Nanymo Bay," a place the Indians called *"Syn-ny-mo,"* which J. D. Pemberton later corrupted to form "Nanaimo".

Douglas's correspondence is largely that of a businessman, matter of fact and to the point, but after he visited Nanaimo in 1853, a new and ecstatic tone echoes in many of his letters. No wonder—the economic potential was tremendous. Even a year earlier he acted like a man seeing the answer to his dreams, when he ordered McKay "to proceed with all possible diligence to Wentuhuysen Inlet, and formally take possession of the Coal beds lately discovered there for and in behalf of the Hudson's Bay Company."[5] What was Douglas afraid of? The Royal Grant of 1849 gave the mineral rights on the island to the company. One possible explanation of Douglas's haste was the potential American threat to the coal fields. As this hardly appears a likelihood at the height of a gold rush, Douglas's haste implies a greater fear of his southern neighbours than usually suspected.

He further ordered McKay to forbid anyone but those authorized by the HBC to work the beds, directly or indirectly. Two days later he again wrote McKay, this time to say that the first group of miners was on the way from Fort Victoria aboard the HBC's brigantine *Cadboro*. Douglas had had no direct involvement with the strike at Fort Rupert, but he was not one to ignore the lessons learned by others. John Muir was hired from his Sooke farm, which he had bought the previous year after his contract at the first mine expired, to act as oversman for the incoming miners, and Douglas wrote McKay, telling him that the miners would follow only the orders of John Muir, and McKay was not to interfere with them, or give them orders except through their oversman.

The miners, all of whom were Muir's sons or nephews (including the two who had earlier decamped for California) reached Nanaimo on September 3 and six days later the *Cadboro* was loaded with 480 barrels of coal and ready to return to Fort Victoria. This was the first commercial load of coal to be shipped from Nanaimo. The mines continued to be worked until 1950 when the last major mine, The White Rapids, closed down.

Building at Nanaimo started almost immediately. The Muirs' house was the first built, followed by less important structures. In June 1853 the bastion, still standing in downtown Nanaimo, was completed by Leon Labine and Jean Ba'tiste Fortier and a crew of labourers. Fortier was such a fine axe-man that he would bet anyone with the money to match him that he could be dragged naked over any of the timbers he produced and not

COURTESY OF HISTORY DIVISION, BC PROVINCIAL MUSEUM

Bastion, still standing in Nanaimo, built in 1853.

pick up one splinter. The bastion's armament consisted of two six-pound carronades. Other houses and a store surrounded by pickets, and under the protection of the bastion, were finished that summer.

Life in this mining village was not as prosperous as might be expected. Late in the fall of 1853, McKay wrote Douglas to say provisions were running short: only 22 barrels of salmon had been packed and the potatoes were "rather dull". Douglas in reply was not sympathetic; the stock at Fort Victoria was no more plentiful, and could not feed the fort's inhabitants. McKay, the miners and their families survived, and were joined by 83 men, women and children, from England the next year. The heads of the families were 22 Staffordshire miners, and their arrival can be said to mark the second stage of Nanaimo's history. Unlike Fort Rupert, a true community existed at Nanaimo.

Vital it may have been, impressive it was not. Pemberton described it in 1860 as a town where the HBC had put up about 40 houses and sheds, and two steam engines, which made it look like a prosperous village, and then went on to say that a large amount of mineral property remained unclaimed. About the same time another visitor saw a town standing "upon a singular promontory. Along the shore are the collier buildings, and about a dozen remarkably sooty houses, inhabited by the miners and the few Hudson's Bay Company officers. There is a resident doctor in the place, and to the left [of the houses] stands the Company's old bastion, on which are mounted the four or five honeycombed 12-pounders, with which the great Fur Company have been wont to awe the neighbouring Indians into respect and submission."[6]

At this time the resources of Nanaimo and the adjoining area were considered by some to be underdeveloped. The means of delivering coal to the waiting vessels was so rudimentary that many ships lay at anchor for up to a month before a cargo could be loaded. What lay behind many of these problems was the American market: it did not materialize. The agents of the Pa-

Nanaimo waterfront, ca *1910.*

cific Mail Steamship Company and other companies asserted that for a number of reasons Nanaimo coal was not economical, even at half the price of English coal. The HBC operated the Nanaimo mines for nine years under the unofficial title of the Nanaimo Coal Company, but coal was never the answer to Douglas's financial problems.

By the time Pemberton wrote of Nanaimo, it was obvious to the HBC men that they could not fulfill their colonization agreement with the Colonial Office. Accordingly, the company began to sell all of its holdings not directly connected with the fur trade. By 1862, the HBC control of the Nanaimo coal fields had passed to the Vancouver Coal Mining and Land Company, a British corporation, for the reported price of £40,000.

Five years earlier the take-over by a private company might have been a landmark move, indicating that the HBC was losing its grip on Vancouver Island. As it happened, the sale made no long-term difference to the island's future; events in 1858 had changed everything. In January 1858, James Douglas controlled all the land and nearly every aspect of life west of the Rocky Mountains and north of Puget Sound; he was, as has aptly been said, the tzar of this territory. Due to events unimaginable to Douglas and the company that January, by the time the coal fields passed into private hands the HBC no longer controlled Vancouver Island, nor the mainland of what is now British Columbia. The company was disappearing into the northern forests as quietly as the small animals on which its fortunes were based.

Alfred Waddington, later to play a role of no little significance in British Columbian and Canadian history, landed at Fort Victoria early in 1858 and "found a quiet village of about 800 inhabitants. No noise, no bustle, no gamblers, no speculators or interested parties to preach up this or underrate that. A few quiet, gentlemanly-behaved inhabitants, chiefly Scotchmen, secluded as it were from the whole world. As to business there was none, the streets were grown over with grass, and there was not even a cart."[7] Waddington came as a businessman to open a grocery, and he remained through the spring and summer of 1858 to watch Fort Victoria change, once and forever.

In one brief summer of hope and dreams, gold did what the HBC and the Colonial Office could not. Gold brought people through Fort Victoria—some 30,000 during the spring and summer of 1858. Since the days of the Spanish, rumours of gold deposits on the west coast had circulated, and still do, but no one could locate gold in paying quantities. During 1852–53, a gold flurry took place in the Queen Charlotte Islands. Some say the first gold discovered on the mainland turned up at Fort Kamloops (today Kamloops) and was bought by Chief Trader McLean in 1852. Two other discoveries, both in the Oregon Territory, at about the same time, are sometimes called the "first" discoveries. Gold was definitely discovered in British territory along the Thompson River in 1856, and a year later an unknown number of American prospectors were active in the area. British Columbia's first true gold rush centred on the lower Fraser River in 1858. Although there were several routes, some difficult and others nearly impossible, most of the miners jumped aboard one of the many ships now making the passage from San Francisco to Victoria.

The village was not prepared for this onslaught. Except for James Douglas, everyone was caught flat-footed. Perhaps suspecting what might occur, Douglas issued a proclamation in December 1857. In it Douglas claimed all the gold that lay in the districts of the Fraser and Thompson rivers for the Crown, and made the taking of such gold without authorization illegal. Those without permission from Her Majesty's Colonial Office to dig or transport gold would be prosecuted. What this came to mean was that every miner leaving Victoria for the bars of the Fraser had to purchase a ten-shilling mining licence, which was good for only a month. This fee was soon raised to 21 shillings (about five dollars US at the time), and to enforce this a British gunboat was stationed at the mouth of the Fraser River.

Strictly speaking, Douglas had no legal power to make or enforce this proclamation. He knew this better than anyone else in Victoria, but the events leading up to the Oregon Treaty were still fresh in his mind; he could foresee that same scenario taking place north of the 49th parallel. So he did what had been in McLoughlin's power to do: he imposed the authority of the Crown from the very outset.

In London the Colonial Office saw the merit in Douglas's actions on July 16, 1858, though warning him in doing so against "using the powers hereby intrusted to you in maintenance of the interest of the Hudson's Bay Company in the territory [the mainland]."[8] The ink on this document was barely dry when the British government made the mainland a Crown Colony with essentially the boundaries it retains today. Only Vancouver Island remained outside the shape of British Columbia. At the request of the Colonial Secretary, Sir Edward Bulwer Lytton, Queen Victoria personally named the new colony "British Columbia" at the same time as the colony was given its boundaries, on August 2, 1858.

Not unexpectedly Governor James Douglas was made Governor of the Colony of British Columbia. Now he could wear two hats, but there was a catch: if he accepted this second position, he had to sever all of his ties with the HBC. When he did so, it was with the promise of a six-year term as governor at what finally amounted to nearly £5,000 yearly—quite a raise from the £1,000 first offered. How much difference his retirement from the HBC actually made is debatable. It has been pointed out that Douglas was neither by birth nor experience democratic, and to the end of his life, he remained at heart the Chief Factor of the Columbia District.

The effect of the gold rush on Victoria was immediate. James Bell, a California merchant writing home to his brother in Scotland, observed: "For years every thing seems to have gone on with these People in the same easy old country style, till the sudden rush awoke them from their lethargy; Land stock and produce of every description went up at once to prices they never before dreamt of." Bell was one of the first of many California merchants to open outlets in Victoria: "When I landed in the middle of July, it presented something of San Francisco in 1849, though of course not so extensive the suburbs white with Tents, while the few streets were alive with a heterogeneous crowd of adventurers, in which every country of the world seemed to be represented."[9]

As far as business was concerned: "It was thought real estate was held at a figure that could not be sustained, yet there has been little depreciation; I paid for the lot on which I built my store, twenty feet by seventy feet deep—two thousand dollars, which is still an average price. Victoria is a free port to goods of every description, from every part of the world; No where is business so little trammeled; I have a business going on there successfully, which has been established now over seven months, yet I have never been asked for one penny, either towards town improvement, or Government expenses."[10]

During the spring and summer of 1858, Victoria's population rose from nearly 500 to 5,000. In 1859 the population fell to 1,500, creating the town's first depression. New Westminster was one cause behind this economic slump. Laid out in 1859,

New Westminster was the capital of British Columbia; Victoria was merely the capital of Vancouver Island. The mainland town, located on the northern bank of the Fraser River, was the terminus for the miners arriving by sea; whatever Victoria might be was purely incidental to these miners. Another reason for the 1859 depression was the location of the new gold fields. The prospectors were no longer working the lower river; the centres of the activities were now far inland in the Quesnel vicinity.

Victoria continued to grow slowly, but it failed to regain the momentum of 1858. An 1860 map of Victoria shows a well-developed townsite, and on December 15 of that year the *British Colonist* noted that the stockade, which surrounded the old fort yard, was rapidly coming down, piece by piece, for firewood. So life continued until the winter of 1863–64.

No doubt even the most optimistic businessman that winter could see the end of the gold rush. Such things do not last long and many of the city's businessmen had witnessed the brief lives of the rushes in California and Australia. Painfully obvious also was the possibility of a future union of the colonies of British Columbia and Vancouver Island. If this happened, New Westminster, with a population larger than Victoria, just as British Columbia's population was many times larger than Vancouver Island's, was a sure bet to be the new capital. Except for its historical and traditional significance, and its abundance of natural beauty, Victoria was not the logical site for the capital. Worse—if Victoria did not become the capital of the united colonies, what would keep the town alive? The fur trade was virtually history; farming and ranching near Victoria were small scale and primitive, compared to the holdings of Americans and eastern Canadians farming the Fraser River delta; there was no industry, and while coal mining was expanding, that wealth now belonged to foreign investors.

The town of Victoria was substantial. "Starting from the corner of Fort and Government Streets, with a radius of three quarters of a mile, the town site covers two-thirds of a circle,

Douglas Street, Victoria, at the corner of Johnson, ca 1875.

stretching round the harbour. The streets in general are sixty feet wide, and cross each other at right angles," and there was "a race-course and cricket-ground" in the "magnificent natural park, called Beaconhill. The Government offices, Supreme Court, and the hall occupied by the Parliament, form one pile of buildings, and are situated some distance from the chief thoroughfare of the town, on James's Bay." The major streets were macadamized and there were wooden sidewalks; the upper section of the harbour was lined with "Large and substantial stone and brick warehouses, well stocked with goods"; there was a theatre that could seat 400 and was "sometimes visited by able and respectable dramatic *troupes,* though it is to be regretted that taste for the noblest form of the drama is not general in these parts"; and there were "Drinking saloons, which abound vastly out of proportion to the wants of the population," that supplied dubious entertainment, but were "much patronised." [11]

Solid as all of this was, it could not survive without a growing population and development. It had to be the centre of
something, but just what was the question nagging away at the
minds of the founding fathers. Thus was born, out of desperation and civic pride, the Vancouver Island Exploring Expedition. Victoria's logic was simple: if gold had "made" the town,
it could save her. Publicly, it was claimed the purpose of the expedition was to explore and map the island's interior, (originally suggested by Governor Douglas in 1862), which was still
almost unknown and, as a journalist of the day wrote: "to un-
fold to the world our hidden treasures".[12]

Nothing suggests many were hoodwinked by such rhetoric.
Up to the spring of 1864 few people, including the HBC, had
shown any interest in the island's geography inside the coastal
fringe. Unless mineral deposits were found on Victoria's door-
step, the town would gain little; another island centre—like
Nanaimo—would arise. Agriculture and logging could do nothing for Victoria's faltering economy in the short run. Only a
gold rush would cure the sick lady's health. Everyone knew that
the expedition would actually be seeking gold, yet the politicians continued the facade by appointing Robert Brown, who
had mysteriously become "Dr. Brown" during his voyage from
Edinburgh to the Alberni Mills at the head of Alberni Inlet, as
Commander and Government Agent for the VIEE.

A surprisingly comprehensive report had been read to the
Royal Geographical Society in London on June 22, 1857, by
Lieutenant-Colonel W. C. Grant, FRGS, Vancouver Island's
first colonist—a man who will be dealt with later. After
Hamilton Moffatt crossed the island in 1852, Adam Horne
made two trips from Nanaimo to the west coast and back in
1856 in the company of Toma Ouamtomy, sometimes de-
scribed as an Iroquois hunter and secret agent for James
Douglas. J. D. Pemberton crossed the island twice also, from
Qualicum to Alberni Inlet in 1856, and a year later from the
Cowichan settlement to Nitinat—one of the early names for the
Alberni Inlet-Barkley Sound area. The latest trip had been made

by Commander R. C. Mayne during May 1861. Nothing significant is known about Horne's trips; Pemberton's reports to Governor Douglas are brief, being little more than expanded field notes; while Mayne's comments are a result of his exploration for a possible route on which to build a road between the head of Alberni Inlet and Nanaimo, one that would connect with another proposed road from Fort Rupert to Nanaimo.

The choice of Robert Brown probably hinged on no more than his earlier and minor explorations of the island on behalf of the British Columbia Botanical Association. He was also not much of a drinking man, and drinking had reached epidemic proportions on the island since 1858. The politicians chose Frederick Whymper as the expedition's artist; Whymper was a well-known local artist, the son and brother of two better-known British artists, who would later gain a certain amount of fame but not fortune as one of the first men to note the presence of gold in the sands of the Yukon River. The remaining choices were hard-headed decisions. Peter Leech and John Buttle were former members of the Royal Engineers; Ranald McDonald was the son of an HBC factor and had grown up in the BC interior; and John Foley was a true prospector, having mined in California, the lower Fraser, and the Cariboo gold fields. Of the other men almost nothing is known, but all were guided by the mysterious one-armed "Toma Antonine" (Toma Ouamtomy), who appears to have known the interior of the island intimately.

It was a curious group, but it was the first expedition to set out to explore the interior. Most of their names still exist on Vancouver Island landmarks, and Brown's map of the island, published in Germany in 1869, was the basis for all future maps of the island. Brown and Whymper wrote about the island in their later, literary years in London, and Brown must be given credit for the first short story set on the island. All of this was in the future, however, as the men made their way up the Cowichan River on June 10, 1864.

After a rough crossing of the island, they reached Nitinat

Lake and the Indian village of Whyac. Here they split into two parties; one crossed overland to Port San Juan, while the other followed the coast. From Port San Juan they travelled together to the mouth of the Sooke River. This they ascended and a few days later, on July 21, John Foley discovered gold on a river the men named the "Leech". Gold had been found earlier below this spot, but not, according to Whymper's journal, in the quantities discovered by Foley.

The Vancouver Island Exploring Expedition proved its devotion to duty by moving on from the Leech River and leaving behind it Vancouver Island's first gold rush. Foley, the only experienced prospector in the group, accompanied the VIEE for several days but, finally unable to resist the lure of gold, returned to join in the rush. The expedition found no more gold of importance, but did locate coal in the vicinity of Comox-Courtenay. It was a rich vein: "one of the finest seams of coal hitherto discovered, at least as far as the outcrop is a criterion, on the Pacific coast."[13] Robert Brown, usually far more optimistic than circumstances and good sense dictated, was for once right. In 1869 11 miners began prospecting in Brown's footsteps, and their work led directly to the founding of Cumberland (or "Union" as it was first known), which later became part of the largest coal empire in the Canadian west.

Meanwhile on the Sooke and Leech rivers a rush was on. Brown had reported the existence of 25 miles of "diggings" or mining country, and predicted the region would employ 4,000 men. From all major nearby points prospectors and dreamers flocked to the area. At the height of the rush during the late summer of 1864, the *Enterprise* entered Sooke Inlet daily with an estimated 100 passengers, and one man watching the overland exodus claimed the road leading out of Victoria was black with moving men.

Prospectors at the Wake-Up Jake claim were finding about $22 of gold daily, while Thain & Company were earning $34 *per diem* with the assistance of a rocker. By one count 227 mining licences were issued by early August. Construction of a

Main street of Cumberland, ca *1910.*

town named Kennedy Flat, in honour of Captain Arthur Edward Kennedy, the new governor of Vancouver Island, began shortly after the initial strike. A newspaper of the day thought the place would appear to be a thriving, picturesque, mining town—if the streets were cleared of brush and stumps. Six stores, three hotels, and other businesses were doing well at Kennedy Flat, a townsite which came to be known as "Leechtown". Kennedy, who had been appointed governor when Douglas's six-year term expired earlier in 1864, reported Victoria's population was nearly depleted by the rush to the new gold fields. The road from Victoria to Metchosin was improved, and the almost-impassable wagon road from there to the tiny settlement near the mouth of Sooke River was rebuilt. From there pack trails were cut in to the Sooke Hills and the "diggings".

It was quite a spectacle, this rush from Victoria to Leechtown, and it must have allowed the city fathers a breathing spell. Their wildest fancies were coming to life before their eyes. The *British Colonist* predicted that before long people would see a series of busy seacoast towns from Esquimalt to Alberni, all of which would be, of course, extensions of Victoria.

Regrettably for all concerned, the Leech River excitement died less than a year after it began. The failure of these gold fields corresponded with the dwindling imports and exports from Victoria's free port, the failure of the Cariboo mines, and an ever-increasing public debt. But there was hope in the offing when Kennedy's appointment as the governor of the colony was announced in London in December 1863.

Governor Douglas's term of office would expire early in 1864, and many saw this break with the HBC and the island's past as the dawning of a new era. After almost 20 years of army service, Kennedy had sold his commission in 1847, then worked for the British government in Ireland until 1851. In 1852 he entered the colonial service and for the next ten years served as governor at various places in Africa and Australia. His vigour and courage when confronted by problems, and his success in dealing with them, earned him the reputation as one of the best governors in the colonial service. Here was a man who might solve Vancouver Island's problems, and when he arrived on March 25, 1864, the press and public welcomed Kennedy with enthusiasm.

CHAPTER SEVEN

Breaking the Land

It has been claimed that John Mackey, left by Captain James Strange at Nootka Sound in 1786, was Vancouver Island's first settler. As the goats he took ashore either soon died from natural causes or for the sake of Nootka diners, the seeds he supposedly had with him were not planted, and Mackey himself spent most of that winter hiding under trees, he can hardly be considered a settler. A settler cames to stay; he clears land, erects houses and sheds, plants gardens and then fields, and raises his family on the land. Thus the Spanish at Friendly Cove, although they did clear land, plant gardens and raise livestock, cannot be thought of as settlers.

During the 1840s and early 1850s, island agriculture was limited to subsistence gardening and company farms. The first farming at the fort (on either side of Fort Street above Government) was subsistence gardening. Later, the large-scale farming on the part of the HBC and the Puget's Sound Agricultural Company was, beyond the immediate necessity of feeding the HBC employees and their families, a business venture. One reason the PSAC took up land on the island was their sinking financial condition south of the 49th parallel. In one way the Oregon Treaty was to their benefit. It was decided that if they could sell their southern holdings to the Americans, and obtain the best available land near Fort Victoria, this would not only revive their finances, it would force later colonists to settle the undeveloped land beyond their own, and this would increase the value of the PSAC holdings.

In 1849, when the island was opened to colonization, the HBC owned 3,084 acres surrounding Fort Victoria, and the Puget's Sound Agricultural Company owned either 30 or 40 square miles of the best land outside the HBC reserve. Douglas's census of Vancouver Island taken in December 1854 is illuminating. The population was close to 774; 151 lived in Nanaimo, 232 at Fort Victoria, 154 in the four farms operated by the PSAC, 84 at farms owned by HBC or retired HBC personnel, and 41 must be subtracted as they lived on San Juan Island. These figures imply that of the 733 people living on the island in 1854, at least 621 were directly connected to the HBC and PSAC. As these companies were one and the same (as maintained by former Governor Blanshard at hearings held in London in 1857), it may be that only 112 people living on the island at this time were economically independent of the HBC. It is not possible to determine from this census just how "independent" many of these people may have been; out of 37 districts listed by Douglas, six (with a combined population of 53) can no longer be identified, and these may well have been connected to the company in ways now forgotten.

Clearly, colonization at this point is not comparable to the settlement of the Oregon Territory. Another major difference between the southern policy and the HBC's was the cost of settling. One pound an acre may not have seemed high to some, but those who felt the price fair were rich men, and rich men could afford to remain in Great Britain. Besides, if one was going to emigrate, why not go to the United States where land was virtually free? Thousands did and not only because of the cost of land: there was "the heavy expense of bringing out him-self and his family, if he had one, in order to obtain a title to the waste lands of this far-away island [Vancouver Island], he must bring out other men or other families."[1]

As if this were not bad enough, and the truth of the HBC's control appears to have been well known in Britain at the time, the southern end of the island was neither mapped nor sur-veyed. Potential colonists were not even able to study the lay of the land before emigrating. No lines of willing colonists queued at the Colonial Office's door; in fact, only one person decided Vancouver Island was the land of the future for a fresh and vigorous young man.

At 24, Walter Coloquhoun Grant had been the youngest cap-tain in the British army. That was in 1846 and Grant's future was assured, yet by 1848, the loss of his personal fortune had forced him to leave the army and, apparently with nothing bet-ter in sight, he began negotiations with the HBC for 200 acres of land. In this he was successful and agreed, as stipulated in the colonization plan, to bring out the necessary men.

Grant's men arrived at Fort Victoria aboard the *Harpooner* early in the summer of 1849. They waited two months for Grant, during which time Douglas found it difficult to keep them on the island (the California gold rush was a magnet for men everywhere), but Grant finally arrived on August 11, 1849. Not only did he arrive broke, when he came ashore at Clover Point he almost immediately shot a cow thinking it was a buffalo. This was an ominous start for his career as a colonist.

The land around the fort was anything but the open prairie Grant expected, not that this mattered to any real extent for it was already owned by the HBC and their interests. Douglas suggested Grant choose land at Metchosin, which was at least close to the developed areas. Instead, he decided to settle at a location Douglas called "*Sy-yausung*," better known even then as "Soke" or "Sooke".

Twenty-five miles west of Fort Victoria, Sooke Inlet was to-tally isolated, and the only other inhabitants were some 60 Indians. Though initially Grant claimed to have had difficulty with these people, in 1857 he maintained there had been no problem in dealing with the Sooke Indians, and the subsequent relationship was friendly. There Grant cleared and cultivated some 35 acres, raised stock and poultry, built houses and barns, and set up a sawmill beside a small and powerful stream.

While still in London, Grant had contracted to become a surveyor for the HBC and this makes him the island's first surveyor, but as he knew nothing, or next to nothing, about surveying, it is not surprising that he tendered his resignation in March 1850. Grant failed to complete even a single survey, according to Douglas, but he apparently did establish the perimeter of John Tod's estate at Oak Bay. A sketch of the southern coast of the island was given to Douglas, but this handiwork of Grant's has not survived.

An impressive array of debts in the colony, isolation at Sooke, troubles with his men and the local Indians, the HBC's lack of interest in his problems as a colonist, high export taxes imposed on his lumber by the company, and a generally depressed economy partially due to the California gold rush, all combined to break Grant's early enthusiasm. Late in 1850 he sailed for the Hawaiian Islands, returned briefly the next year and rented his farm to one of his men, then departed for California. Two years later he returned to the island only long enough to sell his holdings to John Muir of Fort Rupert, then left the island forever. Back in London Grant rejoined the army and died at Saugor, India, in 1861.

Grant's intentions were good, but from the very beginning of his association with Vancouver Island his luck was bad, and his plans always better than his abilities to carry them out. He was an army man and had grown up within a military atmosphere. Grant's early captaincy proves his abilities in that field, but the rude life of Fort Victoria, where he was quite a favourite (even Douglas is restrained in his criticism of the man), bore little resemblance to life at the Royal Military Academy of Sandhurst, his last posting before leaving the army. Still, he was the island's first independent colonist, its first surveyor, and a pioneer in the lumber industry. A detailed *Description of Vancouver Island,* read by Grant before the Royal Geographical Society in 1857, remains an interesting document. It is also said that Grant imported the broom (locally called "Scotch" or "golden" broom) now growing everywhere along the roads of southern Vancouver Island.

By the end of 1850 the only other independent settler on the island was John Tod, so some authorities claim. When he bought 100 acres of land at Oak Bay, he was on leave from his position as a chief trader with the HBC. Two years later, at the age of 58, Tod retired to what is usually referred to as his "Oak Bay Estate". From 1851 to 1858 he served as a member of the Legislative Council of Vancouver Island and was, like his fellow members, very much a company man. That a man with Tod's affiliations can be termed a colonist is open to question, and certainly one long-time contemporary did not see him as such. Former Chief Factor Roderick Finlayson wrote; "After Grant came Cooper."[2]

Captain James Cooper was English and went down to the sea early. By the time he was 23 he was working for the HBC's marine service and by 1849, when he was 28, Cooper was captain of the HBC's barque *Columbia.* For reasons that are not clear he decided to take up land on Vancouver Island, so he sailed from England as a passenger with his family and sections of a small iron vessel aboard the *Tory,* which reached Fort Victoria on May 14, 1851. Governor Blanshard wrote that the *Tory* landed some 120 people at the fort, only two of whom were not HBC servants. The second person was Thomas Blinkhorn, an English stock-raiser, who had worked in Australia from 1837 to 1849, and was now Cooper's partner. On Section 1 of the Metchosin Land District, they established Bilston Farm, part of which fronted on Witty's Lagoon.

Cooper's iron vessel, the *Alice,* 45 tons burden, was the first iron vessel built (or assembled) on Vancouver Island. Her owner's first venture was to open up a cranberry and potato trade

with the Fraser River Indians. As the HBC had complete trading privileges with the Indians by law, Douglas soon put a stop
to Cooper's enterprise; this apparently soured Cooper for the
rest of his life, since as late as 1878 he was still unable to say
anything good about the HBC on Vancouver Island.

The two men took up 300 acres and from 1851 to 1857
Cooper called himself a colonist. According to some the farm
was a success until 1856, when Blinkhorn died; Cooper, talking
about it years later, said he did not think the farm at all successful. In 1855, there were only five people on Bilston Farm: two
adults and three children. From the outset the erstwhile HBC
hand fought an uphill war with his former employees until it
was common knowledge that the company stifled Cooper's at-
tempts to farm at Metchosin. This opinion was not entirely
unjust; both Grant and Cooper had spent all of their money,
but due to HBC interference, the work came to nothing.

Now that colonists were arriving on the island, another element of society began to change. So far as is known, life at the
fort was largely a bachelor society. Charles Ross had brought
his wife and family to the fort in 1843, but the three younger
children, Walter, Charles and Elizabeth, were almost immediately sent to school in England. As Ross's wife, Isabella, is almost never mentioned during the earliest period of the fort's
history, she, like the other Indian and half-breed wives of the
HBC men, probably kept to herself. Governor Blanshard was a
bachelor, as was Roderick Finlayson until 1849 when he
married one of the half-breed daughters of John Work.
Although Amelia Douglas was also of mixed blood, several features set her off from the other wives. When the Douglas family
arrived at Fort Victoria, Amelia had been married for 18 years;
she was the daughter of a chief factor and the wife of a man
who was markedly successful, and had spent years as one of the
important women at Fort Vancouver. If James Douglas's rising
star did not put her in a special light, where she moved with
ease, her five good-looking daughters would have done it in
Fort Victoria society.

These women were certainly the first at Fort Victoria, yet they came as HBC wives and daughters, and remained throughout the fort's earliest years part of a society in which their roles were dictated by their husbands' positions with the company. Also, as these women were all raised on, and accustomed to, life on the frontier, their presence at the fort did not mark a departure from the old order. This only began happening when the first European women arrived with their husbands.

The first such woman to arrive from outside an HBC background was Emma Frances Staines, the wife of the newly appointed Fort Victoria chaplain and school-master. The Reverend Robert John Staines and his wife reached Vancouver Island on March 17, 1849. In a letter dealing with his appointment, Staines described his wife as "perfectly qualified to take every department in the usual course of a gentlewoman's education, including music and French, of both which she is *perfectly mistress*, and Italian and German sufficiently to read and translate."[3]

Like many of the other early arrivals at the fort, the Staines were shocked by what they saw. At this time there were no streets, and the traffic cut up the roads so badly that, if the ground was wet, men and women had to wear sea boots to make their way through the deep mud that all too quickly turned to gumbo. Finlayson saw the couple ashore, and was ashamed of the conditions, so he had planks laid down to enable the Staines to walk safely to the fort. There they expressed "deep surprise" as "they looked around wonderingly at the bare walls of the buildings," before telling Finlayson what the HBC had promised them in London.[4] The Staines were thought of highly as teachers, but as Helmcken wrote: "She [Mrs. Douglas] and Mrs. Staines did not chum at all—there being too much uppishness about the latter, she being the great woman—the great complaining—and the great school mistress and I may here state, that she really was the best schoolmistress ever seen since in Victoria."[5]

Reverend Staines's life at the fort might have gone well had he not attempted to live on both sides of the line. As man, chaplain, and teacher he was well liked, initially; his downfall began when he took up land near Mount Tolmie, and later purchased some 400 acres in Metchosin. Subsequently the London offices of the HBC received an anonymous letter, which Douglas attributed to Staines, complaining of "illtreatment at the hands of the Company" and "injustice," the HBC's monopoly and the absence of a church building. Douglas refuted these allegations point by point, calmly; then came other problems that led Douglas to describe Staines as a "fomenter of mischief and I believe a preacher of sedition."[6] All the disagreements came to a head with Douglas's appointment of his brother-in-law, David Cameron, as chief justice.

At a public meeting on February 4, 1854, a decision was made to send Staines to London to lay a formal protest before the home government. Four hundred dollars was raised on the spot to defray Staines's expenses. For reasons known only to himself, Staines did not sail for more than three weeks, and this was his last error. Some time between February 22 and March 19, the *Duchess of San Lorenzo*, with Staines aboard, foundered off Cape Flattery, and this unhappy event spelled the end to the organized protest. After selling her property in Metchosin, Emma Staines departed Vancouver Island forever on January 16, 1855. Nothing more is known of her, though as the first European woman to come to Vancouver Island with the intention of remaining, she deserves to be better remembered.

More important in the workaday history of the island is Annie (or Ann or Anne) Muir who arrived on June 1, 1849. She and her husband, John, and their large family first went to Fort Rupert, then Sooke, where they bought Grant's property and sawmill. There, or in the vicinity, the family and many of their descendants have lived ever since 1851. Little is known about Annie Muir, but she certainly played a significant role in the life of one of the major families on early-day Vancouver Island. As coal miner, farmer, businessman, and politician, John Muir contributed more to the island's growth than any other private citizen among the first settlers. Muir and his family created the pattern for successful, family-owned firms that would be so common in the business world of Vancouver Island throughout the latter half of the 19th century.

In 1852, James Deans, later to make a name for himself as a writer of no small talent, claimed there were only seven settlers in the Fort Victoria area: James Yates, James Cooper, R. Anderson, R. Scott, James M. Reid, W. Thompson, and himself. To this list must be added six Muirs at Sooke, Thomas Blinkhorn, Thomas Munroe, James Sangster, R. J. Staines, William Fraser, John McGregor, William McDonald, and a few settlers at farms that can no longer be identified. Around this time the Puget's Sound Agricultural Company established their four well-known farms: Viewfield, Constance Cove, Colwood or Esquimalt Farm, and Maple Point or Craigflower, all in the Esquimalt area, and operated by Donald Macaulay, T. J. Skinner, E. E. Langford, and Kenneth McKenzie, respectively.

Viewfield was established in 1850 and never did well. In 1855 only 35 of the farm's 600 acres were cleared; there were 14 Europeans on the land, but nine of these were children. This was the poorest of the four and it did not survive beyond 1860. Constance Cove Farm was little better off and when it was taken over by the HBC in 1865, T. J. Skinner and his family moved to the Cowichan Valley.

Colwood, named after E. E. Langford's old residence in Surrey, was the farthest of the four PSAC farms from Fort Victoria. In 1855, 190 of its 600 acres were cleared, and 30 Europeans lived there. Langford's time on the island began with the same shocked surprise expressed by many others. His stay was not pleasant, some say because he expected too much and was used to luxury, but the real crux of the matter lies at Langford's feet—the man was something of a fool. He was appointed magistrate by Douglas and proved to be inept; he ran for and won a seat in the first Legislative Assembly in 1856, only to be disqualified; he was one of Douglas's staunchest opponents yet the HBC (or PSAC) employed him, and in one year he borrowed eight times his own salary from the HBC. Finally the company had him removed and Langford and his family returned to England in 1861.

Historically, Craigflower appears the most important of the four farms. It survived the longest and as the manor and school still stand, this lends more credibility to Kenneth McKenzie's abilities than they deserve. The farm's economic story was as chequered as its manager's financial statements; it was closed in 1866 and sold piece-meal.

By 1855 settlers began spreading out from the fort. The Muirs were already at Sooke, and by the late 1850s other families began moving into that area, as well as Metchosin. In the other direction the Saanich Peninsula had its first settlers by 1858, when Angus McPhail and William Thomson (or Thompson) took up land near Mount Newton. Both were "freehold" farmers—in short, squatters who did not pay for their land. McPhail was a former HBC employee who took up his land at Saanich in 1855. Thomson, a close friend of McPhail's, came to Fort Victoria the hard way: he was aboard the brig *William*, wrecked at the mouth of Nitinat Lake on June 17, 1854. All hands with the exception of the captain and cook made it to shore, and from there the men reached Fort Victoria with the help of Indians living at Whyac. After this, Thomson worked for the HBC until he squatted near McPhail's freehold.

Six other men were farming at Saanich by 1858. These were Henry Simpson, Duncan Lidgate, George Deeks, John Coles, Leon Morrel, and John Bull, but little is known about their work on the land. Bull died in 1860, Coles in 1869; Morrel may have drowned in the Leech River during the gold rush into that vicinity; and Deeks and McPhail were gone by the early 1870s. Whatever their relationship to the land, all of these men were settlers in the western tradition of North America, not the financially independent colonists the HBC hoped would settle on the land.

It may be wondered why the company allowed freeholders or squatters on land that only nine years earlier had been so expensive and tightly controlled. Certainly the gold rush to the lower Fraser River was behind the slackening reins. Suddenly the island had a credible population, and it was obvious to all that these men were not going to obey the rigid rule of the HBC. Its grip on the land, already proven wrong-headed, was the first to give way. The Colonial Office wanted the island colonized, and the growing population on the island, as well as on the mainland, put a high premium on farm produce.

Between February 14, 1859, and January 19, 1861, James Douglas as Governor of British Columbia issued four land proclamations. At first the price of surveyed land was set at ten shillings per acre. A second proclamation, on January 4, 1860, made it possible to pre-empt 160 acres at that price, but the fourth, in January 1861, lowered the price to four shillings two pence an acre. A similar land proclamation was issued by Douglas for Vancouver Island on February 19, 1861. In part it stated a single man could pre-empt 150 acres, a married man whose wife was resident in the colony could take 200 acres, and each of his children (also resident and under 18) gave the pre-emptor the right to an additional ten acres. A married man with five children could take 300 acres, not inconsequential in locations like Saanich or the Cowichan Valley, where the land was as rich as the Fraser River delta.

After the first influx of settlers into the Saanich Peninsula region, there is little chronological sequence to settlement on the east coast of Vancouver Island. Fort Rupert and Nanaimo had existed from 1849 and 1852, but the local histories of these areas fail to record the existence of settlers during the 1850s and 1860s, though in the case of Nanaimo this must be an oversight. Up and down the east coast of the island men were wandering—miners, businessmen, churchmen, fly-by-nighters, fishermen, prospectors, whisky smugglers, men who had "gone Indian," and probably a few settlers—but their lives, like the paths they took, are lost forever. The story of east-coast colonization begins seriously in 1862 in the Cowichan and Comox valleys.

Something of a land rush did take place in the Cowichan-Chemainus locality during 1858–59. Nineteen speculators bought a total of 9,880 acres, and each buyer was given "Cowichan Scrip"; a document that gave the owner the right to claim the land he wanted. In this case the buyer also paid for the cost of surveying his property, but few had to, as they turned around and sold the land to miners. The Cariboo gold rush was not unlike any other gold rush: few men made more than wages, and most worked for wages. Almost all of them, winners and losers, came to Victoria for the winter. There, without the money to go farther, and realizing their dreams of Cariboo riches were just that, they looked around for other methods of making a living. Many saw a future for themselves as farmers now that the land was cheap enough; most did not remain on the land, but land was an immediate solution to their problems. The only one of the 19 who bought "Cowichan Scrip" to take up his land was J. A. Grahame, who paid £75 for 75 acres near what is now the town of Chemainus. As it seems he did not move onto his land until 1859, he was not the first settler in the area. This honour goes to Samuel Harris who appears to have settled down at Cowichan Bay early in 1859; apparently he had spent several years exploring the area before deciding he wanted to live in the district.

By 1864 over a hundred settlers may have been living in the Cowichan Valley. Of 52,658 acres surveyed in the area, 45,000 were "superior in quality, and the remaining 7,600 good for the general objects of agriculture."[7] By another estimate, the extent of agricultural land available surrounding Cowichan was 100,000 acres. These "estimates" cannot always be taken at face value. Almost everyone who wrote about the amount and quality of the land was involved in speculation, and most were also involved in the governing elite, which gives a certain undeserved credence to their statements. The majority of these men were HBC employees or former company men. They were the only ones to have the ready cash necessary to purchase large sections of land and some, like James Douglas, were buying blocks of land from the very beginning of their stay on the island. They might not like colonists or "aliens," (one of Douglas's early terms for non-British settlers) and they might not know (or want to know) how to manage a colony, but they were willing to make a dollar if the chance arose. They were betting on the future and the gold rushes made it all worthwhile.

In 1862, when the first large group of settlers moved into the Cowichan district, Samuel Harris, now an Indian agent and constable, pre-empted a block of land at tidewater and laid out a townsite. This he named Harrisville with typical frontier modesty, and built himself a house; next door he erected a tavern, the John Bull Inn, which kept him busier than he probably wanted to be. Harris not only sold liquor in the John Bull; it was something of a grocery store as well, and church services were held in the building as late as 1864.

The population of Vancouver Island was in a constant state of flux during the late 1850s and throughout the 1860s, and it is quite impossible to say, beyond the major families, who was living where. Two private censuses taken at Cowichan are wonderful illustrations of this point. In January 1863 there were 18 men living in the area, and by 1869 there were 71 residents. Only five of these 71 are on the earlier census; five years later on the Voters' List only three of the original 18 appear, and only 47 of the 71. Confusing—and then as it turns out some of the people listed as Cowichan settlers in 1869 actually lived in Chemainus, and several others were among the earliest black settlers on Saltspring Island.

However, beyond any doubt the Cowichan settlement began in 1862. Two years later it was still finding its feet, judging from comments made by members of the Vancouver Island Exploring Expedition. Mail was delivered to the area by ship as early as March 1863, but as there was no post office in the Cowichan-Chemainus district until 1872, the settlements cannot have been thriving. It is easy to see why: most of the land was covered with timber of every size and shape, and where

there were meadows or clearings, there was also water. Falling
and bucking trees, burning brush and limbs, digging out stumps
and digging ditches was brutal and mindless labour, and when
the land began to produce, the result was never large enough to
pay the bills. Then there were transportation problems: Victoria was the major market, but there were no roads to the
town and only a fortnightly steamer. The bright side of all this
is that the work and logistics failed to stump many good men.

John Newel Evans moved into the Cowichan Valley in 1870.
His unpublished memoir describes the problems faced by the
pioneers, yet until the end, his point of view was a happy one.
When Evans died he was 98; this was in 1944, the same year
that the poet, philosopher, writer, and farmer, Eric Duncan,
passed away in Comox. Duncan reached Comox in 1877 and
the work he found there was endless and hard, yet he lived to be
86. Many of the pioneers on the east coast lived to surprising
ages, considering their life-style. Duncan maintained that the
air of Vancouver Island was good for a man.

Comox, which Duncan watched grow from a ragged collection of farms into one of the loveliest communities on Vancouver Island, was Cowichan's exact contemporary.

COURTESY OF HISTORY DIVISION, BC PROVINCIAL MUSEUM

Comox Harbour and Mount Arrowsmith.

The HMS *Grappler,* following the request of Governor Douglas, landed the first official group of settlers on the beach of Port Augustus (now Comox Harbour) in early October 1862. On October 10, 1862, the *British Colonist* reported: "Some thirty-five settlers have taken up claims in the vicinity of the Courtenay River and express themselves as delighted with the prospect."[8] Eric Duncan wrote that "There were two bands, one of gold miners and sailors which came up from Australia, and another of emigrants from the British Isles which sailed around Cape Horn."[9] This implies they came directly to Vancouver Island as settlers, which is not the case; most were disgruntled miners from the Cariboo who, like so many others, found themselves high and dry in Victoria. Farming was their second choice. Substantiating this interpretation of the events is a later statement of Duncan's—all but two were bachelors. The first group reached Comox on October 1, the remainder on October 25.

In 1864 the locality was said to have 30 or more square miles of agricultural land. A visitor at the time wrote: "Although we had been informed that there was some fine land there, the extent and beauty of what we saw quite surprised us."[10] The harvest of 1864 was excellent and the farmers were pleased with their oats, barley, wheat, peas, and potatoes. Potatoes were the chief crop everywhere in the beginning, and those who could afford the luxury hired Indian women to dig them up. The women came to work with a man whose job was to sit and watch, make sure they worked and were paid, and cook their lunch. On these occasions the women wore several skirts, the hems of which they sewed together, and into these "pockets" went many a large potato, but this was apparently none of the overseer's business.

Throughout Duncan's memoirs, Comox and its people are described in such a way as to imply stability; certainly a foundation was there that Cowichan lacked, and this creeps into all the early descriptions of Comox. There is no one explanation for this, though distance from Victoria and the Puget Sound

Threshing crew at Comox, ca *1900.*

centres may be one reason. There were two other contributing factors. The men Duncan speaks of are often older than many early settlers; Grant and Cooper, near Victoria, were both in their 20s, as were the majority of the first Fraser Valley pioneers. Also, there was little speculation, no brilliant plans for the future; Comox's story was one of solid, day-to-day work, which all knew would lead to something.

Whatever their differences, the two districts had one similar problem: the lack of roads. In 1872, $5,000 was spent on Comox's roads, according to the government figures. Duncan claims that even as late as 1877, "None of the roads were graded then, even surveyed highways were mere tracks in the open and trails in the woods," and "there was very little grading anywhere."[11] Adding to the misconceptions caused by the government's report, the official map of British Columbia in 1871 shows a road connecting Comox, Nanaimo, Cowichan and Victoria. Almost everything officially reported about this "road" is fiction; in fact, it was an unblazed trail wandering about the country. It was so bad that a civil servant and his *guide* got lost on the way from Victoria to Cowichan trying to follow it. The Comox settlers did not use this road, which was apparently navigable only by seasoned travellers on foot in good weather. Boats were the only relatively sure means of travel on the east coast of Vancouver Island well into the 1880s.

All this would be by the by if the government's published accounts were not so misleading. Even after the turn of the century, politicians allowed themselves, and speculators of all hues, to push the truth to the edge of collapse. As will be seen later, there was no end of "mega-projects" planned for the northern half of the island, and everyone had a hand in the pot. No one wanted to admit the truth: the east coast was truly isolated, with no roads, no nearby towns, and no businesses already in place. The truth would drive future investors away.

Comox village and wharf, ca *1910.*

The fortnightly vessel that visited Comox goes without a name in Duncan's writings. He missed the ship on his arrival at Victoria, but managed along with several others to make the trip to Nanaimo aboard the *Emma,* a small tug. What ships ran along the east coast, carrying the mail, delivering goods and picking up produce, is largely unknown. The *Governor Douglas* was the first steamer built in British Columbia; she made her trial run in 1859 but, like many others of the gold-rush era, she was built for inland navigation. Her voyages appear to have been limited to the Victoria-Fraser River run. As the HBC controlled the northern trade well into the 1860s, and there was an HBC trader at Comox, the company's vessels, which now included the *Otter* (the first propellor-driven ship in BC waters) and the steamship *Labouchère* as well as the *Beaver,* may have provided east-coast service between them. By 1880 several American vessels, such as the well-known *Ancon,* on the Puget Sound-Alaska run, were stopping at Victoria, Nanaimo, and Comox. The curious feature of these ships is that they carried tourists, sight-seers who got off at Victoria and Nanaimo to look at the locals, and "Kodak" the scenery. Tourists only supplemented the revenue of these vessels. Their primary purpose was supplying the Alaskan canneries with men and goods, but it would appear they also served the east-coast ports of the island. Whatever ships they were, all writers of the period agree that their arrival was a holiday as everyone gathered on the beach or wharf to collect their mail, do business or gawk, or simply visit neighbours.

Many of the Scots who came to Vancouver Island referred to it as the "back of the world". Apparently this term was a common one for Vancouver Island in Scotland at the time. Be that as it may, many of the earliest settlers came from areas of Great Britain that were in many respects far more isolated, and the life a great deal more difficult, than anything experienced by island pioneers. James Bell hinted at this in his letter from Victoria in 1859, when he wrote his brother: "These people [former HBC traders and factors] being originally from the north and west of

Scotland, of the poorest class, As might be expected, their ideas of Farming are very primitive."[12] As Bell himself was a Scot, this cannot be taken as a racial slur. Many of the pioneers may have thought they had died and gone to heaven when they reached Vancouver Island's east coast. Eric Duncan certainly did.

Born in the Shetland Islands, Duncan was 21 when he left his home island for the first time. In the days of his childhood the wheel was almost unknown on the islands; most of the houses were rude cabins with a fireplace in the centre of the house where the farm animals lived on more or less democratic terms with their owners. The land he grew up on was owned by a proprietor and rented on a yearly basis.

Isolation may have been independence, but hard work gave the lives of these people a shape that can only rarely be glimpsed. The pioneers were too busy to write. Owning books was a needless luxury, and the thought of writing them attached itself to few Vancouver Island pioneers. Some, such as Grant, did write after they left the island, but few of those who remained wrote; of these Eric Duncan left the clearest picture.

"I came back to Comox for good in time for the haying which was all scythe work then, even in the open fields. The hours were longer than at the sawmill, but there was much more variety in the work. We started to gather the cows about 4:30 A.M. and we did not stop field work till 6 P.M., doing milking and chores afterwards. But we took an hour for dinner." This was in the fall of 1878; earlier that year Duncan had gone to Nanaimo to work "at the Nanaimo sawmill, then run by a Yankee named Carpenter. The wages were $30 a month and board, but when we were idle, as happened often, board was deducted at $1 a day. And Carpenter managed it so that at the end of a month we never had more than $10 coming to us." Duncan describes a typical day, but says nothing about the brutal labour. "The whistle woke us at 5 A.M.; breakfast at 5:30, and start work at 6. Whistle blew for dinner at 12, work resumed at 12:30 and continued till 6, when we had supper and were free for the rest of the day."[13]

There was another side of life at Comox that, like the tourists coming ashore to sightsee, is quite unexpected. The settlers had no time to fish, but the fishing in the area had a certain renown elsewhere. Judges and lawyers came from Victoria to camp along the banks of the Puntledge River and spend their holidays fishing, so Duncan claims, which makes it sound as though it was an area closed to others. Probably any business or professional man from Victoria, who loved fishing, could not long resist the lure of the Puntledge.

If life was calm at Comox, and it undoubtedly was, events elsewhere were changing the entire appearance of the Pacific slope and Vancouver Island. In Victoria and New Westminster politicians were intimately involved in far-from-pleasant confrontations with London, Ottawa, and Washington, DC. All along the east coast of the island the Indians were fighting a guerrilla war with the changing times, and to the southeast of Victoria on San Juan Island, where the Puget's Sound Agricultural Company was farming and colonizing, the American settlers were refusing to abide by British laws.

CHAPTER EIGHT

Manifest Destiny

Only rarely are pioneers thinkers; the vast majority are dreamers whose dreams are limited to finding a place for themselves under the sun. For decades the North American west was the place where dreams could come true; land was free, talent at a premium and, for a few years at least, the future was more important than the past. As few people are more conventional and conservative than the pioneer, usually sooner rather than later the inevitable sets in: laws are drawn up and enforced, schools and churches built, towns erected and named, governments founded, and public servants elected. In the Pacific Northwest this process resulted in political subservience to the east and the near-demise of the indigenous cultures.

On the shores of Garrison Bay, San Juan Island, less than an hour by fast boat from downtown Victoria, there stands a marker with one of the strangest legends in the Pacific Northwest. "English Camp. In 1859, the killing of a pig on San Juan Island brought England and the United States to the brink of war over the issue of territorial rights here. By agreement, both nations' troops were permitted to occupy this area while the problem was studied. British soldiers established camp at Garrison Bay, just west of here, while American troops camped at the southern end of the island. Peaceful arbitration of the dispute in 1872 placed the San Juan Islands within the territorial United States. In October of that year the British garrison was abandoned."

The problem began in the vague wording of the Oregon Treaty. Everyone concerned knew what the 49th parallel meant, but what did "to the middle of the channel which separates the continent from Vancouver's Island; and thence southerly through the middle of said channel" mean?[1] The first channel is the Strait of Georgia, but there are two channels connecting it with the Strait of Juan de Fuca. To complicate the problem further, between these two straits there is a group of islands. One of these is San Juan Island to which Douglas sent sheep and herders shortly after he moved from Fort Vancouver to Fort Victoria. As a Briton, he quite naturally considered the international boundary to be the centre of Rosario Strait on the east side of the island group. This gave the HBC control of three large islands and literally dozens of smaller ones. The Americans decided the line ran through Haro Strait, west of the islands, so in their minds *they* gained control of all the islands.

Throughout the late 1850s there were problems between the British and American settlers on San Juan Island, as was to be expected. Something was bound to occur that would bring about a major confrontation, but no one in his right mind expected it to come about the way it did. On June 15, 1859, one Lyman Cutler, an American settler, shot a pig belonging to the HBC. Cutler offered to pay damages, but he refused to pay the $100 demanded by the HBC. One thing led to another until Cutler got tired of the affair and warned the HBC that if they bothered him again he would shoot their messenger.

Cutler and the dead pig disappear at this point. A month before the shooting episode, the Americans among the island settlers had petitioned the military commander in Oregon for protection against the northern Indians, who had killed several settlers. When this commander, Brigadier-General Harney, visited the island, the islanders petitioned him again. He also learned of the murder of the pig. Shortly afterwards Captain George E. Pickett and Company D, 9th Infantry, landed at Griffin Bay, San Juan Island. Late in July, Pickett issued a proclamation that in part read: "This being United States Territory, no laws, other than those of the United States, nor courts, except such as are held by virtue of said laws, will be recognized on this island."[2] Within days Pickett and his company found themselves on a hill looking down the gun barrels of two British war steamers.

Washington, DC, was appalled by Harney's actions and dispatched General Winfield Scott to the coast to straighten the matter out. During October and November 1859, Scott and Douglas agreed on a joint occupation of the island, and joint action to repel any Indians who might attack it. Due to the Civil War the two countries did not meet to discuss the international boundary until 1868. They could not agree and the question was handed over to Emperor William of Germany. In 1872 he chose the Haro Strait division, thus awarding the area now known as the San Juan Islands to the United States.

As there were only 184 male settlers on the various islands, and these were mostly Americans, it does not seem that Britain lost much at the time by the boundary decision. Out of all the verbiage written about this "Pig War," as it is usually called, one fact does emerge clearly: the men who signed the petition and presented it to Harney were genuinely worried about Indian attacks.

San Juan Island lies not quite ten miles off the coast of Saanich. It is a beautiful island and was bound to attract early settlers. What these people failed to realize at the time is that the island lay directly in the path used by northern Indians on their way to Victoria, Puget Sound, or Port Townsend. Romance and legend have it that these northern people were the Haida—the ancient warriors of the North Pacific. That hundreds of these

Haida were among the visitors is undeniable. One early writer claims 1,500 Haida visited Fort Victoria in 1854 to see what the whites were up to. Among the coastal peoples the Haida were not particularly highly thought of, either as warriors or sailors. Probably any coastal Indian with the wherewithal to own a canoe and organize a crew headed for Fort Victoria or Puget Sound. Curiosity, trading, whisky, travel—all were attractions in such a venture, and so was attacking Indian or white settlements.

One apparently wild statement made in 1914 places 3,000 Indians at the fort in 1859: 2,000 Haida, and the rest Bella Bella, Tsimshian, and Tlingit. Supposedly they were holding a convention on the shores of Victoria Harbour. Essentially, this statement is correct. When a head count was made in April of that year, it was discovered that there were 1,545 Indians camped within shooting range of the fort. The man making the count found 574 Tsimshian, 405 Haida, 223 Tlingit, 111 Salish or Bella Bella, and 217 made up of three unidentifiable northern groups. Shortly afterwards, 690 more northerners arrived at Fort Victoria which, along with the 600 or so local Salish, puts the total very close to 3,000. However, the people were not holding a "convention"; they were drinking and fighting, pimping and selling slaves, and having a good time—just as the white sailors, sealers, loggers, and fishermen would 40 years later when Victoria's red-light district winked at men all along the Northwest Coast.

Everyone enjoyed the spring and summer of 1859. Business was booming, especially the whisky trade. Somehow Douglas managed to maintain the peace, so there were no major incidents. Three years later the story had quite a different ending. Thousands of people were again gathered at Victoria when smallpox broke out, and Douglas ordered the Indians to return home, hoping that dispersion would help stay the probable results of the outbreak. If anything, this made things worse: it spread the disease and as a result a third of the coastal Indian population died in 1862.

Smallpox was not a dreaded menace in the 1840s and 1850s: the Indians were the menace. No little wonder for they outnumbered the whites; they knew the country, and it was theirs. People always fight with desperation on home soil. It is amazing, considering contemporary events south of the international boundary, that there were no Indian wars either in British Columbia or on Vancouver Island—not even skirmishes or guerrilla battles of a prolonged nature.

Between 1848 and 1879 the Americans fought eight major Indian wars in their Pacific Northwest, and an unknown number of police actions must be added to this figure. North of the border, the Chilcotin "War" of 1864 is almost an isolated incident. Commenting on this action, old John Tod in Victoria said that in the old days under the HBC such an affair would have been dealt with by a handful of men. The truth behind this has already been seen: Finlayson quickly and effectively dissuaded the Indians from attacking Fort Victoria in 1844.

Leading the 1844 attack was Tsough elam, a Cowichan chief. As "Tzouhalem" or "Tzuhalem," Tsough elam has become a man whose importance rivals Maquinna's. Fascinating and bloody stories circulate still about this chief and his deeds; historians and poets, writers of fiction and local history, have added touches of colour, and today a mountain behind Genoa Bay bears his name. He was "among the most notorious Indians of the region during the 19th century. His cruelty stemmed from the early loss of his mother and brother kidnapped and then drowned by invading Haidas. His own people feared him and he was exiled to live in the caves of Mt. Tzuhlam. He was finally beheaded while trying to steal a wife on Kuper Island."[3]

Sadly, for those who love stories, much of the tale of Tzuhalem-Tsough elam is based on a mistake. Finlayson, who should have known, refers to him as a chief with a large following, and his sway over the Songhee at Fort Victoria is evidence of his authority. Yet this may in part have been due to the absence of Chee-ah-thluk, the undisputed Songhee chief. In any case, the bloody deeds, the near-fortress-like sanctuary on Tzuhalem Mountain, the captive harem of 14 wives, his belief that every man was his enemy or each was fair game, which led to his banishment by his fellow Cowichan, and the young men said to have followed him, can all be traced to the story of Tsoqelem, an outlaw who was supposed to have lived in the 1840s.

It is not conceivable that such an outlaw, detested even by his own people, could camp near Fort Victoria among the Songhee (in a large house no less), and command a sizeable force of men. Nor is it likely that such a man would make a gentlemanly peace with Finlayson as did Tsough elam. The Cowichan chief is a man whose existence is documented; Tsoqelem may have been a real man but the Indians telling stories about him in the 1890s thought him part of their folklore.

Less colourful, but more indicative of the changing times are the Songhee chief Chee-ah-thluk, absent at the time of Tsough elam's attack on Fort Victoria, and the Haida chief, Captain John. Both are unhappy illustrations of how the whites at the fort were altering the traditional ways.

Formerly chief of the Cadboro Bay people, who soon after the establishment of Fort Victoria moved to Victoria Harbour, Chee-ah-thluk came to be known as "King Freezy". The "King" was "principal chief in the early days of the Hudson's Bay establishment" and "held undisputed sway over the tribe for many years." Chee-ah-thluk gained his nickname from his frizzy hair, an inheritance passed on to him from his Hawaiian (Kanaka) father or grandfather. He was a "peaceable old chap," and "was completely under the control of the Hudson's Bay Company to whom he rendered himself valuable by being at all times ready in consideration of a small donation of blankets &c. to exert his authority in quelling any disturbance that broke out or was impending among his subjects."[4] In other words, the leading Songhee chief was a half-breed yes-man. No wonder he was detested by the Haida, who shed no tears when "King Freezy" drowned, drunk, on November 11, 1864.

COURTESY OF HISTORY DIVISION, BC PROVINCIAL MUSEUM

Songhee land in Victoria Harbour, ca 1890.

This was the heyday of the whisky traders. The HBC, and later the Legislative Assembly, had outlawed the sale of alcohol to the Indians, yet the officials turned their backs to what was taking place at the Indian camp, now located along the shores of James Bay opposite the fort and growing village. "The so-called whiskey was the vilest stuff that the ingenuity of wicked-minded and avaricious white men ever concocted. What it was composed of was known only to the concocters. I was told that it was made of alcohol, diluted with water, toned up with an extract of red pepper, and colored so as to resemble the real thing. It was conveyed to the reserve under the cover of night by boatloads." The men who made and sold this rotgut were, according to a newspaper editor of the time, "men who went to church regularly or occupied a good position and were immune from the visits of constables."[5]

Captain John, most likely the son of a Russian fur trader and a Kaigani Haida woman, was an Alaskan. He could read and write English to some extent, but "his language was a puzzling maze of Russian, English, Chinook and Indian." Prior to his arrival at Fort Victoria, he had lived in St. Petersburg and London, and sailed on HBC and Russian vessels. By the late 1850s he was known to Victorians as the "King of the Haidas," despite the fact he does not seem to have been a chief. "At one time it was estimated by the Hudson's Bay Company" that he "had three thousand warriors under his command."[6] This can be doubted, but as a leader Captain John was the centre of much of the local trouble between the Haida, HBC, and Tlingit. Although he did control his men, whisky controlled Captain John, until he became a quarrelsome alcoholic. His end came shortly after the Haida fired on the *Royal Charlie* as she sailed out of Victoria Harbour. No one was hurt, but the HBC acted swiftly and arrested Captain John and another chief. As the men were being searched at the jail, they drew knives and were shot on the spot, and there they died.

Alcohol was not always the source of the problem. In 1850 four deserters from the *England* jumped ship and managed to get aboard the *Norman Morrison,* believing she was sailing for California and the gold fields. Instead she sailed for Fort Rupert. Shortly after her arrival there, the *Beaver* steamed in behind her; the men, thinking she was after them, jumped ship again. One of the sailors was soon apprehended; no one knew of the whereabouts of the others until three Kwakiutl men, Killonecaulla, Tackshicoate, and Tawankstalla killed them near the mouth of the Shushartie River, on the northeast coast of Vancouver Island.

After a good deal of fruitless action, described in an earlier chapter, the HMS *Daphnae* arrived in 1851, a year after the HMS *Daedalus*'s departure, and her crew set fire to the murderers' home village. This seemed equally pointless at the time, but having lost their canoes and homes and goods to this attack, the tribesmen tried to talk the killers into surrendering. When this failed, the wanted men were shot by their own people—at least two were. The third may have escaped and a slave was killed to take his place in the bottom of the canoe that the Kwakiutl towed to Fort Rupert in hopes of collecting a reward.

Whether or not the self-appointed law-men were rewarded is not recorded. It did turn out that the murderers' intent was honourable enough when they first sighted the deserters. Seeing the men on shore, the Kwakiutl approached—but only to warn the white men of the possibility that Haida warriors were in the area. The white men, misunderstanding everything, threw rocks at the canoe, while one man waved an axe. Ordinarily this might have not meant much, but one of the rocks smashed into the canoe. To understand what happened next, one must consider the geopolitical situation.

These Kwakiutl were from Newitty or Nahwitti, a name sometimes implying the northern tip of Vancouver Island, but properly, Newitty was a village on Hope Island. To the north lived the Bella Bella and mainland Kwakiutl and, though Kwakiutl themselves, the Newitty fought these mainland people, as well as the Kwakiutl living southward on the east coast of the island. To the southwest lived the Nootka. Thus the Newitty had learned that if they were not the quick, they were the dead. Instead of either passing on or going ashore to calm the whites down, the three high-strung and nervous men chased the whites into the timber and killed all three. The bodies of Charles and George Wishart were placed in a hollow tree. Fred Watkins' body was tied to a rock and sunk somewhere at sea.

A year later and far to the south, Governor Douglas himself led the action following the apparently pointless murder of Peter Brown, and the results were immediate and successful. Brown, one of two shepherds stationed at Lake Hill (near Swan Lake Park, Saanich), was shot and killed before noon on November 5, 1852, while his partner, James Skea, drove the sheep out to pasture. Douglas immediately set about seeking the identities of the murderers, and soon learned one was a Cowichan, and the other the son of a Nanaimo chief.

On the morning of January 4, 1853, Douglas, aboard the

Beaver, towing the *Recovery* and the boats of the HMS *Thetis,* and accompanied by 130 Royal Navy sailors and marines, set out for the Cowichan village. Describing the events in his journal, Douglas is unusually wordy: "Arrived at Camegin [Cowichan Bay] this morning—great excitement among the Indians who shunned the vessels. I despatched [a] messenger to the Camegin chiefs inviting them to a conference, in which I hope to be able to prevail upon them to surrender the murderer quietly and without a recource to coercive measures."[7]

Later that day the messengers returned. The Cowichan agreed to meet Douglas at the mouth of the Cowichan River the next morning. Douglas and his men arrived first, and then came the Indians: "They had a very imposing appearance as they pulled slowly towards us, chanting their warlike songs, whooping like demons, and drumming on their canoes by turns with all their might. They landed a little beyond, and rushed up the hill, in a state of the wildest excitement, shouting and dashing their arms about, like people who expected to be immediately attacked. This was a most trying moment for the troops could hardly be restrained from firing a volley among them, which would have been attended with the most fatal effect. The excitement over, the murderer was produced by his friends armed cap à pie [from head to toe] and was heard in his defence, which went to declare that he was innocent of the crime laid to his charge."[8]

After some talk, and Douglas's promise to give the accused a fair trial, the Cowichan handed the man over. Douglas then "addressed the Indians who were there assembled, on the subject of their relations with the Colony and the Crown. I informed them that the whole country was a possession of the British Crown, and that Her Majesty the Queen had given me a special charge, to treat them with justice and humanity and to protect them against the violence of all foreign nations which might attempt to molest them, so long as they remained at peace with the settlements."[9]

The Nanaimo man was harder to capture. He heard of Douglas's approach and took to the woods. On January 16, he was finally caught, due largely to fresh snow that made tracking easy. The next day the two men were tried on the cold deck of the *Beaver*. Their trial began at 10 A.M. and they were hanged at Gallows Point, Protection Island, before 3 P.M.

Good causes lay behind the increasing number of similar incidents during the 1850s and 1860s. Europeans were reaping what Europeans had sowed. For decades the maritime fur traders had treated the Indians in the typical American fashion of the period, killing them for reasons however large, small, or non-existent. These traders had taken Indian women aboard ship by force, held chiefs hostage, and engaged in a slave trade; they were as dissolute as they claimed the Indians to be. Now the coastal people were turning on the Europeans in revenge. Happily for the whites, righting past wrongs was never a concentrated effort, and only seldom even a village effort.

As stated earlier, the pre-European population of the British Columbia coast was probably close to 50,000 people. How many more lived in Puget Sound and Southeastern Alaska is not known. What is known is that most of these people were mortal enemies. In 1853 the Haida may have numbered 6,000, but there were two major groups (not including those in Alaska), now referred to as the Masset and Skidegate Haida, divided into dozens of villages. Many of these were continually at war with one another and with groups to the north, south and east.

The Haida "war" pattern was similar to all such efforts on the coast: night attacks, guerrilla battles, or the occasional large-scale strike, but for the most part one attack was the result of another. Revenge, the eye-for-an-eye code, was all-important to every one of these people. Many whites were killed for revenge, but not because of what they had done personally. It does not seem to have mattered to the coastal people who was killed in revenge, just so long as revenge was taken. As a consequence, whites were murdered for deeds done by Indians and vice-versa.

What was different in the Colony of Vancouver Island, with

its white population and HBC headquarters, was James Douglas's iron hand and his blend of HBC and British justice. His concerns were not totally based on judicial rights and wrongs; everyone of the day feared a unified attack by the Indians. As the settlers and traders were outnumbered many hundreds to one, they had every right to be nervous. From the very beginning Douglas knew that as long as he took advantage of each isolated incident, never allowing the guilty to go unpunished, he could prevent the possibility of a strong leader emerging to lead the many groups to unification and war. That such a unified effort was an impossibility and need not have worried anyone at the time only became visible in the 20th century.

Too many people speaking too many languages in a huge area made unification highly unlikely, and without a strong leader, who had proven his ability to fight the settlers effectively, it was only a common nightmare for many whites. Douglas's gunboat diplomacy, and smallpox, only increased the odds against unity. After the epidemic of 1862, the first of several, came the churches. An already-divided people was separated further by the variety of Christianities and their missionaries that spread along the east and west coast of Vancouver Island. The dislike and distrust among the various churches was intense. Father Brabant, long a resident priest on the west coast of the island, wrote as late as 1895: "Everything we asked for was promised by the [Indian] agent. I returned to my Mission rejoicing in the thought that the efforts of the Protestant ministers would be unsuccessful. If we could keep the children from perversions, our position was safe."[10] Each missionary saw his local problems in the light of his own candle, and few on Vancouver Island had more than flickering solutions.

One intelligent and sensible early missionary was Thomas Crosby, a Methodist. His "fists and voice were his sword," and almost single-handedly he "took on the whiskey dealers and slave traders, and cut a swath wide as Moses." From the beginning he knew that learning the languages of the people he dealt with was one key to a solution. Next came schooling— and education was not limited to the classroom; "Later on I followed up this work of education among the tribes on the Nanaimo and Fraser rivers, teaching them not only how to improve their homes, but to till their ground·and plant orchards, and in every way take their place among their white brethren."[11]

None of the first island missionaries travelled as widely as did Crosby. Nor did any rail as loudly as he did against the demon of alcohol: "For years the natives of the Pacific Coast of British Columbia have been exposed to the temptations of the white man's whiskey. The traders on ships in those early years thought it to their advantage to take a good supply of rum with them in the traffic of furs, and the poor people became so in-

Indians shucking clams, Winter Harbour, ca 1912.

fatuated with it that while it lasted they would not even go out
after the pelts. Finally Sir George Simpson forbade the sale of
liquor at any of the trading posts."[12]

Regarding the HBC and the Russian American Company's
agreement to stop their liquor trading in 1842, the historian
H. H. Bancroft comments: "It is needless to say that the liquor-
loving savages did not relish this arrangement. But for their
own safety, to say nothing of profits, the Europeans were forced
to this course. For while intoxicating drink was freely sold it
was unsafe for white men to appear at any distance from their
forts except in armed bands."[13] Even though little evidence has
arisen in recent years to prove Bancroft's point wrong, the overall generalization remains unfair. The HBC was never actively
involved in the whisky trade on the coast to any extent.

The first recorded sale of liquor to the Indians occurred at
Nootka in 1792. The French vessel, La Flavie, supposedly
searching for the missing La Pérouse expedition, traded brandy
and clothing for sea otter skins. Later the same year the American ship Boston probably traded in a like manner. By 1800 the
maritime fur trade had altered drastically; now only American
ships were involved and these people were always willing to
give the Indians what they wanted, no matter the consequences.
In 1808 the Russian government complained about the trade in
whisky and firearms. On her second voyage to the coast the
Columbia carried nearly 1,000 gallons of spirits, plus half a ton
of powder and 200 muskets. When the Boston was captured by
the Nootka in 1803, Jewitt says she had about 2,000 gallons of
rum in her hold. The problem came to such a pass that 30 years
prior to the 1842 agreement, the Russians and the North West
Company had agreed to "abstain from giving the Indians any
spiritous liquors".[14] Regrettably, this did not affect the
maritime trade.

On the outside coast before 1842, the whisky trade harmed
only the drinkers and the traders. After 1843, with the establishment of Fort Victoria and the slow colonization process developing along the shores of Puget Sound and the east coast of

Vancouver Island, the innocent became involved. If it were not for the needless deaths of a number of Haida warriors, the *Laurel* incident would be pure comic opera.

Off the shores of the Saanich Peninsula in May 1861 the *Laurel* sold two barrels of whisky to Chief Jefferson and his Haida canoe-men. Only after sailing away did the Haida discover the whisky had been diluted with gallons of salt water. Immediately the Haida doubled back to the *Laurel,* which had been unlucky enough to lose her wind, and stripped her of everything worthwhile. No one aboard was hurt. Nor did the Haida attack any of the people at Beggsville, one of the pioneer settlements on Saltspring Island, when they raided the storehouses of Jonathan Begg and Edward Mallandaine. In fact the Indians even warned one white settler, a man named Sampson, away from the scene.

Douglas, learning of the Haida "attack" on the *Laurel,* sent the HMS *Forward* out to investigate. At Nanaimo Lieutenant-Commander Charles R. Robson, of the *Forward,* retrieved various items taken from the *Laurel* by the Haida and traded to local residents; here he was told of the Saltspring Island incident. Convinced that the Haida could now be legally considered pirates, Robson took up their trail. On May 17 the Haida were located several miles south of Campbell River at a place still known as Willow Point. By this time Robson also knew that some 300 people accompanied Chief Jefferson. Robson "sent Constable Gough and Mr Horne, both well known to them, and unarmed, on shore, with a message to say that the Magistrate of Nanaimo was on board, to enquire into the nature of certain robberies and to desire the chief to come off. Failing to do so, they were to be informed, that they would be fired on."[15]

The Haida laughed at this, so Robson moved the *Forward* close in and fired over their camp, but this only drew return fire. Next the ship's guns were lowered, and fired at the canoes. Some of the cannon-fire was wide of the mark for two Haida were killed and several others wounded as they lay hiding in the forest. Spurred on by this encouragement, Chief Jefferson and his men gave up. He and four others were arrested and taken to Victoria to stand trial. Of this engagement Douglas wrote: "I entirely approve of Captain Robson's proceedings in regard to the Hyder Indians who fired upon and insulted Her Majesty's flag—and set the civil authorities of the Colony at defiance—The punishment inflicted upon them was the result of their own rashness and was merited and necessary."[16]

While the Haida were being held, the authorities learned of the watered whisky. This was enough to change their opinion of the matter. The crew of the *Laurel* had only received their just deserts for a lousy trick. On the promise of Chief Jefferson and his men to behave themselves in the future, the "pirates" were released.

No one will ever know to what extent alcohol, or the demand for alcohol, contributed to the Indian "wars" on Vancouver Island's east coast. Bill Brady was killed at Bedwell Harbour, Pender Island, and his companion, John Henly, badly wounded, in early April 1863. These men took five Cowichan into their camp for the night and as there were two women among the Cowichan, one or both may have instigated the attack. Another attack in the Gulf Islands, this time on a settler and his married daughter, also in 1863, goes unexplained. The survivors of such incidents, when there were any, certainly were not going to admit they were whisky traders. It was the impression of Robert Brown, leader of the 1864 expedition into the centre of the island and still travelling the coast in 1866, that many of these settlers were "a useless set, disappointed miners & loafers of all sorts "—riffraff ready to trick the Indians whenever the opportunity arose, but just as quick to lie to the authorities as they pleaded for assistance from the "murdering savages" whenever the Indians evened the score.[17] Two incidents cited by Thomas Crosby—the murder of two Cowichan chiefs near Nanaimo by white men and the murder of James Hamilton in the Nanaimo vicinity—were caused by alcohol.

Drastic and effective as Douglas's gunboat diplomacy was in

Queen Charlotte and Johnstone straits, and the Strait of Georgia, it could only work to a limited extent. It was more effective in the case of the Indians than the whisky traders who were behind many of the problems. The entire area is a labyrinth of islands and winding waterways which, in Douglas's time, was practically uncharted. Much has been written about the gunboats and their successes, but as far as the traders were concerned, this was a no-man's-land. For every whisky trader caught, undoubtedly dozens continued unmolested.

Another problem of this period was slavery: not the traditional slavery of captives held by conquerors, though this continued to vex the missionaries and authorities, but slavery that resulted from Indians selling their female children. Crosby states: "And so when the miners came the natives willingly sold their daughters, ranging from 10 to 18 years of age, for a few blankets or a little gold," and then he goes on to explain from the perspective of 50 years on the coast, "For years these wretched, deluded people have visited our towns, our mining and lumbering and fishing camps, bringing their bright-eyed, happy little girls with them, and after having made a lot of money in this foul method, have returned to make a great potlatch and ostentatiously give away hundreds of dollars of their ill-gotten gains."[18] Who bought these girls, Crosby does not say: probably miners, fishermen, hand-loggers and drifters—men who wanted feminine company during an isolated winter along the coast.

Writing in 1864, Robert Brown makes an interesting point: "We speak of the immorality of these Indians, but the only whites with which they have any communication have been the vilest of whiskey sellers in Victoria & elsewhere, or the traders with no regard for aught but their own gain, or a corresponding class who visit their villages for similar purposes. No sooner is the anchor down than the demand for women & bribes are held out to Mothers to prostitute children of the most tender years." He also maintains there was little prostitution among any of the Vancouver Island people except at the Alberni Mills and Victoria. And "The large amount of prostitution exhibited in Victoria is not due to the neighbouring tribes, but to the Haida, Tshimshian, & other tribes."[19]

Douglas's unique style of diplomacy, and the European vices, were not as disastrous in the long view as were the summer congregations of Indians at Fort Victoria. This caused the unholy spread of smallpox in 1862, and it broke down the traditional hunting and gathering cycle. The Vancouver Island people became totally dependent on European goods, which in turn made them an easy mark for any one of the many small trading vessels cruising along the coast. When Indian prostitution earned husbands and fathers and brothers hundreds of dollars every summer, the potlatch and the entire system of prestige based on wealth (and this was the backbone of the social system) collapsed.

Gilbert Malcolm Sproat, resident manager of the mills at Alberni in the early 1860s, wrote from Alberni Inlet: "I seemed all at once to perceive that a few sharp-witted young natives had become what I can only call offensively European, and that the mass of the Indians no longer visited the settlement in the former independent way, but lived listlessly in the villages, brooding seemingly over heavy thoughts. The fact was that the curiosity of the savage had been satisfied; his mind was confused and his faculties surprised and stunned by the presence of machinery, steam vessels, and the active labour of civilized men; he distrusted himself, his old habits and traditions, and shrank away despondent and discouraged." From this point on they "began soon to disregard" their "old pursuits, and tribal practices and ceremonies."[20] He goes on to remark the increase in mortality among the Indians and the high death rate that continued to grow for the five years he was at Alberni Inlet.

The hell the Indians of Vancouver Island were living through might have been better dealt with, or better documented, had not events elsewhere drawn the attention of the island's leading minds. The first event in a series that was to have more reverberations than any one incident since the first Fraser River gold rush in 1859 was the retirement of Governor Douglas in the spring of 1864.

As already mentioned, Arthur Edward Kennedy, later to be Sir Arthur, replaced Douglas as governor of Vancouver Island. Initially welcomed by all, Kennedy soon found himself unwelcome insofar as the Legislative Assembly of Vancouver Island was concerned, because they saw him as a hindrance to a merger with BC. As a governor Kennedy was efficient and practical: public accounts were audited; the civil service was improved; the Common School Act (promising everyone a free education) was passed; and real estate taxes were collected. This was by the by in the assembly where Vancouver Island's stale economic present and future overshadowed all but the looming question of union with British Columbia. The pinnacle of Kennedy's career in Victoria was reached in 1864, when the assembly, led by Amor De Cosmos (who had been the thorn in Douglas's side and was now in Kennedy's) agreed to union with British Columbia under any terms considered appropriate by the Colonial Office. Because of this resolution the assembly voted to pay Kennedy's staff and the rent on his official residence, and even withdrew $50,000 for a government house—out of a total budget of $390,000. The move was not popular and it was not done for Governor Kennedy; the assembly was looking to the future, with Victoria as the capital of the combined colonies. Kennedy remained on at Victoria until 1866. When he submitted his budget of $193,000, the *British Colonist,* which was the voice of Amor De Cosmos, one of the owners, suggested Kennedy was mad. Actually it was De Cosmos (plain William Alexander Smith from Nova Scotia until he changed his name in California by an act of legislature) who lived on the narrow edge dividing madness and genius. It is said that the act, which changed his name to "Lover of the World," was almost amended by the California legislature to read "Amor De Bacchus". "De Bacchus" suited De Cosmos better in 1865 when, in opposition to Kennedy's budget, he introduced a muddle-headed scheme to eliminate taxes and borrow money for government expenses.

The position of Governor of British Columbia, left vacant by Douglas's retirement, was filled by Frederick Seymour, a colonial administrator since 1842. From the beginning he was accommodating and popular, except with De Cosmos, but New Westminster looked better on paper than it did to the eye; there was intense rivalry between the two colonies and "the extreme inconvenience of the position of two Governors of equal authority close to each other yet far from home."[21] Seymour agreed to finish Douglas's dream—the Cariboo Road, on which £10,000 was still owed for work done in 1863.

As Vancouver Island had virtually no income, early in 1866 the Bank of British North America refused to extend the island's $80,000 overdraft. While visiting London at this time Governor Seymour discovered that everyone concerned with the two colonies (from the HBC to the Colonial Office) was resolved that they must be united. Fearing the power of Victoria and the men there, British Columbia was against union and so was Seymour, but he bowed to the pressure and managed to make a number of suggestions. One was that instead of a federal union, Vancouver Island should be incorporated into British Columbia. Others of Seymour's suggestions that were adopted were that the laws of British Columbia be extended over Vancouver Island, that the form of government be modelled upon British Columbia's Legislative Council, and that New Westminster be named as the capital of the new colony.

The bill to unite the two colonies was rushed through parliament without debate at the end of the 1866 session. Seymour returned to British Columbia, a sick man with a wife of less than a year, to a sour welcome in Victoria. When Governor Seymour issued the proclamation of union on November 19, 1866, James Douglas wrote: "The ships of war fired a salute on the occasion—A funeral process, with minute guns would have been more appropriate to the sad melancholy event."[22]

Seymour was now governor of the enlarged colony of British Columbia. As his office gave him the power to proclaim New

Westminster the new capital, he might have done so, but his popularity was on the down grade and his fear of using his powers arbitrarily convinced him to allow the question to be voted on in the Legislative Council at New Westminster. This was a mistake. The Victorians detested Governor Seymour and were determined to place the capital in Victoria come what may. A combination of drink and trickery won the day for Victoria on March 28, 1867.

The day after the decisive vote at New Westminster, the British North America Act was passed by the British Parliament. The act provided for the confederation of New Brunswick, Nova Scotia, Lower Canada, and Upper Canada, and for a railroad to link the regions. On July 1, 1867, the Dominion of Canada came into existence.

When Vancouver Island became part of British Columbia, its debt was $293,698. The mainland was no better off with a debt of $1,002,983. Seymour's health and popularity were rapidly waning, both problems to some extent due to his drinking. His opposition to confederation was increasingly unpopular. Seymour's strongest opponent in this matter was Amor De Cosmos who, having one of his brighter years, knew that British Columbia was doomed if it continued to starve and struggle on as an isolated British colony.

In Victoria, where ideas were thrown about at random, there was growing interest in BC withdrawing from its relationship with Great Britain and joining the United States. In an editorial of April 25, 1867, the editor of the *British Colonist,* D. W. Higgins, listed six arguments in support of the Annexation Movement, then summed it up: "Is it any wonder that a transfer of the Colony to the United States under the arrangement proposed would be hailed with satisfaction by many of our people."[23] This movement was largely restricted to Victoria and to counter the Annexationists, De Cosmos proposed a resolution in the Legislative Council advocating "immediate entrance into the North American Federation [Canada]."[24]

The Home Office was against amending the BNA Act to in-

Dr. John Sebastian Helmcken.   *Sir Arthur Kennedy.*

Sir Frederick Seymour.   *Sir Anthony Musgrave.*

clude BC because there was just too much uninhabited distance between the two areas. Many British Columbians were against confederation for personal reasons: "The government officials, the Hudson's Bay agents and the Yankee adventurers," according to Sir John A. MacDonald, one of the Fathers of Confederation, "have conspired together to defeat confederation and have been for the time successful."[25]

In 1869 two things happened to bring confederation closer. Governor Seymour died and was replaced by Governor Anthony Musgrave, a known supporter of confederation and a former governor of Newfoundland. Also, during this year the HBC transferred all of its rights to the land between Canada West and the Rocky Mountains to the Dominion of Canada.

After a long debate, British Columbia joined the Dominion of Canada on July 20, 1871. This was ultimately the result of the dominion's promise of a transcontinental railway, on which construction would begin in not more than two years and would be completed in not more than ten years. The immediate benefit to British Columbia was responsible government.

The years of promise were now over. Call it manifest destiny, or the tide of progress, either way the wave had rolled the length of Vancouver Island. The HBC was gone, Vancouver Island was now only a geographical unit within British Columbia, and in turn BC was a Canadian province. Colonization was working, settlements were established, and farms were developing. Although Victoria, like all of BC at the time, was suffering an economic slump, the coal-mining town of Nanaimo was relatively prosperous. The wave had broken the back of the indigenous culture, but few cared; what counted was that the honest, hard-working Canadian had his place in the sun. Now it was time to settle down and make the promise pay.

CHAPTER NINE

Rogues, Red Lights and

Rum

Approximately 5,000 people lived in Victoria and its vicinity in 1872. From the city it was a six-hour trip by steamer to New Westminster; three hours to Port Townsend, the only centre of any consequence in Puget Sound at the time; and about a three- or four-day trip to San Francisco. As the only major port north of San Francisco, Victoria was the distribution point and the centre of foreign trade for British Columbia.

"Victoria" in the 1870s meant Victoria and Esquimalt. Ships drawing less than 18 feet found Victoria Harbour suitable for their requirements, but larger vessels used Esquimalt Harbour, some three miles by road from Victoria. With its ample and protected harbour, Esquimalt seemed destined to become the western terminus of the Canadian Pacific Railway when it reached the west coast. Already Esquimalt was the naval base for the British ships patrolling the Northwest Coast; the base had a naval yard and hospital, and the island's first free public school was opened there in 1863. Although Esquimalt had the harbour and its own prosperity, Victoria had the banks and businessmen, the government offices and civil servants; when Victorians dreamed and talked of the future, Esquimalt was understood to be an extension of Victoria—the centre of trade and transshipment for British Columbia, if not western Canada.

"Victoria is more than prosperous—she is solid. From her business blocks to her Government buildings—all is stability. Her business firms are solid, and what cannot be said of some of Oregon's thoroughfares, even her roads are solid. Wherever you find the English doing business there will you always find a volume of business to be done, and wherever the English element is predominant there will you always find prosperity."[1] Such views of Victoria, and this one is from an Oregon magazine of 1885, were written and published widely in the years between Confederation and World War I. So many were published, in fact, that the unsubstantiated optimism of travellers and journalists came to be accepted as hard fact.

She was "solid" but to many, Victoria was something of a never-never land. The Marchioness of Dufferin visited the city in August 1876 with her husband, the Governor General of Canada, and wrote of their arrival with graceful honesty. "Then we stepped ashore, and were received by Sir James Douglas and a number of residents, and got into the carriage which was to drive us to Victoria [they landed at Esquimalt]. We grew into an enormous procession before we reached that city, numbers of carriages and riders joining us. At one point along the route there rode out from the wood a party of magnificently-dressed archers, such as you have *not* seen off the stage: green-feathered hats, green velvet coats, breeches, big boots, bows, arrows—really very handsome-looking people. They formed an escort the rest of the way. Further on we picked up a band of horsemen with red ribbons across the breasts—a company in green—bands—some militia—an army of small boys, each carrying a bright-coloured flag—my 'bodyguard.' The men who wore the coloured sashes saluted in a curious fashion, by putting the hand to the mouth."[2] Thus they continued on into Victoria, where the Governor General made a speech, and his wife observed that the feeling in Victoria was pro-British and anti-Canadian, due to broken promises regarding the transcontinental railroad.

Interestingly, the Marchioness of Dufferin does not comment on the British element in Victoria, though she does broach the subject from a fresh angle: "We have a Chinese cook, who is, I grieve to say, highly British, having cooked for six Governors, but he is very good in his homely way."[3] Twenty years later a visitor argued that Victoria "is said by some writers to be an essentially American city. I cannot agree with them. To my mind it is the most English one I have visited in America. Many American customs prevail there; but, apart from these customs, I doubt if there is a place on that continent containing more people so essentially English, who in language, appearance, and actions differ little from their countrymen in Great Britain."[4]

The fantasy of Victoria being "a bit of old England" developed during these years, but not from the pens of well-travelled American and British writers, who knew better; the promoters of the idea were newspapermen looking for material—or colour—for their stories. That the climate was very similar is indisputable, and it was true that some of the farms near Victoria resembled British farms. One thing was true of all the pioneers in the Pacific Northwest: as soon as possible they built homes and towns exactly like those they had left, and more often than not gave them the same names. Yet a few British visitors "felt" something here that they realized ran deeper than these obvious superficial similarities. It was not until Eleanor Caroline Smyth, who lived in Victoria during most of the 1860s, came to write her memoirs almost half a century later that an observer caught the heart of this resemblance. "Little Victoria, the capital, must have been not unlike our own infant settlements in Britain of a thousand and many more years past, in that it was a wooden town of unpretentious buildings which, except where it faced the sea, was hemmed in by vast forests whose outer fringe only had been explored, and in which roamed fierce packs of timber wolves."[5] It was the spirit of the place, not what man was building on the place, that made British visitors think of home.

The "bit of old England" idea persisted, and the likeness became more specific in 1903 when a writer claimed: "On the southern and eastern parts [of the island], holly, ivy, broom, gorse, heather, privet and other old country shrubs thrive to perfection and all the old-fashioned English flowers are seen in the gardens and fields as though to the manor born. The picturesque oaks complete the verisimilitude."[6] Others at this time saw much more of England in Victoria than just landscape and plants, but as their views are mingled with talk of "Empire" and "British blood," their objectivity is open to more than one question. Even Rudyard Kipling, the empire's staunchest soldier of the pen, who saw much of England locally, did not compare Victoria to the homeland. "To realize Victoria you must take all that the eye admires most in Bournemouth, Torquay, the Isle of Wight, the Happy Valley at Hong Kong—the Doon, Sorrento, and Camps Bay; add reminiscences of the Bay of Naples, with some Himalayas for the background."[7]

One must write about the myth of Victoria at some length for, while the English facade did exist, in reality the city and island had many faces, few of which are ever discussed. It never was the calm and beautiful, British and "solid" city of legend. "A walk through the streets of Victoria," wrote a visitor in 1872, "showed the little capital to be a small polyglot copy of the world. Its population is less than 5,000; but almost every nationality is represented. Greek fishermen, Kanaka sailors, Jewish and Scotch merchants, Chinese washerwomen or rather washermen, German and Yankee restaurant-keepers, English and Canadian officeholders and butchers, negro waiters and sweeps, Australian farmers and other varieties of the race, rub against each other, and apparently in the most friendly way."[8]

Yankees came to Vancouver Island, as did men from every part of the British Empire, but there were others, too: South Americans, Chinese, and Europeans. Of these Europeans the most prominent and successful were Germans. Joseph Lowen, one of the earliest miners, founded the Victoria Brewery and a flour business. Louis Erb, once Lowen's partner, started the soon-to-be-famous Phoenix Brewery. Leopold Loewenberg was one of Victoria's first real estate men, and long the city's most eligible bachelor. On May 20, 1861, the *British Colonist* announced the formation of the Germania Sing Verein: "Victoria Harmonie:—a number of our German residents have recently formed themselves into a singing club."[9] When the Germans won the Franco-Prussian War, the club ran a notice in the newspaper: "The German society, one of the most popular and respectable of our national societies, will hold its annual gathering. We have been requested to state that the occasion is not one of thanksgiving, and least of all is it connected with or commemorative of 'the victory'. Indeed, so free is it from anything of the kind that Frenchmen will be found mixing in friendly sociality."[10]

Black Americans also came with the gold rush. Mufflin Gibbs opened the first store in Victoria, Lester & Gibbs, Dealers in Groceries, Provisions, Boots, Shoes, &c., to compete with the HBC. Another black American was a lawyer, and others were barbers, restaurateurs, store-keepers, and draymen. One visitor thought these people "a most orderly and useful and loyal section of the community," and considered most of them superior to Englishmen of equal rank.[11] Another thought them "far more steady, sober, and thrifty" than the "whites by whom they are so much despised."[12]

By the 1870s the blacks and Germans were often important figures in Victoria's very fragile economy. When necessary, both groups were quite capable of out-Britishing the Britons, many of whom were only synthetically British—sons of the empire, not of English soil. Such was not the case with the Chinese, who came with the first wave of gold-seekers in 1858.

Throughout the gold-rush years there were those who complained of the Chinese presence. That the Chinese would work for lower wages than their European counterparts bothered many miners a great deal less than did their success in the gold fields. The Chinese miners were renowned for their ability to find gold in locations already worked over by white miners, and most of it was shipped back to China. The estimates as to how much gold they found vary; some writers claim it was worth millions, but the fact is no one knows. Complaints aside, democracy in British Columbia included the Chinese. That this soon ceased was due in part to population. In 1870 the population was 36,247; 70.8% were Indian, 24.9% white, and 4.3% Asian. In other words the whites were outnumbered three to one by men who lived outside European society. Later figures are equally revealing. Between 1851 and 1901, 78,603 people immigrated to BC; of these 19,388 were English, 17,164 were American, and 14,516 were Chinese. The next-largest group was the Scots and Irish totalling 10,411, and then came the Japanese, of whom 4,515 arrived. Many whites, particularly of the small business and labouring class wondered if British Columbia was going to be a "white man's country."

In 1886 the BC government passed three acts dealing with the Chinese: one made it impossible for Chinese to own Crown

A Chinese funeral in Victoria, at the corner of Government and Johnson streets, ca 1892.

COURTESY OF HISTORY DIVISION, BC PROVINCIAL MUSEUM

A street in Victoria during Chinese New Year, February 1900.

land, another regulated the Chinese population, and a third, which was disallowed, attempted to prevent their immigration. The Dominion government took even stronger steps: in 1885 it created a $50 tax on every Chinese person entering Canada, and by 1903 this tax had been increased to $500. W. S. Caine, a visiting Member of Parliament from England, painted a clear picture of the lot of the Chinese in Victoria in 1888. "Cooking, laundry, gardening, and housemaid's work, is all done admirably and thoroughly by the Chinese, against whom there is a great deal of unjust prejudice, because they are the only cheap labour to be got. Many of these Chinamen come from Hong Kong, and are as much our fellow-subjects as the British Columbians themselves, and out to possess equal rights of citizenship."[13] Unable to settle on the land, the Chinese congregated in Victoria, where they worked as menials.

Interestingly, although everyone concerned agreed that Victoria had a substantial Chinese population, no one agreed as to their numbers in the city—or on the island for that matter. One government census counted slightly more than 4,000 Chinese in British Columbia in 1881. In 1884, according to one Victoria historian, there were 15,000 Chinese living in Victoria. If this is an accurate figure, there were 3,000 more Chinese in the city than Europeans; no wonder the "yellow peril" was such a reality to so many Victorians of the day. The whites were outnumbered (and no one bothered to count the Indians living in Victoria at this time). The statistics did not make the British the "predominant" race in the city, so Victorians ignored the truth and talked all the louder about the scenery and British immigration.

The confusion surrounding the ethnic-social conditions on the island prior to 1914 is not clarified by the histories and guidebooks, as nine-tenths of these books were written by tourists for tourists, or by civil servants for promotional reasons. One writer describes a guidebook that reached "rhetorical ecstasies when it speaks of 'the quietude of the city and orderly inhabitants,' but what the book says is true. The inhabitants are not only orderly; they are correct."[14]

Only three years prior to this observation, part of this "orderly" and "correct" population rioted on learning of the sinking of the *Lusitania* in May 1915. After doing an estimated $30,000 damage to the Blanshard Hotel (previously known as the Kaiserhof), owned by H. Kostenblader, a naturalized British citizen, the crowd marched on Government House. Only when the Lieutenant-Governor and his wife, said to have close German ties, were threatened did the government call out the troops, and the decision was not a popular one. Many Victorians saw the Germans getting no more than they deserved. This attitude, which continued privately and publicly, prompted many Vancouver Island Germans to move to the United States.

Another side of Victoria and Vancouver Island life ignored

by the majority of writers was described in no uncertain terms by one Oregon writer in 1885. "In the minds of the average Oregonian the name Victoria is at once associated with the thoughts of defaulting cashiers, postmasters and refugees from justice in general. No sooner do we hear of a bank suspension in Oregon or Washington Territory, of some postmaster's ingenious methods of duplicating accounts, of some conniving rascal who has cheated an unfortunate widow out of her last dollar, than we read in our Victoria dispatches of the safe arrival in that city of those distinguished individuals."[15]

Many of these criminals were returned to US ports as quickly as they arrived in Victoria, often by the same ship. Yet for every man or woman returned, there is a story of the "shady character" or "mysterious lady," who appears in Victoria, well-to-do but without known means, remains for varying lengths of time, then disappears. Over the years literally hundreds of articles have appeared in Vancouver Island newspapers concerning these men and women. So little is known about many of them, that it is safe to say the curiosity of Victoria's residents wove mysteries where little mystery existed. It was a small town, 20,219 in 1900, and there was always gossip. Stranger than the stories of Russian princesses living in seclusion in the upper suites of the Empress Hotel, sons of rich German barons living as hermits on the shores of Cowichan Lake, or con men on the lam hiding out as labourers in logging camps, is the apparently well-documented account of William Clarke Quantrill's last years on Vancouver Island.

Quantrill led a troop of Confederate irregulars during the Civil War. In 1863 he received a captain's commission and a year later, leading 450 men, he raided Lawrence, Kansas. There he and his men killed 150 or more men, women, and children in what has become known as one of the most infamous actions during the war. In 1865 his band of men, now much reduced in size, was attacked by a federal force and virtually wiped out, and Quantrill supposedly died in prison. In 1907, the *Victoria Daily Colonist* ran an article under the title "Guerrilla

Interior of a logging camp cookhouse, ca 1900.

Chieftain's Home at Quatsino," and in part it ran: "Bill Quantrill, leader of Quantrill's guerrillas in the American Civil War is alive on the North Coast of Vancouver Island, under the name of John Sharp. That is the statement made by people who should be in a position to know. Among them is J. E. Duffy, a prominent timberman who recently became interested in timber limits at Quatsino. He met the so-called 'John Sharp' and recognized him at once as Quantrill. Duffy was a member of a Michigan troop of cavalry which cut up Quantrill's force, and had no difficulty in recognizing his man."[16]

The Seattle papers, and undoubtedly many other US papers, reprinted the story. Shortly after the article appeared, the *Tees* sailed for the west coast of the island; aboard her were two strangers bound for Quatsino Sound. There they went ashore briefly. A few hours later, the *Tees* now on her return voyage to Victoria, Sharp was found dying, a bloody iron poker lying nearby. The men apparently disembarked at Victoria and left on the next boat for Seattle, as they were never seen again.

Every decade or two there occurs a year that stands out, a benchmark of sorts. In looking backward, 1907 is one such year. Sharp-Quantrill was killed at Quatsino Sound; a fire swept Victoria's red-light district clean; and it was the last year that opium factories operated legally in Victoria.

On July 23, 1907, a fire began in a blacksmith's shop at the corner of Herald and Store streets. Burning out of control, it soon engulfed the Albion Iron Works and then, fanned by a southwest wind, it swept the length of Herald and Chatham streets between Store and Government. As the ashes were cooling, firemen counted over 97 buildings destroyed and more than 250 people homeless. However, there is no record of the city's churches taking up collections for the destitute, as so often happened. Almost all the "people" burned out in the fire were prostitutes, and the loss of the bawdy houses was not mourned. They opened up again, as they always do; the one-dollar houses on Chatham Street, the two-dollar houses on Herald.

Just when this area developed into a red-light district is not known. Stories of sailors enticing Indian women into the bush east of Johnson Street date back to the 1850s, and as the area was fronted by wharves in the 1880s, certainly by that time the streets closest to the waterfront were a thoroughfare for sailors. In 1892 the *British Columbia Directory* lists the residents along the south and north sides of Chatham and Herald in its street directory; almost all the residents are men, but someone listed only as "Susan" and "Mrs Jesse" did live next to the Albion Iron Works, while the occupants at numbers 24 and 28 Herald are "cabins". The "Victoria Directory" section (a listing of the residents' full names and occupations), almost never names the men resident along Chatham and Herald. This oversight is as suggestive as "Susan" at Number 12 Herald, or the close-by "cabins"—certainly a euphemism, for much of the business in that district was negotiated in cabins.

Only at a half-century remove can the area be thought of as colourful. It was a skidroad, one of the first in the Pacific Northwest; a place where prostitutes and their pimps, small-time criminals and derelicts gathered around cheap hotels and boarding houses; where sailors, loggers, miners and fishermen gravitated to drink and carouse their way through their savings; and it was a place that the police preferred to ignore as the bouncers employed by the saloons and bawdy houses could do the policeman's work more quickly and quietly, and with much less paper work. Another aspect of Victoria's first skidroad was white slavery, which was rampant in the decades immediately prior to 1914. European women were imported to New York and Montreal, and then sold to dealers on the Pacific coast for sums ranging from $15 to $500 and the trade in Chinese girls was even more lucrative. In Washington, Oregon, and California, these girls sold for amounts ranging from $500 to $2,000, and sometimes the prices went as high as $3,000. As Seattle and San Francisco were later ports of entry in this trade, it stands to reason that Victoria was one of the first—particularly as Asian women could not land in the US after the Chinese Exclusion Act of 1882. Before the 1890s, Victoria was the closest North American port to Asia. It is likely that throughout these years Victoria, as Vancouver was known to have been after the turn of the century, was a major distribution point for San Francisco and Los Angeles clearing houses.

In the 1880s, before the mushroom growth of Vancouver and Seattle, Victoria had the largest red-light district on the Northwest Coast. Considering that the period corresponds with the middle years of the reign of Queen Victoria, the newspapers understandably said little if anything about one of the city's claims to fame. Even in the years since, very little has been written about this area, known as the "Restricted Area," stretching along Chatham and Herald from the waterfront to Government Street. One reason for this silence is that writers have nowhere to go for information. The police thought the district too tough to patrol or were bought off; this explains the high rents in the area. At a time when a family could rent a house in Victoria for $50 a month, madames were paying up to $500 a month. There are other reasons for the lack of information, and for similar silences surrounding the red-light trade in Seattle, Vancouver, Ocean Falls, and Prince Rupert. Businessmen who were, or became, leading citizens were financially involved in prostitution. In a society where single men outnumbered eligible women ten or more to one, young and attractive prostitutes became "eligible" and then the wives and mothers of a new generation. Silence, initially bought or sold, then maintained by financial and political pressure in many cases, is now complete, as perhaps it should be, if it were not for the loss to history.

After the fire of 1907 the Restricted Area was soon back in business, only to be closed down forever three years later. A Victoria columnist, writing in 1910, tore a strip off the people behind the closure. "Now you religious persons have closed up 'the restricted area' and you have the infinite gall to make a 'kick' because your wives and daughters cannot walk down the street without being accosted." He goes on to say: "When I first came to Victoria six years ago, any girl could walk down the street and if she were respectable there was not a man who would dream of accosting her." He predicted the "breaking up of the Chatham Street sheep-fold would result in the scattering of the sheep throughout the residential area". And not long afterwards he happily informed his readers that "The trademark of these unfortunates may be seen any night on Rockland Avenue, Burdette and Linden, and even on the Fairfield estate."[17]

Drinking was another story. Hardened miners of the 1850s and 60s, men who had spent their lives in mining camps and towns, commented on the amount that Victorians drank. It was the practice then to nip in for a quick one whenever a man met an acquaintance on the street, and this began early in the morning and continued until no one was left standing. By 1885 even the locals were complaining of the goings-on inspired by drink. The girls working Broad Street would rent carriages and drive out to the Ship Inn at Esquimalt and carry on all too loudly for any listener's comfort. Two decades later a Montreal newspaper referred to Victoria as a "sin den" with a population that drank too much for its own good.

A Miss Murcutt, speaking in Victoria at an 1908 temperance convention, spoke of an anonymous town where there lived not a dozen girls over 15 who were still "pure". The *Colonist* took this personally and asked for the name of the town and the source of her information. Outside the hallowed convention hall, and outside the doors of the *Colonist*, a joke had it that Victoria had many, many churches and only three saloons—to every church.

If whisky created legends prior to prohibition (1917 to 21 in British Columbia), few are remembered; opium had quite different results. One of Victoria's legendary attractions was the opium dens in Chinatown—opium smugglers lived and worked

Tobacconist's shop, ca *1900. Note bar at the back.*

in the tunnels honeycombing the rock under Fisgard Street; housewives stopped off at these dens to smoke; young European girls became addicts and lived out their now-brief span of years in the dens—most of these stories are still current in Victoria, in spite of the fact there never was any factual support for these tales.

In 1892, two opium factories were doing business in Victoria; Kwong on Lung & Co., "opium merchants," at 32 Cormorant Street, and Sing Kee & Co., "importers and dealers in opium," a few doors away at 24 Cormorant. On July 27, 1886, Lem Chung & Co. paid their $250 fee for a licence to sell opium on Cormorant Street; it is thought that 13 other opium dealers were in business at this time. Most of these, it is claimed, closed down between 1887 and 1894, when the US passed a series of acts to restrict and control the importation of opium. No such acts existed in Canada, and it would seem that at least six dealers continued processing opium in Victoria. After the Canadian Pacific Railway reached the west coast, US papers claimed the railway was the greatest factor in the spreading opium trade. In 1908 the Opium and Narcotic Drug Act was passed by the Canadian government. This spelled the end to a lively trade and is said to have cost Victoria businessmen some $200,000 yearly.

Little was done to stop the importation of untaxed opium into the United States from Canada. In 1904 the trade involved 300 people and $2,000,000 of opium annually. This industry was based in the Pacific Northwest, particularly within the Victoria-Vancouver-Puget Sound triangle. As it was not illegal in British Columbia to import or export opium, and as it was a source of government revenue, the authorities turned their backs on the problems it was causing south of the border. There the government agents were quite helpless, for the hundreds of miles of waterways in Puget Sound were a smuggler's paradise. An hour out of Victoria and quite literally a fast sloop or schooner could disappear, not to be seen again until, its cargo landed, it sailed innocently back into the open water of the

Strait of Juan de Fuca.

Smuggling opium was only a new feature of an old and established business. As early as the 1850s, Canadian wool and wool products and British whiskies were smuggled south. Vancouver Islanders grew a little grim with the smugglers when sheep thieves began working on the island. Smuggler's Cover on Cadboro Point was named in honour of these nocturnal capitalists, San Juan Islanders, who landed at the tiny cove. These smugglers were small-timers compared to the men smuggling opium and, later, Chinese from Vancouver Island to Washington. The Chinese usually paid their own way for the trip across the Strait of Juan de Fuca. Supplying transportation was lucrative, but it could not compare to the profits from smuggling opium.

Best known of all the local smugglers was Lawrence Kelly, a British seaman who, after jumping ship at New Orleans, fought in the Civil War, only to disappear from sight after 1865. He reappeared in Puget Sound in the 1870s where he soon became known as "the King of the Smugglers".

It would seem that Kelly did well enough when he started smuggling—at first it was easy to out-sail the slow and undermanned US government vessels—but Kelly hung on to sail when the government changed over to steam and after that he was not much of a challenge once sighted in open waters. On his release from a federal penitentiary in 1910, Kelly retired to a veterans' home for confederate soldiers in Louisiana.[18]

Kelly's legend lives on, but not as "the King of the Smugglers"; today he is frequently spoken of as "Pig Iron Kelly". Kelly demanded prior payment from the Chinese he planned to smuggle into the United States. This meant that to make a profit he did not even have to complete his side of the arrangement. Kelly kept pig iron in his bilge, and it was not there for ballast. If a revenue vessel closed in on him, Kelly tied an ingot or two to each of his passengers and tossed them overboard. There was little trouble involved in this for he only carried a few men at any given time. When the government vessel asked Kelly to heave-to, the evidence was gone; gone except for the smell of incense and opium that the stories claim lingered in his hold, and still linger in the legends along with his deadly efficiency.

Another smuggling activity in these decades was carried on by men such as "Poker" Jack Quail and Billy Lyons. British seamen unhappy with their lot at Esquimalt would pay good money to be transported from the island to the tall and uncut timber of the Olympic Peninsula. They never lacked for customers and Quail and Lyons made a handsome living accommodating sailors.

There were other characters working out of Victoria at one time or another who, if their stories were known beyond sketchy details, would provide a deep look into the darker side of Victoria the Good. Men like "Bloody" Fritz Hansen, sometimes better known as "Bully" Hansen, who bragged he killed a man with his fists on every one of his voyages and Sapaniza, a half-Chinese, half-Filipino smuggler, once known along the entire Pacific coast of North America as "the King of the Opium Ring" were in and out of Victoria at various times. The man with the strangest legends surrounding him was Captain Alex McLean, the man that Jack London used as the prototype for Wolf Larsen of *The Sea Wolf*, though the two men never met. If anything McLean was deadlier than the fictional Larsen. Hansen killed a man each voyage; McLean returned from at least one voyage without a crew. Unlike the other smugglers and pirates and worse, McLean called Victoria home. He lived in the city from 1880 to 1910 and was among the leading captains in the sealing industry that was for years based in Victoria.

Life in Victoria was not as black and white, as good and bad, as these pages may suggest; there was also a gray middle ground. Not all the prostitutes lived in the cribs and cabins of the Restricted Area, just as the local business was not all conducted in the solid brick buildings on Fort and Douglas streets. There were meeting places for people from either side of Government Street: restaurants, usually, where privacy was guaranteed, while men and women dined and talked business. The Poodle Dog Restaurant was one such place, and while its notoriety is still talked of, just what went on there and what business was dealt with, is unknown.

The Poodle Dog, then at 49 Yates Street, was the meeting place for Tom MacInnes and Alex McLean on three occasions between 1897 and 1914. Twelve years after their final dinner together, MacInnes wrote of their time together but why they met, as they were not friends, is never explained. During the years they met, both were "men about town" in Victoria, and here the similarities end. Tom MacInnes was a lawyer who was acting as secretary for his father, Thomas Robert MacInnes, Lieutenant-Governor of British Columbia (1897–1900), at the time of their first meeting. Later MacInnes would be one of Canada's most popular poets. In 1897, Alex McLean was wanted by the US government for bilking them of $50,000; the Russians were after him as a poacher in their sealing grounds; and the French government wanted him for piracy (poaching their oyster beds for pearls) and various other acts, possibly including murder, in the South Pacific.

Whatever their reasons for meeting, this brief description of the early part of their first evening together is one of the few solid pictures of Victoria's netherworld. "The Poodle Dog of that time, of course, is no more. Wine was cheap; love was free. Louis Marboeuf was of the old school, in which cookery was reckoned with the fine arts and dishes were prepared with the same care one gives to the structure of a sonnet. They had a ravishing way of cooking mussels, which were then in season. And we were told that two fine blue grouse had just been received. There was no law against serving them. I looked around to see who else might be there. And in one dim corner of that dim kafay I saw Vanilla. Her glance and smile were enough to light it up for me; I had known her elsewhere as one of the quality; but she was then living quietly and in reduced circumstances. But her troubles had only left her sweeter than in her earlier years; as one may find a ripe hot berry in July sweeter by far than the tart impudence of the berries in early June. I introduced the captain and the three of us dined together."[19]

That night McLean gave Vanilla a French pearl, and in 1914, when the two men dined together for the last time, McLean was wearing the woman's pearl as a tie pin, the pearl clenched by five golden claws. That first evening together, as described by MacInnes, is a picture of a world gone: gone even as they met the last time. The Victoria known by McLean since 1880 no longer existed: sealing was over; smuggling was too dangerous to be worthwhile; the Restricted Area was closed down; and Vancouver had usurped Victoria's place on the west coast of Canada.

In 1871, Seattle had a population of 1,107; Vancouver did not exist, and Victoria's population was estimated to be 3,270. Ten years later the populations of Seattle and Victoria had increased by some 2,000 each, and Vancouver was a village of 300 but by 1911, Seattle had grown to a city of 237,194 and Vancouver's population had exploded to 100,401 while Victoria staggered along with 31,660.

Although out-matched by Vancouver, now the terminus of the CPR, Victoria fought the mainland city every inch of the way in their battle for supremacy in BC. It was a losing battle; due to a variety of reasons, the CPR's direct contact with Vancouver being the major one, the island city lost most of the Klondike gold-rush trade to Vancouver. Two railroad schemes were planned, both of which would connect Victoria directly with the Kootenay mining area: the first, the Victoria and Eastern Railway and Navigation Company, was taken over by the CPR in 1898, and Victoria's rights cancelled by the federal government; the Coast-Kootenay Railway Company died in the bud. The Dominion Assay Office was built in Vancouver; the Victoria-owned-and-operated Canadian Pacific Navigation Company was bought out by the CPR and part of the headquarters moved to Vancouver; and then the end came in 1900 when the Victoria branch of Bank of British Columbia was sold to the Bank of Commerce. A year later Vancouver was the centre of provincial banking, and Victoria was just another city in British Columbia.

By 1905–06 the financial centres of the logging and fishing industries were in Vancouver, as was the mining centre. Residents north and west of Nanaimo had very little reason to visit Victoria. After spending months in the bush or at sea, men wanted entertainment; having closed the Restricted Area, Victoria was not a place for single men bent on having a good time. Vancouver was, and so was Seattle; both cities were impressed by money, unlike Victoria, where the proprieties, though as outdated as Queen Victoria and her era, were all important.

Such conditions might have existed forever, but on August 4, 1914, the guns opened fire. As Canada was not independent, but merely a self-governing colony within the empire, when Great Britain declared war, Canada's role began at once. That August a "detachment from the 5th (BC) Regiment of Canadian Garrison Artillery embarked," first for Vancouver, then to Valcartier and the Canadian Expeditionary Force.[20]

Although Royal Navy men-of-war had begun using Esquimalt Harbour as an anchorage in the 1840s, the only shore buildings were coal sheds on Thetis Island. The first permanent buildings were erected in 1857 and the base, now known as Canadian Forces Base Esquimalt, continued to grow, albeit slowly, until the 1880s and 1890s. A boom in these years, caused by the construction of the graving dock, saw the hospital and prison built, as well as residences. Great Britain's 1902 alliance with Japan caused drastic budget cuts; now that Japan could, if necessary, look after Britain's interests in the Pacific, London turned her naval interests on Germany's growing power.

On May 4, 1910, Canada initiated its own naval service, and on November 9, 1910, Great Britain turned over the Esquimalt base to Canada. Two days prior to this formality the Canadian cruiser HMCS *Rainbow* anchored in Esquimalt Harbour. Less than four years later, and only days before the United States declared its neutrality on August 5, 1914, the forces at Esquimalt were strengthened by the arrival of two submarines.

The *Iquique* and *Antofogasta* did not belong to the Canadian navy, at least not when they cruised into BC waters. Learning that Germany had two cruisers somewhere in the Pacific, and realizing that the antiquated *Rainbow* would not be able to protect BC shipping, Premier Richard McBride acted quickly. A Seattle shipyard had built two submarines for Chile, which could not pay for them, and the premier bought the vessels for $1,500,000. He was criticized locally for this unauthorized action until a pleased Dominion government took them over on August 7, 1914. Renamed the *CC-1* and *CC-2*, they served locally until 1917 when they sailed for Halifax, thus becoming the first Canadian naval vessels to make the passage from the Pacific to the Atlantic using the Panama Canal.

At various times during the war, rumours pitted the HMCS *Rainbow* against the German vessels, but no such battles ever occurred. Esquimalt's major activity during the war was as a

The Rainbow, Iquique *and* Antofogasta *in Esquimalt Harbour.*

training centre, and 20,000 men passed through the base's gate. As the locale was considered extremely healthy, the base also served as a recovery centre for the wounded. Victoria, "still relatively small and tightly-knit, responded generously. Private homes were opened up for those from out of town who needed a good meal and a family setting, convalescing soldiers were given special seats at local cultural and sporting events, while organizations such as the Victoria Patriotic Fund staged theatrical performances to aid the troops."[21]

Between 1914 and 1918, 8,000 men and women from Victoria saw service overseas. They returned to a city that had almost doubled in size since their departure. In 1918 Victoria was a city of 60,000 people, and she could and did brag of her 47 miles of paved streets, 60 miles of boulevard, and 132 miles of concrete sidewalks. The city was riding a wave of post-war prosperity, and though she may have lost out financially in many respects to Vancouver, Victoria was still the first and last port of call for ships passing through the Strait of Juan de Fuca. Victoria had every right to brag; by 1918 she was a 20th-century city but this growth had not been without its cost to the remainder of Vancouver Island.

CHAPTER TEN

Selling the Island

A very good macadamized road connected Victoria with Esquimalt by 1872. The road westward to the farming communities of Metchosin and Sooke had seen few improvements since the brief gold rush to the Leech River in 1864. Prospectors continued to seek the mother lode in the Sooke Hills, and while some of these men were making wages, no one was getting rich. Beyond Sooke on the west coast there was virtually no white population, though a few traders continued to do a small business in skins and oil. The extensive complex known as the Alberni Mills, located at the head of Alberni Inlet, was little more than a collection of empty buildings in the overgrowth, now almost a decade old.

On the northeast coast there remained some hope that new coal deposits would be found in the Fort Rupert area, but the fort itself was eking out its last years as a trading post. Comox, Cowichan, Chemainus, and Saltspring were considered to be small and prosperous agricultural communities, very pastoral in nature. The settlements of Lake (Lake Hill) and Saanich on

Hayward & Jenkinson sash-and-door factory, corner of Broughton and Langley streets, Victoria, ca 1875.

the Saanich Peninsula continued to thrive and flourish, mainly due to their proximity to Victoria. Nanaimo was a town of local importance that grew as the coal-mining industry expanded. Nearby on Newcastle Island, a recently established quarry was supplying stone to the contractors building the Federal Mint in San Francisco.

A Vancouver Island visitor in 1898 was not impressed by Victoria, a city that she claimed had no local market and very little money, though the city could afford to import eggs from the US—78,853 dozen for $13,000, on which $3,942 was paid in duty. Everywhere she looked she saw shabbiness. "The water-supply in the town is a disgrace; the roads are rough and uneven, the gutters stink, the wooden side walks are frequently so out of repair that they are positively dangerous." The bridges were considered unsafe; cows were allowed to browse on the streets, and as the ditches were never cleaned, they sprouted a "rank growth". "The British Columbian government make no free grants of land, and furthermore, exact a royalty upon all timber sold (even as cordwood) off the land." These charges, it was maintained, were required to pay for the business of government, but this logic, considering "the erection of the magnificent and costly pile of Government buildings at Victoria," could not stand on its own two feet for any visitor "who looks up at these buildings [the Legislative Buildings] and then turns round to find the squalid wretchedness of the town, and goes away into the backwoods to find the settlers struggling with the enormous initial difficulties of the country."[1]

This visitor was Frances MacNab, an English tourist whose real name was Agnes Fraser, and her tour of the island took her from Victoria to the new settlement then developing at Alberni, where she visited the mines, before crossing the island by stagecoach to Nanaimo. After a few days in the Nanaimo district, Fraser returned to Victoria by canoe. She possessed a healthy sense of humour, something she found lacking in most of the men she encountered, but her humour could not soften what she found outside Victoria—economic depression, poverty, and settlements that were in her eyes nothing more than collections of wretched shacks. Fraser's opinions are supported by a good deal of contemporary evidence and it all adds up to one conclusion: the flowering hoped for at the time of Confederation had died in the bud.

Men had seen a brilliant future for Vancouver Island in 1871: Victoria would be the capital of the province, the terminus of the Canadian Pacific Railway, and the greatest port north of San Francisco. Realistic as these dreams were in 1871, nothing worked out as planned. So many things backfired that, economically, Vancouver Island was left in the lurch until the turn of the century. Everyone knew that Confederation was a gamble; what no one could have foreseen was how the combination of a series of weak governments in Victoria, the old island-versus-mainland controversy, the complicated island-versus-Victoria situation, and the one-family control of the island's railroad and most of the coal mines would raise the odds against Vancouver Island's future development.

Between 1871 and mid-December 1915, British Columbia

elected 16 different governments. The briefest administration was that of Premier Joseph Martin, February 28 to June 14, 1900; the longest Premier Richard McBride's, June 1, 1903 to December 15, 1915. One recurring theme in all of these administrations was the island-versus-mainland fight, which had begun with the establishment of the Colony of British Columbia in 1858. In the first elected legislature, with John Foster McCreight as premier and attorney-general, there were 12 members from Vancouver Island and 13 from the mainland. At this time there were no political parties at the provincial level; members gathered around certain leaders. Governments based on personal loyalties are always weak and in BC's case the situation was made even more unstable by the island-mainland rivalry. This situation ceased to a degree after 1894, when Premier Theodore Davie created new constituencies based on population; prior to this an agreement had given the mainland one more member than Vancouver Island.

Vancouver Island was well represented in all of these governments. Its members were, of course, interested in maintaining Victoria's dominant position in the economic and political arena. This idea was based on the credo that what was good for Victoria was good for Vancouver Island. In the confusion of creating a provincial government and, until 1903, the political chaos caused by governments changing on the average of every two years, the island members failed to realize that Victoria's only concern was Victoria.

There is little evidence that Victoria entertained any real and lasting interest in economic or social problems outside what later became known as Greater Victoria. The island towns depended on Victoria as a centre—all the roads supposedly led to Victoria; but Victoria depended on them for nothing as they had nothing to offer her. Nanaimo did not fit into any of the island patterns because it was economically independent, and the owners of the coal mines owed Victoria nothing. Little did Victoria care what Nanaimo thought: Victoria-Esquimalt had been promised the terminus for the transcontinental railway. Her fortunes were secure and then the inconceivable happened: the construction of the railroad began on the mainland, and not on the island as Ottawa had promised.

The Terms of Union stated: "The Government of the Dominion undertake to secure the commencement simultaneously, within two years from the date of Union, of the construction of a railway from the Pacific towards the Rocky Mountains, and from such point as may be selected, east of the Rocky Mountains towards the Pacific, to connect the seaboard of British Columbia with the railway system of Canada; and further to secure the completion of such railway within ten years from the date of the Union."[2] This promise, and the economic boom that it forecast, led BC into Confederation, and for many these financial considerations were all that made union worthwhile. Although the promise was vague as to the railway's location, the federal government passed an order-in-council in June 1873, stating "Esquimalt on Vancouver Island be fixed as the Terminus of the Canadian Pacific Railway and that a line of railway be located between the harbour of Esquimalt and Seymour Narrows on the said Island."[3] This order was based on the assumption that the railway would reach the Pacific via Bute Inlet.

By 1875 it was becoming obvious to many islanders that the Bute Inlet route would not be chosen. Distrust mounted after the Esquimalt and Nanaimo Railway Bill was defeated in the Senate. Islanders began discussing secession; when Lord Dufferin visited Victoria in 1876 with his wife they were greeted with a large welcoming arch, which he refused to pass through, as it bore a slogan threatening separation. On August 30, 1878, the secession question was voted on in the BC legislature; the result was 14 to 9 in favour of separation. The resolution was forwarded to London, but was lost somewhere along the way, and when it finally arrived in January 1879, nothing was done as the mood had changed in BC.

The first contract for laying rail in the Fraser River valley was let early in 1880 and this, as far as the mainland was concerned, put an end to the secession movement. The islanders had to face the fact that Victoria would not be the western terminus; however, they still wanted the island railroad and the graving dock since, under the Terms of Union, "Canada had agreed to guarantee the interest at five per cent for ten years on £100,000 to aid the scheme".[4] This matter was not settled satisfactorily until 1884 when an act was passed that "provided for a grant of about 2,000,000 acres of land by the province, to be supplemented by a grant of $750,000 from the Dominion as aid to the construction of the island railway".[5] The same act provided for the construction, completion, and operation of the graving dock by the Dominion government.

The money and the land for the railway were handed over to the Dunsmuir Syndicate, which agreed to build the railroad within three years. At this time Robert Dunsmuir and his sons, James and Alexander, controlled most of the coal mines on Vancouver Island and they were certainly among the richest men in British Columbia—but more of this in the next chapter. Their deal with the federal government to build the Esquimalt and Nanaimo Railroad has been called a bit of canny bargaining on the Dunsmuirs' part, and also a "scandalous giveaway"; it gave the company not only approximately one-fifth of Vancouver Island, and three-quarters of a million dollars, but also the control of all the potential coal fields on the east coast of Vancouver Island.

Construction of the E & N Railway began in 1884 and it was completed to Nanaimo in 1886. A year later a link was built to Wellington, some five miles northwest of Nanaimo. In 1888 a connection was constructed to Victoria, via what is now known as the Johnson Street Bridge, and the first passenger train arrived in Victoria on March 29, 1888.

The arrival of the CPR at Vancouver had sealed Victoria's fate. In 1901 the *Colonist,* usually optimistic to the point of foolhardiness, could only say: "No one will claim that Victoria is enjoying a boom, and the amount of building in progress is not strikingly large, but the number of vacant houses in this city

COURTESY OF HISTORY DIVISION, BC PROVINCIAL MUSEUM

Robert Dunsmuir.

is very small, and so is the number of vacant business places. This is a good sign.'''⁶ No longer the centre of anything in the province by 1900, Victoria turned her attention to Vancouver Island. Nothing else had succeeded, but she could still be the island centre. Even this was no easy task as shown by a 32-page brochure, *Vancouver Island,* published by the Esquimalt and Nanaimo Railway Company in 1905, the same year the company was purchased by the CPR. It is a sales brochure for "A Promising Field for Farming, Fruit Growing, Dairying, Mining, Lumbering and Fishing in the Esquimalt and Nanaimo Railway Belt." What is striking about the book is its lack of interest in Victoria, a city seldom mentioned and never described in its pages.

The E & N, whether under the control of the Dunsmuirs or the CPR, owed no debt to Victoria. The Victoria & Sidney Railway, opened in 1894 and operated by private individuals, was also relatively independent of Victoria. In the Duncan-

Cowichan area, a nationally and internationally known sportsman's paradise was developing, largely due to the efforts of a few local entrepreneurs and later the E & N publicists. Nanaimo was a company town controlled by the Dunsmuir family, and later various national and international interests. None of these businesses depended on Victoria, nor did the Dunsmuirs, whose finances were tied to US interests.

The Dunsmuirs rose from the working class. In a few quick years they rose above any class then existent in British Columbia. Just as Victoria controlled the southern reaches of the island, Robert and James Dunsmuir controlled the area between Ladysmith and Courtenay.

Their island coal mines employed the Chinese when other businesses refused to do so, but the mine bosses gave them the worst jobs (sometimes jobs so dangerous that whites could not be forced to do them) at starvation wages—and these were often skilled labourers whose ancestors built the Great Wall of China. Other nationalities worked in the mines, but they could come and go. As the Chinese could not take up land, the coal mines were the only jobs available to most of them. Among the other nationalities, a certain percentage always settled on the

COURTESY OF HISTORY DIVISION, BC PROVINCIAL MUSEUM

Chinatown at Cumberland, ca 1910. *Only one cabin stands today.*

land, but as they did not settle in groups and were usually considered "Europeans" by the government, little is known of their
ethnic backgrounds. Exceptions to this rule were found at Duncan ("Duncans" at that time), which was first known as an
English settlement, and Saltspring Island, with its black settlers.
In both cases the predominance was a development, not a plan.

Except for the Europeans living in the major centres, any
census return before World War I is questionable. A large
majority of the white males were bachelors, as were the Orientals, and these men were constantly on the move; many fished
or logged or prospected during the summer, only returning to
Victoria or Nanaimo in the winter. The English novelist Morley
Roberts, who laboured in BC during the 1880s, remarked:
"The fact of the matter is that the whole of the Slope, the Pacific
Slope, is only one Main Street. It begins to dawn on a man on
the Slope, that in a very few years he might know everyone from
the Rocky Mountains down to Victoria and to Seattle and
Tacoma and Portland and San Francisco."[7]

Such movements as described by Roberts, and the lack of
sound details concerning the ethnic groups, make an accurate
history of the labourers' contribution to the settlement of the
east coast virtually impossible. However, two settlements, the
result of the "Dream of Freedom," as it has been called, are well
documented.

Nationalistic colonization schemes were common in western
Canada throughout the latter half of the 19th century. Many of
them were British, but the only two such schemes to develop on
Vancouver Island were European and the failures of both,
though for strikingly different reasons, illustrate the then-
current problems on the island.

Cape Scott is probably the least likely spot for a colony on
Vancouver Island. The northwestern edge of Vancouver Island
is as rough as any part of the Northwest Coast; without harbours, nearby settlements or passing steamers, its isolation in
1894 was awesome. Rasmus Hansen, a Dane working on a halibut schooner out of Puget Sound, fell in love with the cape:

"love" at any rate explains why he dreamed of establishing a Danish colony there. It sounds like a pipe dream, yet two years later the nucleus of a colony was in existence and some of the men, led by Nels C. Nelson, were exploring the land and conditions at Cape Scott. Good farming land did èxist in the area, if it was cleared and drained, and there was already at least one settler at nearby Shushartie Bay. In spite of the storms and fog dominating the north end of the island, the weather was generally mild.

Satisfied with what they had found, the Danes agreed, in a letter in 1896 to the Minister of Immigration in Victoria, to create a Danish colony on three townships at and near Cape Scott—if the government would build roads within the area, construct a dyke, and provide a school teacher. In 1897 the first colonists arrived on the *Willapa,* and that same summer the Canadian Pacific Navigation Company extended service to the new settlement. By 1900 there were 90 settlers at Cape Scott, and from there its history as a colony is downhill. The government found reasons not to build substantial roads. The men built the dyke, thus creating several acres of pasture land at the very head of Hansen Bay, without government assistance, but experience proved the land better for dairy herds or raising stock than farming, which never amounted to much more than truck gardening. To make matters worse, the men were forced to work in mainland or island logging camps or canneries to support their colonization effort. Shortly after the turn of the century the district was opened to pre-emption, and this ended the colony as such. By 1907 the remaining colonists had moved to the San Josef Valley, a few miles away on the west coast, where there was a harbour and land better suited for farming. Theo Frederiksen, among the first of the original settlers, remained behind with his family and continued to live at the cape until 1942.

The colony died but the idea of settling the area lived on. In 1908 what can only be called a settling rush began in the Cape Scott-San Josef Bay-Holberg region. Many of these people were

honest settlers, but others may have been lured into the area by
the promise that the cape would be connected to Nanaimo by a
railroad in the near future. Once this took place, Cape Scott (so
real estate brochures claimed) would be the gateway to Alaska.
By 1917, Fisherman Bay, a few miles north of Cape Scott, had a
hotel, a post office, and two stores, as well as a Dominion Government Telegraph office. By 1930 the population at the tiny
settlement was down to 200, which included all the settlers between Shushartie and San Josef bays. Nothing promised by the
government in 1897, or by the government and land promoters
later, ever materialized. Isolation killed this settlement twice.

Isolation, the government's refusal to keep its promises,
World War I (when most of the male population returned to
Victoria or Vancouver or London to enlist in a war effort from
which they did not return) spelled the end to various western
Canadian colonization efforts. The only island colony to sur-
vive all that fate threw at it, albeit in a different form, was
Sointula on Malcolm Island, across Broughton Strait from Port
McNeill.

Like many of the colonies in western Canada of the day,
Sointula was the result of economic problems in the western
world and the equally wide-spread labour-management strife.
Unlike the others, the idea of Sointula was Canadian born (the
organization of Cape Scott was planned in the United States, as
was the north-coast colony at Bella Coola), created by Vancouver Island problems. After the completion of mainland construction projects, Finnish labourers found work in the island's
coal mines. These mines were owned by James Dunsmuir who,
though he had begun life himself as a labourer, had no patience
with the increasing demands for a fair day's pay for a fair day's
labour. The Finns thought him a slave-driver, as did everyone
else working in his mines. When it became obvious to them that
he was introducing whisky into the towns to stifle their voices,
they sought a solution. Willing and able to act (unlike the
Chinese helplessly caught in the middle of a totally foreign
culture), the Finns asked Matti Kurikka, a Finnish writer and

editor, who had already attempted to establish a community in Australia, to come to Vancouver Island and lead them in the establishment of a utopian colony.

Led by Kurikka, the first pioneers reached Malcolm Island on December 15, 1901. The first official meeting of the new community was not held until the following June, whereupon it was quickly decided that Sointula would be a true utopia—everything would be shared. A three-day celebration was held, but the dreams and plans of those June days were stillborn. The miners, plus other Finns from the United States and Europe, were constantly in need of funds; farming, fishing, and logging, as well as a construction project on the mainland, failed to provide the necessary revenue. A fire killed 11 people, mostly children, in 1903. Kurikka was inept, debts piled up, and the population dropped from 238 in 1903 to less than 100 two years later. The colony's last meeting was held on May 27, 1905, and its assets liquidated.

A few of the original settlers did stay on at Sointula. The close-knit community continued to grow, and by 1910 the population was again over 100; by the end of World War I the population was 300, and the settlement was described as a farming and ranching centre. The first co-operative store in British Columbia was organized there in 1909, and is still operating. More important, and to the entire Northwest Coast, was the invention of the gill-net drum by Sointula fishermen. This revolutionized gill-net fishing, as no longer did the nets have to be pulled into the boat, hand over hand.

Remote as Cape Scott and Sointula and the many other coastal villages were from London and Vienna and Berlin, they too were affected by the events of August 1914. Every village on the island had its volunteers who went overseas, while at home, industry boomed for the first time. Fishing, logging and mining were all vital to the war effort. There were other side effects from the war: the cost of living rose 18% in 1917; strikes were almost a daily affair; union membership almost doubled; and labour considered a general strike in late 1917 to protest military conscription. The quiet island world north of Victoria was no more.

Another outcome of the war was prohibition. Supposedly it was imposed nation-wide as a war policy, but the acts (each province had its own) were not repealed at the end of the war; in fact, Quebec did not pass its prohibition act until 1919. These acts may have assisted the war effort, though how they did so is an open-ended question. In reality prohibition was the result of a strong temperance movement that had slowly gained strength throughout the 19th century. The British Columbia Prohibition Act came into force on October 1, 1917, and its effect was devastating. In Victoria, 80 hotels and saloons were forced to close. At the time there were three breweries in Victoria, three in Nanaimo, and one in Cumberland; just what happened to them is not known. Records suggest they began brewing near beer and certain other records suggest they were allowed to continue brewing beer for the export market. Whatever the case, the island's cities and villages lost the revenue from the hotels and saloons—the men who had wintered in Vancouver and Victoria found the climate south of the border more relaxing. Liquor was smuggled in from the United States and every man with a still, homebrew, or wine vat became a criminal.

In 1919 prohibition came into effect in the United States. Two years later BC repealed its prohibition, and almost immediately the Canadian rum-runners went into business—and a big business it was—supplying the needs of southern drinkers. Sailing out of Vancouver or Victoria, the rum-runners were legal businessmen in Canadian and international waters. The *Malahat* transported 60,000 cases at a time on her regular run to California, where American rum-runners would meet her outside the three-mile limit to buy and transport the cases to shore. Few of these ships were ever caught. It was good business, and one that continued until 1933, the year that the US repealed prohibition.

After 1921, the breweries failed to gather the momentum

they had lost during the dry years, and the hotels failed to reopen, and these factors contributed to the economic difficulties faced by the soldiers and sailors returning to the island at the end of the war. It was the "selling of tourist Victoria" that was the largest single contributor to the economic record for Victoria and Vancouver Island between 1918 and 1939.

The year that Victoria officially entered the tourist trade can be pinpointed exactly—1901. It was the idea of Herbert Cuthbert, a Yorkshireman and a resident of Victoria since 1891. During most of these years he had pleaded for an agency in Victoria to promote tourism, but his arguments fell on ears more interested in schemes to build railroads, to market island products on a world scale, and to somehow keep Victoria in her rightful place under the sun. By 1901, it was obvious to even the most loyal of Victorians that something had to be done to bolster the city's economy. Almost immediately after this realization, funds were found to create the Tourist Development Association. For the next 15 years Cuthbert directed this organization, but then he quit to move to Seattle. It seems that Cuthbert's ideas worked, and although the city appreciated his work, the city fathers found no pleasure in paying him for his efforts.

In 1918, the Tourist Development Association was reorganized and became the Victoria and Island Development Association. This association was based on the concept that tourists could create an interest in an area. In turn this "interest" could lead to an influx of people and money that, logically, should attract industry. Victorians knew they could sell the island's beauty; it was the one thing that had remained consistent. Los Angeles, which was then beginning its phenomenal growth, was used as an example of a city created by successfully marketing a climate—and that was about all that Los Angeles had had in the beginning. Advertising that would attract tourists was the scheme developed by the association. Once the tourists returned home, they would become salesmen for the island. To see the island once was to love it forever was the rationale.

Regrettably for everyone concerned, the United States was experiencing the largest boom in its history, and that activity did not extend to Vancouver Island. On the island people were

Tourist pamphlet map, pointing out Victoria's desirable climate.

discovering that you cannot eat beauty, and there was a constant flow of emigrants to California. Victoria's population grew by only 300 people between 1921 and 1931, and the increase elsewhere on the island was far from impressive. Philosophically the Victoria and Island Development Association was at odds with reality. Tourists did return to Vancouver Island to settle, but generally, these were people who had already made their money elsewhere. This class settled on the island because of the beauty and though a boon to local businesses, the last thing it wanted was industry. Despite the overall failure of the association's long-range schemes, they did succeed in luring tourists to Victoria.

It was the day of the auto and the auto camp where travellers could "rough it" in their tents. These were not unlike the federal and provincial camp grounds so popular currently. Victoria opened an auto camp on The Gorge near Curtis Point, which would eventually accommodate 400 cars and their passengers. The first year only 1,509 cars used it, but 1,227 were from the United States and they brought in an estimated $45,000 to the local economy. "Follow the Birds to Victoria" and see "a bit of old England" was the association's song. Tourists could reach Victoria via the Triangle Route—Seattle-Vancouver-Victoria—inaugurated by the Canadian Pacific Railway in 1904, when the *Princess Beatrice* made the first run. In 1922 Captain Harry Crosby, an American coastal businessman, began the Sidney-Anacortes ferry. The *Harvester King,* a slightly remodelled power scow, began running in April, and that June she carried 600 cars and 3,000 passengers.

It was estimated that 355,000 visitors reached Victoria in 1925, and in 1929, 33,605 cars landed at Victoria and Sidney. Obviously there was money in tourism. The CPR added the *Princess Marguerite* and *Princess Kathleen* to its Triangle Route in 1925; at the same time the Puget Sound Navigation Company, which was also making the triangle runs, increased its Seattle-based fleet. In 1928 another ferry system reached Victoria, the Edmonds-Victoria Company, and the *City of Victoria* began daily runs between Seattle and Victoria via Edmonds.

Victoria visitors certainly did not see much of England in Victoria and district, but few complained as they did not know what to expect; having seen something foreign they were satisfied. A folding map issued in 1935, and entitled *Where To Enjoy Yourself In Victoria & Vicinity,* lists 43 "Points of Interest". As most of these "Points" hardly reflected England (and what's more, similar spots could be seen anywhere in Puget Sound), obviously once the tourist was off the boat he was fair game. The points include Bazan Bay, Colwood, Elk Lake, Langford, Sooke, Shawnigan Lake, Telegraph Beach, and Whitty's Lagoon.

The brochure describes the Empress Hotel, built in 1908, as "the largest hotel in British Columbia", Beacon Hill with "small lakes with Royal Swans from the King's Preserves, Windsor Castle", the Parliament Buildings, and the "English" Residential Section on Moss Street: "It will be noticed that in this area of the city, sidewalks are built on only one side of the road, to the right, and there are many scenes resembling old English lanes".[8] Butchart's Gardens was one of the final attractions to the motorist, and the cost of admission was 50¢.

After 1929 tourism decreased substantially, yet by 1936 it was on the increase and the numbers of tourists continued to grow right up to 1939 and the onset of World War II. During this last decade fewer people were bringing their cars to the island, one reason being the condition of the roads outside Victoria and vicinity. As the selling of Victoria was all important, even though the Victoria and Island Development Association allegedly was interested in the entire island, there is little detail as to the effect of tourism on the areas north of Shawnigan Lake.

Government statistics throughout the period from 1914 to 1939 are unreliable. Yet, from the welter of facts and conflicting opinions, a few images emerge quite clearly. The most notable of these is that by 1919, everyone on the island was interested in the tourist trade. Victoria was connected to

The third Willows Hotel at Campbell River, ca 1914.

Nanaimo and Campbell River by the Island Highway; Nanaimo, in turn, had a ferry link to Vancouver. Parksville, a few miles north of Nanaimo, was the turnoff spot for the Canadian Highway that crossed the island to Alberni and Port Alberni. Most of the eastern centres were on the E & N Railway line, as well as being regular stopping places for steamers. The island highway system, the Olympic Highway that ran to Port Angeles from Olympia, Washington, and the Pacific Highway that connected Portland, Oregon, and Vancouver, British Columbia, was known as the "Georgian Circuit"—"An International Auto Tour in the Pacific Northwest". It was claimed in 1919 that "You might tour over the whole American continent for twelve months and at the end of that time if you came to take stock of what you had seen, you would recall the International Georgian Circuit with the greatest amount of pleasure."[9]

The condition of these island highways was the source of complaint by many tourists. In 1919 the Department of Public Works stated "It is proposed to improve it [the Island Highway] by re-surfacing, bettering the location, while at or near Victoria there will be an amount of hard-surfacing or permanent roadway." This, and the proposal to improve "curvatures, widening of the road and placing guard rails at the most dangerous portions" of the Malahat Drive imply that most of the Island Highway was yet under construction.[10] The road leading out of Nanaimo was "rough, then; the buses, primitive. Short stretches of blacktop soon gave way to a gravel surface which, in turn, as the buses rolled farther northwards, became a dirt track."[11]—but this description dates from the late 1920s, after many improvements had been made.

Vancouver Island towns used every means available to advertise themselves; thus a BC directory of 1919 reads in part like a tourism promo book. "When the visitor arrives in the Al-

Cowichan Lake road, 1921, showing wooden culvert.

Ladysmith, ca 1910, with St. Joseph's Church and school on the right. Note stumps.

berni Valley he realizes what the feelings of the poet, Tom Moore, were when he viewed the Vale of Avoca, in County Wicklow, where the waters of the Avon and Avoca meet"—thus began the description of Alberni—where "all that is necessary to the mind and body of mankind" could be found. Cowichan Lake was "one of the finest lakes in the province" and visitors on the way to the lake "will pass through one of the finest stands of big timber to be seen in the west." Ladysmith (only incorporated in 1904) and Nanaimo used strong language when describing their fine harbours and industrial strength. In Parksville, which considered itself a "tourist centre" because of the nearby fishing spots and its road connections with the island's interior and northern villages, and had more than doubled its population since 1913, "There is a pleasing lack of disfiguring, blackened stumps, and green meadows and creeper-covered houses give the impression of an English village."[12]

"English villages" were important at this time, as already noted. One of the tourist brochures issued in Victoria after the war had as a cover illustration a thatch-roofed cottage. If tourists asked the location of the cottage, no one recorded it. Nor did anyone at the time admit the photograph had been taken at Alberni in 1886.

Almost without exception, the descriptions of east-coast villages had something to say about a wonderful view, points of historical interest, fishing and hunting and, when all else failed, the climate. Only on the west coast, relatively new villages, such as Tofino, Ucluelet, Quatsino, and Holberg, seemed utterly immune to the tourist fever raging through the remainder of Vancouver Island. The fact remains that tourism, no matter how large or small the immediate revenue might be, was supposed to induce immigration, which would be followed by industry. This did not happen.

The population of Alberni increased from 850 in 1919 to 998 in 1929, while close by, Port Alberni grew from 940 to 1,150; Comox and Cowichan Bay failed to increase at all; Courtenay, which had grown up as a service centre near Comox, went from 600 to 1,000; while Nanaimo, reputed to have a population of "upwards of 10,000" in 1919, dropped to 9,000 ten years later. Harder hit was the electoral district of Parksville, which lost 700 people in the decade. Some towns just hung on. Crofton was one such place; when the Britannia Mining & Smelting Company's smelter was closed there in 1908, many thought this spelled the end of Crofton, the company town. Yet in 1919 it had a population of 150 and retained that population into the 1930s, relying on fishing and logging to pay the bills.

Statistics are one thing, peoples' lives another. The second-wave settlement at Cape Scott was essentially dead by the early 1930s, yet in spite of the back-breaking work of clearing land, the isolation, and the sea that never seemed to stop roaring in their ears, 50 years after leaving "The Cape," men and women who spent their formative years there could look back wistfully.

It had been a good life in many respects, simpler and reward-
ing—and it might have even amounted to something had the
government kept its promises. Others came to visit and
remained for a while, and when it came time to leave, this was
the biggest step in their lives.

One such visitor, though not to Cape Scott, was Negley Farson. He and his wife reached Cowichan Lake in 1921, supposedly for a short visit, but ended up falling in love with the
lake and the fishing, so there they stayed for two years. Twenty
years later he would write about their life on a houseboat on
Cowichan Lake: "It was a delectable life. There were no
mosquitos to contend with, no pests, no neighbours (unless we
wanted them), we owed no one in the world any money; I cannot imagine why we left it."[13] He left the lake, he as much as
says elsewhere, because the life was too good—Farson wanted
something more. Yet even when he had become a well-known
foreign correspondent for American and British newspapers, a

Courtenay, ca 1910.

novelist with an international reputation, and no mean writer on sport fishing, he looked back fondly on life on Vancouver Island where he and his wife could live for months on $100.

The provincial government, which had created such problems by its frequent changes, eventually stabilized itself to some extent, largely due to the introduction of party politics in 1903, when Premier Richard McBride formed the first Conservative government—one that remained in power until 1915. Between this date and 1941 six governments came to power, and two of them remained in power for a combined period of 18 years. They were the governments of Premiers John Oliver and Thomas Dufferin Pattullo.

Oliver considered the Old Age Pensioners Act, which he talked the BC legislature into passing, the crowning achievement of his career. This act of 1924 was the first such legislation in Canada. Oliver was extremely popular in Victoria, and all the Vancouver Island women must have thought highly of him when, in 1921, he appointed Mary Ellen Smith to his cabinet as Minister Without Portfolio. Smith was not only the first woman to be elected to the BC legislature: Oliver's appointment made her the first woman in the British Commonwealth to hold a cabinet post. Another action that did nothing to harm his popularity was his opening of government liquor stores; called "John Oliver's Drug Stores" they were to provide a major source of the government's revenue in the next decade and a half.

The achievements of the government of "Duff" Pattullo are not so much individual acts as general programmes. By borrowing huge sums of money from the federal government he kept road construction going throughout the Depression; his government provided relief camps, assisted agricultural areas with much-needed legislation, created apprenticeship programmes in the trades, took a step towards controlling public utilities by creating the Fuel Control Board, and planned to introduce a health-care programme.

By the late 1930s the worst of the Depression seemed over. In

1936, 37,372 cars landed on Vancouver Island from Washington, but no matter what these facts said, or how loudly Premier Pattullo's government talked of the improving times, Victoria spent $608,000 on relief; that same year the city was officially $16,000,000 in debt. The 1930s were a perplexing decade on Vancouver Island. The island was a major tourist wonderland, Victoria had a fledgling movie industry, the towns continued to hold their own, if not grow, yet the island did not develop as expected. Of course the Depression is one reason behind this lack of growth, but two other factors contributed to it in no small way.

Many of the countries that were logical export markets for Vancouver Island goods were too poor to pay island prices. The island's closest neighbours, the mainland and Washington, already had an abundance of everything that the island had to offer. The Far East was one of the island's earliest and consequential markets, but a variety of wars and revolutions, and then Japanese expansion, kept this area closed to Vancouver Island trade throughout the first decades of the 20th century.

After 1918 there was also a policy developing on Vancouver Island and the mainland to import goods from eastern Canada and the United States rather than rely on provincial suppliers. Exports were supposed to expand with the island roads and railroads, but instead, the transportation systems only increased imports.

Economically unstable though these decades were as Vancouver Island came of age politically and socially, there were bright aspects on the horizon. Island industry was far from nonexistent; however, its story is so varied, its episodes isolated from one another to such an extreme, and certain elements such as logging and fishing so much a part of the future, that the industrial history must be the final chapter of the history of Vancouver Island's first 90 years of British-Canadian development.

CHAPTER ELEVEN

Industrial Convolutions

The history of British Columbia can be separated into four relatively distinct periods. These are: Fur Trade and Exploration (1740s–1860s), the Gold Rush Era (1840s–1890s), Urbanization and Industrialization (1870s–1920s) and Metropolis (1920s–   ).[1] Generally speaking these eras are applicable to Vancouver Island, if the dates are shifted slightly. On the island the Fur Trade continued as an economic factor until 1911, when the federal government outlawed sealing. The Gold Rush Era did not begin to affect the island until 1858, and the search for gold continued to be an aspect of island life through the next 80 years. The last island gold rush took place at Zeballos during the late 1930s, and by 1939 the town boasted of a population in excess of 1,000 inhabitants. Urbanization and Industrialization (a period characterized by small cities and company towns) began in the 1860s and continued with few exceptions until the declaration of war in 1939. Economically, Metropolis is characterized by post-industrial services, and socially by large towns and cities, so the term has little meaning when applied to Vancouver Island.

Resource exploitation was the basis of the first three periods in the island's history, and the result was not a happy one. None of the wealth accumulated by the maritime fur traders, who flourished between the 1780s and 1820s, remained on Vancouver Island. The establishment of Fort Victoria and Fort Rupert did little to change this, for most of the Hudson's Bay Company profits were forwarded to London, only a fraction remaining in the hands of men such as James Douglas and Roderick Finlayson. The earliest gold rushes certainly changed Victoria's economy, but after the boom years of 1858–62 it went bust within a few short years. Tons of gold may have passed through Victoria, but despite the stories of city fathers with chests of gold buried in their basements, almost none of it remained as investment.

The third period of island history begins while Victoria was still an HBC fort, and continues through the gold-rush years and the decades following when the slowly growing town fought to dominate Vancouver and the province. Agriculture, which began side by side with the construction of Fort Victoria, is the first industry of this era. Over the years many writers have given the honour of being the first industry to logging. There is a case for this: Captain Cook's men did go ashore to fall trees, and Captain John Meares did cut and load spars in 1787, but this was hardly an industry. Agriculture begins in 1843 and continues without a break; the lumber industry did not begin until 1848.

The story of the earliest farms, those of the Puget's Sound Agricultural Company, has already been outlined; the conditions relating to farming between the 1860s and the appearance of the *First Report of the Department of Agriculture* in 1891 are hazy. Even at this late date the author of the report began it with an apology: "The absence of any material from which to form comparisons; the difficulty of procuring reliable data makes the writing of "an interesting and intelligent report a matter of much difficulty."[2] It is worth quoting H. T. Castley, who was farming in the Duncan area in 1891, for his views sum up the odds and bits known about one aspect of farming before the turn of the century. "Most of the men who hold land around here are of the labouring class, and are obliged to work for wages during the best part of the year in order to earn money to support them through the winter months, therefore, agriculture is in a very backward state. The land is all very heavily timbered, and the best pieces, when clearing has been accomplished, all require to be drained before they can be profitably farmed. The only places that can be called farms are those that were taken up by the first settlers. They had the first chance of the land, and, as a matter of course, took up the best pieces, and those that were easiest to clear. These advantages, combined with the number of years the occupiers have been employed on them, have resulted in a few tolerable farms being made."[3]

Castley began farming near Duncan in 1886, the same year a visitor wrote that "for men possessing even a small capital there were few more profitable investments than a cereal farm or cattle rancho within her [BC's] borders."[4] Accurate as this picture is for the mainland, on the island cattle were not raised in any large numbers, and grain was limited to the southern end of the island, particularly the Saanich Peninsula where "The remarkable fertility of the soil and equable climate renders the successful cultivation of all grain, root crops, hops, and fruits, both hardy and half hardy, an easy matter in most seasons."[5]

On Vancouver Island it was estimated that there were not more than 300,000 acres of farming land available, and by the late 1880s less than 15,000 were under cultivation. Some felt this first figure, supplied by the Canadian government, was an exaggeration. One early settler wrote: "Of all the poor apologies for an agricultural country, V.I. exceeds anything that I have as yet beheld. Its surface is diversified with rocks, and for a change, swamps, and swamps and rocks."[6]

In the late 1890s the industry began to perk up. As the local agricultural production had been insufficient to meet the demands placed on it by commission merchants in Victoria, these merchants had come to rely on farm produce from Washington, Oregon and California; these sources were reliable in both quality and quantity. At the end of the century, as a result of the growing population and the end of a long depression, the US market began to consume all of its own agricultural production. This, and rising prices, threw island merchants back on local producers.

Another reason for the booming demand for local production was mining. Coal production had an immense impact on the economy of British Columbia. The value of mineral production in Canada between 1886 and 1910 was estimated to be $1,130,000,000. Of this total, BC produced $310,000,000, or between 27 and 28 per cent. Coal and coke, most of which was produced on Vancouver Island, contributed $104,000,000, or roughly one-third of the mineral production of BC during this period.

Minerals—not agriculture and not logging—opened up the

Coal miners at Ladysmith, date unknown.

island during these years. A 1911 gazetteer lists 25 of the "most important" places on Vancouver Island. At best this list is arbitrary, but it does illustrate the economy. Of the places listed, the farming community of Jordan Meadows in the mountains behind River Jordan did not develop as expected; Bamfield was a trading post; Esquimalt, even then, was considered a suburb of Victoria; Clayoquot was essentially a government life-boat station and telegraph office; Campbell River was a resort and sport-fishing centre, and Duncan was listed as an English residential centre. Chemainus was the site of the Victoria Lumber Company, and a "town dependent upon the manufacture and export of lumber"; Hardy Bay (Port Hardy) was "a prospective terminal for railway lines and a steamer landing"; Cowichan was a railway station, as well as a large and important farming district; Gordon Head, Metchosin, Sooke, and Sidney were agricultural areas, while Shawnigan Lake was known for its hunting and fishing. Victoria was considered the island centre. The ten remaining places: Nanaimo, Alberni, Comox, Courtenay, Crofton, Cumberland, Fort Rupert, Goldstream, Ladysmith, and Nootka were closely linked to mining and/or prospecting. To this list should be added Mount Sicker (55 miles from Victoria and several miles from Chemainus), and Wellington and Extension, both on the east coast.[7]

Even these lists do not accurately portray the extent of mining activity on the island. For instance, in the Alberni District 239 Free Miners' Certificates were issued in 1898 and 441 claims recorded. Some of these claims were no fly-by-night affairs; the Nahmint Mining Company, working at Hayes Camp, near Nahmint Bay, was organized in 1898 with $100,000 capital, and development work consisted of 600 feet of tunnel and 150 feet of shaft work. Shipments in 1898 totalled 120 tons of ore containing copper, gold, and silver. The company had constructed two miles of road, a wharf, various buildings and a boarding house large enough to accommodate 30 men.

Margaret Mine near Sooke, ca *1917.*

In the West Coast of Vancouver Island Mining Division, 106 claims were recorded and several were preparing to ship ore, mostly copper, by the fall of 1898. In the Nanaimo District, which included the islands and a few mainland points, 566 claims and a vast amount of extensive development were reported. Activity was slower in the Victoria Mining Division with only 392 claims reported, and work on the Mount Sicker properties had all but ceased, due largely to the Klondike gold rush.

At the conclusion of 1898, the BC government had realized revenues amounting to almost $30,000 from the sale of mining leases and certificates, various rights and recording fees. The economic health reflected by all these figures continued unabated until, in 1918, Vancouver Island shipped gold, silver, lead, copper, and zinc worth $4,772,954 — and this was a war year. Impressive as these figures are, coal remained the undisputed king of island minerals.

Coal production on Vancouver Island rose from 10,000 tons, valued at $40,000, to 1894 when it reached a pre-war high of 1,012,953 tons with a value of $3,038,859. In 1918 the mines produced 1,666,211 tons of coal, which sold for an average of five dollars per ton; as well, they produced 24,887 tons of coke valued at seven dollars per ton. The production for this year would have been larger had it not been for a shortage of manpower, caused by the war in Europe, and labour problems that seriously interrupted the output.

One source of the "labour problems" was the number of Chinese employed in the island coal mines. At the Canadian Collieries (Dunsmuir) Ltd. mines, which employed 1971 men, more than a third of the men working underground, and slightly less than half of those employed above ground, were Chinese. Wages were also a source of trouble. The Canadian Collieries did not make public the wages it paid the miners, but in one Nanaimo mine white miners were paid from $5.50 to $8.13 daily; white labourers earned from $4.96 to $5.50; while the wages for boys working above ground ranged from $2.25 to $3.92. The Chinese were paid from $3.30 to $3.74 daily. Another problem was safety; safety precautions, if they existed, were not enforced, and conditions were generally bad both below and above ground. During 1918, 21 miners were killed in the east-coast mines, 20 seriously injured, and 16 suffered slight injuries. According to information published that year, 5.6 men out of every 1,000 employed in the mines were killed; 5.6 men for every 80,254 tons of coal mined.

At the Nanaimo mines the labour problems had slowly increased from the strike in 1877, when miners demanded a 20¢ increase in wages — and the military was called in by the owners to evict the miners from their homes when they refused to go back to work—to one in 1890 as the miners fought for an eight-hour day. In 1903, labour declared a war on the Dunsmuir interests. That year conditions reached such a state that Mackenzie King, later prime minister of Canada, was sent out from Ottawa by the federal Department of Labour to study the problems.

Nine years later a strike began at Cumberland. Gas explosions in the mines—explosions that had killed 373 men between 1884 and 1912—were behind this strike; the miners wanted to discuss the gas conditions with the management and the latter refused. The strike spread, and by 1913 the Nanaimo miners were striking and rioting. Acting Premier W. J. Bowser promptly dispatched 1,000 soldiers from Esquimalt on August 13, 1913, and there they would stay, claimed Bowser, "until the bitter end."[8] That they did, keeping the peace and escorting non-striking miners to and from work, right up to the eve of World War I.

Canada's first general strike was called on August 2, 1918, to honour Albert "Ginger" Goodwin, a "radical leader"—in other words a socialist union man. Goodwin had been active in the 1912–14 island strike, then moved to the mainland where he was actively involved in the union movement. In 1917 Goodwin was conscripted but pleaded ill-health, and when that failed he headed for the hills behind Cumberland. Locally, the police knew where he was hiding and it was only a matter of time before they caught him. On July 26, 1918, he was shot while resisting arrest—this was the official story. Many then and now believe Goodwin was a victim of the government and the mining interests (often one and the same).

Goodwin is one side of the business-versus-labour struggles. The Dunsmuir family is the other side; if coal was king, this family was the ruling deities. Power was money and once Robert Dunsmuir began making money, everything he touched turned to riches. Dunsmuir's uncle, Boyd Gilmour, was the oversman at the fledgling mines at Fort Rupert in 1851 when

Cumberland, after the gas explosion of October 16, 1908.

the 26-year-old Robert indentured himself to the HBC and, with his wife and three children, joined him there. After refusing to join his fellow miners in a strike at Nanaimo in 1855, Dunsmuir the loyal employee was given a Free Miners' Certificate and began working an abandoned shaft.

Three years later he became resident manager of the Harewood Coal Mining Company at Nanaimo; when this company was taken over by the Vancouver Coal Mining and Land Company in 1862, the company made him mines' supervisor. In 1869 Robert Dunsmuir discovered the Wellington seam and, four years later, he founded Dunsmuir, Diggle Ltd. By 1878 this company was producing more coal than the VCMLC—88,361 tons to the other's 82,135. The next year he bought out the interests that were working at South Wellington. By 1881 Dunsmuir could claim his operations were worth $245,000, yet two years later Dunsmuir bought out the last of his non-family partners for $600,000.

One writer maintains that "What distinguished him above all the other promoters, the majority of whom failed to secure sufficient start-up capital, was his astute move in turning for support to the naval officers who had both an awareness of the value of the coalfields in the region and the financial means to make substantial investments."[9] The naval officers were seven of the original partners in Dunsmuir, Diggle Ltd.; his sons, James and Alexander, were also among the original partners, and he trained them to be his future subordinates. Dunsmuir lived most of the year in Nanaimo, so nothing happening at the mines escaped his attention and he was able to make all the management decisions. As the company prospered so did the family.

Robert Dunsmuir was, or was well on his way to being, BC's leading capitalist when he undertook to build the Esquimalt and Nanaimo Railway. This agreement not only gave him one-fifth of the island, as already noted, but "all coal, coal oil, ores, stones, clay, marble, slates, mines, minerals" in or under the land.[10]

On May 1, 1905, the Dunsmuirs sold the E & N to the Canadian Pacific Railway for $2,330,000, which included the land grant. In 1910, alarmed by the increasing use of California oil, James Dunsmuir sold his coal enterprise to MacKenzie and Mann of the Canadian Northern Railways for a reputed $7,000,000. Between 1908 and his death in 1920, he officially lived at Hatley Park, now Royal Roads Military College, which he had built at a cost of $4,000,000, but he spent much of his time fishing at Cowichan Lake. He apparently showed little interest in anything else during his last years. As one of his sons drowned when the *Lusitania* sank in 1915, and the other was living in disgrace outside the country, these circumstances may explain his state of mind.

The coal mines continued producing huge amounts of coal—1,277,533 tons in 1928—but due to the increased consumption of oil and the use of electricity, demand began dropping. Island production dropped to 988,805 tons in 1930; by 1938 it was down to 684,398 tons. What this meant to the island towns is clear from the employment figures: the mines employed 3,093 men in 1928; 2,771 in 1930, and 1,841 by 1938. A few of these now-unemployed miners may have started farming locally, but this seems hardly likely as agriculture was not doing well.

Logging, not farming, was the alternative for many men. After a slow start, compared to the development of the logging industry south of the border, logging and sawmilling began to realize their potential after 1918.

The HBC constructed the island's first sawmill in 1848 in the area now known as Millstream in Esquimalt. In 1850 the Vancouver's Island Steam Sawing Mill and Agricultural Company planned a mill, but the idea fell through. The Vancouver's Island Steam Saw Mill Co. was a local private venture put on paper in December 1851, but despite many prominent shareholders, including James Douglas, there is no proof it ever operated, though it seems to have been constructed. A fire in August 1859 reduced the plant to ashes and nothing remained but debts.

Captain Walter Coloquhoun Grant's attempt to set up a saw-

The first sawmill at Shawnigan Lake, with W. E. Losee, the first owner and operator, in the dugout canoe, 1891.

mill at his homestead at Sooke was another local venture to fail in the 1850s. John Muir and his sons bought Grant's establishment in 1853 and made it pay, shipping more than 1,290,000 feet of lumber in 1869. The Muirs sold the mill once, in 1864, but were operating it again by 1867; in 1875 a fire razed it to the ground at a total loss of $20,000, but it was rebuilt and operated until 1892.

William Banfield (after whom the village of Bamfield is inaccurately named) was one of the earliest men to visualize the potential for logging on the west coast of the island. He reached Esquimalt in 1849; after moving to the outside coast he traded with the Nootka until one of them killed him in 1862. In a letter to the Colonial Secretary in London, Banfield reported that the timber stands around Barkley Sound were large and valuable, but he did not think them large enough to compete in quality or quantity with those in Puget Sound. This warning, voiced earlier by men watching the growth of the mills in the sound, would haunt Vancouver Island logging interests for decades.

The creation of the third sawmill on the island can be traced directly to the vision of Captain Edward Stamp, a ship's master and future Victoria businessman, who first saw the head of Alberni Inlet in 1857. Early in 1860 Stamp gained permission from Governor Douglas to claim 2,000 acres on the land where Port Alberni now sits, and to log a further 15,000 acres. The capital for this complex was supplied by James Thomson & Company and Thomas Bilbe & Company, London firms.

The *Meg Merrilies* landed nine labourers at the proposed site of the new settlement in June 1860. In September, the same schooner landed Captain Stamp and Gilbert Malcolm Sproat, the island representative of the London backers. The mill began working in May 1861 and was described at that time as having "been erected in a most solid fashion, and at a heavy outlay, by English labourers, and with English machinery."[11] The mill contained two sets of saws that were capable of cutting some 18,000 feet of lumber daily. At this time there were about 70 men working either in the mill or on the townsite, for it was a flourishing little settlement. Two schooners and two steamers were operated by the company; the *Diana* transported cargo to and from Victoria and as well she served as a tug. The enterprise was more than just a sawmill for they traded with the Indians, and shipped spars, salted fish, fish oil, and furs, as well as lumber.

The best year for the Alberni Mills (it was also known as Stamp's Mill and Anderson's Mill) was 1863 when it exported 11,273,000 feet of lumber and 1300 spars. During this year it also shipped another million feet of lumber to Victoria. The exports in 1864 were lower, yet the drop in scale was not large enough to suggest what would happen by the end of the year.

The mill was forced to close because of a lack of timber. Sproat outlined the problems in a letter to the Colonial Secretary: "It requires a large tract of land anywhere to furnish 20 million feet of logs every year for the use of a Mill, but especially in a country so totally unsuitable for large Sawmills as this Island owing to the broken character of the country and the Smallness and Shallowness of the Streams."[12] The reference to the streams implies the loggers were driving their logs down the Sproat and Somass rivers from Sproat Lake (then known as Kleecoot Lake). In this letter Sproat claims the original timber grant only contained enough timber for a year and a half. This is not a ridiculous claim; in the days before steam and gas machinery, a great deal of the timber would have been totally inaccessible. He also regretted to the Colonial Secretary that the mill had not been built in Puget Sound, as was suggested, and prophesied that no mill as large as the complex he operated would ever again exist on Vancouver Island.

The settlers in the vicinity, probably all mill employees, left shortly after the mill closed down. In 1866 a caretaker was the only resident; two years later the machinery was sold to the Puget Mill Company when all efforts to reopen the mill failed. The buildings stood empty until 1879 when a fire got away from some Makah Indians camped there, and burned the buildings to the ground.

Henry S. Shepard began building a mill on the Shawnigan River just above its mouth early in 1861. Prior to starting operations with his mill, for there is no record of the mill producing lumber before 1863, Shepard sold it to William Sayward, a carpenter and lumber merchant from Maine via California. He arrived in Victoria in 1858, perhaps as a prospector, and soon opened a lumber yard. In 1863 Sayward's mill cut 1,666,000 feet of lumber, which was shipped to Victoria; two years later Sayward had expanded and was exporting lumber to San Francisco. During these years the Spring Vale Sawmill operated in Esquimalt; also, two small, water-powered mills were cutting lumber in the Chemainus-Ladysmith district, but few details are known concerning their production and owners.

Logging was difficult. Elsewhere in North America the timber was relatively small; this meant that men and horses could move the logs to a river's edge, and from there they would be driven downstream to the ocean or mills. It was hard work, but not impossible. In the northwest the combination of huge logs and rough country, with few rivers suitable for log drives, made logging almost impossible before the invention of powerful equipment. Vancouver Island logging, as everywhere else in the Pacific Northwest, can be traced through three stages of development. First came hand-logging: along a strip no wider than 500 feet from the shoreline men fell the trees towards the water, then used a variety of jacks and wedges and levers to roll or slide the logs into the ocean. The next step involved oxen or horses, sometimes as many as 24 to a team, which hauled the logs along a skidway or skidroad to the water. As the skidroad's length increased, so did the operator's overhead; worse was the time factor—no one hurries an ox. In the third stage railroads were introduced to haul the timber from the sidehill to tidewater.

The importance of Vancouver Island logging before 1918 has been exaggerated for the sake of romance. Generation after generation of island boys grew up knowing there was nothing quite as glorious in the world as being a logger. Histories have

COURTESY OF HISTORY DIVISION, BC PROVINCIAL MUSEUM

Logging with oxen, late 1880s.

continued this spell with tales of Seattle Red, Big Jack Mulligan, Curley Hutton, and the man known as Eight Day Wilson. Little has been written about the facts and figures for good reason—they are not impressive when compared to those of Puget Sound, and they must be compared, if Vancouver Island logging is to be seen in perspective.

The main problem was competition. In 1914 the sawmills of British Columbia were estimated to have an annual cutting capacity of 2,500,000 board feet, yet in 1913 they only produced 1,157,000 feet. In the American northwest the mills cut 6,800,000,000 feet in 1914, and their capacity was estimated to be 13,600,000,000 feet. Other problems were markets: high freight rates made it difficult to sell BC lumber in eastern Canada, and only one-fifth of locally cut lumber was bought within the province, most of the rest going across the Pacific. Shipping to foreign ports in 1913 only amounted to 28,170,000 feet while the US exported 1,818,520,000 feet: each year between 1900 and 1915, BC exports fell, because of growing US production.

However, there was a brighter side. In 1900, the industry was Canadian controlled and the investments amounted to only $2,000,000. Ten years later, due to American investment, the industry's value had climbed to $65,000,000. After the San Francisco earthquake in April 1906, 925,000,000 feet of lumber were required to rebuild and most of this was ordered from British Columbia. This was also the year that the Fraser River Lumber Company began operations; later it would be known as the largest sawmill in the world.

Vancouver Island benefitted from the capital investment and the growing demands for lumber in a limited way. In 1900 the only large sawmill on the island was at Chemainus. There was a logging camp near Chemainus, and a large camp at Rock Bay on the northeast coast about 30 miles from Campbell River. The Vancouver-based B.C. Mills Timber and Trading Company owned this camp; by 1919 it was large enough to have a post office and school, and ten years later a hospital, hotel and telegraph office. The biggest boom in these years came with the railroads. The Chemainus Mill which, after changing hands numerous times, was to be known as the Victoria Lumber and Manufacturing Company until 1944, supplied 12,000,000 feet of lumber during the construction of the E & N Railway—one of the owners was a son-in-law of Robert Dunsmuir. It has been claimed that the first mill to use a railroad locomotive in its logging operations was the Chemainus Mill and this was as early as 1900; within 20 years locomotives were in use by all the major logging companies on the island—and they had begun to spring up everywhere. In 1918, within the Vancouver District (the island and the lower mainland) there were 111 sawmills and in the entire province 221, double the number existing in 1902. By 1929 there were 341 mills in BC, 254 of them in the Vancouver District. Every town and settlement, on the average, had at least one logging operator at this time; some, like Vic-

toria, Alberni and Lake Cowichan had three or more. Alberni
had six businesses manufacturing and dealing in lumber and
shingles; Duncan had five; Ladysmith, three; Nanaimo, six;
and Victoria 13. It would appear that each town on the island
had one or more mills.

The forest industry peaked in 1928, when its value came to
$93,787,000. The next year it was down slightly to
$93,301,000, and then it slid drastically until it reached
$35,157,000 in 1932. The wide-spread Depression was the
major reason behind this drop in sales, as well as the already-
mentioned Japanese expansion in the Pacific that closed many
market areas, but coastal conditions were also factors.

In 1938, for example, "The Coast logging-year opened under
the usual handicap of difficult seasonal weather conditions, ag-
gravated each year by the small, but accumulating, effect of

Floating logging camp, Chamiss Bay, Kyuquot Sound.

receding timber frontiers."[13] By May the industry was working at about 70% of normal, then the camps were closed for nearly three weeks in July and August because of fire hazards.

One often-overlooked aspect of the forest industry on Vancouver Island is the pulp industry. The first pulp mill in the province was constructed on the island. Built some time after 1892 on the Somass River near Alberni, the mill was owned by Herbert Carmichael and William Hewartson, but as it made paper from rags rather than from wood, this unlikely venture was closed by 1896. By the summer of 1917, 300 men were employed at Quatsino Sound laying the foundations of the Whalen Pulp & Paper Co. Ltd. Port Alice, the company town built near the mill, had a relatively constant population as in both 1919 and 1929 it had 600 people and was, until the 1940s, the only successful pulp mill on the island. A pulp mill built at Beaver Cove, near Alert Bay, in 1918 was Port Alice's only brief competition, but it closed after about a year's operation. Then the local residents, if any of them had been employed by the mill, went back to logging and fishing.

In a time-honoured scheme of things on Vancouver Island, a man goes fishing when there is no work to be had in the mines or woods. Fishing was important, not only as an escape from the problems on land, but because it fed the family. Even as early as 1874, when the total BC catch amounted to something less than $100,000, the Dominion Commissioner of Fisheries estimated that fish worth twice this amount entered the kitchens of the province.

The first step in the industry as it is known today took place at Fort Langley on the Fraser River. Archibald McDonald, commander at Fort Langley, wrote to Governor Simpson on February 10, 1830: "In my last Communication I touched at some length of the prospect of curing [salting] salmon, from the 20th of August to the 13th of the next month we were fortunate enough to procure upwards of 15,000; enough to make up more than 200 Barrels". This sample, McDonald admitted, "will not stand the Test of a foreign market, and trust by next

Season, we shall be provided with a good Cooper, that will know something of fish curing."[14] It was not until the years immediately following 1867 that the canning process was developed to the point where it was trusted by the public. This was the greatest advance in the salmon industry up to that time, and would remain so until the invention of the fish trap in the 1880s.

The hunting of seals would not seem to be a "fisheries product," but so it is listed in government yearbooks. As it began in a very small way about 1855, sealing predates the salmon fisheries by almost two decades. Shortly after arriving in Victoria in 1853, Captain William Spring entered into a partnership with Hugh McKay, a cooper, for the purposes of trading with the Indians and curing salmon for the then-lucrative trade with the Hawaiian Islands. Exactly when Spring and McKay entered the sealing business is not known, though they were certainly involved in it during the 1860s. "Prior to 1881 most of the vessels would go on very short cruises, but, as the habits of the seal became better known, they began to equip for longer voyages, sailing far south of the Columbia to meet the north-bound herd and follow it up the coast."[15] In 1881 the *Ariel* took 131 seals during one day, while another American vessel, the *Juanita*, killed 500 seals in 2½ days. These sealing schooners hunted along the Northwest Coast with Indian hunters. Two years later the ships began to range farther afield. Captain Cathcart and Daniel McLean, the older brother of Alex McLean, took the *City of San Diego* into the Bering Sea during the summer of 1883 and returned to Victoria with 900 seals in October of that year.

Working for Captain Charles Spring (William Spring's son) of Victoria, Daniel McLean took the *Mary Ellen* into the Bering Sea in 1885, accompanied by Captain Alex McLean commanding Spring's *Favorite*. The *Mary Ellen* established a record take with 2,309 skins that year, but the *Favorite* was a close second with 2,073; the combined value was $35,000. By 1890 the combined kill of Victoria-based sealing vessels amounted to

COURTESY OF HISTORY DIVISION, BC PROVINCIAL MUSEUM

Sealing schooner, 1890s.

43,315, and two years later the kill was set at 45,385. At this time four-fifths of the sealing industry had its headquarters in Victoria, and was said to employ over a hundred vessels, 952 whites and 500 Indians.

The peak year for this industry was 1894 when 97,474 skins were landed at Victoria. The value of these skins, and the trade to Victoria businessmen, is not recorded, though in 1902, when the kill came to only 16,301, the value of the skins alone was $337,660. By this time the industry was on its last legs; the depletion of the seal herds, which the schooners now went as far as the coasts of Japan and Russia to hunt, was nearly complete. Canada, Japan, and the United States outlawed sealing in their Pacific waters in 1911.

During the earliest years of the sealing industry, the canning of salmon was beginning in a small and quiet way. "The first recognized salmon cannery in British Columbia was built in 1870 at Annieville, some three miles below New Westminster, by Alexander Loggie, Alexder Ewen, James Wise, and David Hennessy." And the same source maintains that "From 1878 to the beginning of the World War the number of failures of canneries and salteries was extraordinary. The history of this period of 36 years is replete with stories of bankruptcies of companies, destruction of plants, frequent abandonment of canneries, and removal to new locations."[16] Greater than the difficulties of catching the salmon, and preserving them properly, was the timing of the runs.

The spring salmon begins to appear around the mouths of streams and rivers in early June and this run continues until some time in August. The sockeye, rightly called the king of all salmon for canning purposes, appears in July and runs until September, which is approximately the same period as the migration of the coho. Late in August the first pink or humpback appears, followed by the chum or dog in early October.

Another problem is the size of the run. One early writer wrote: "If the size of the run of fish in the Fraser River for a given year is dependent upon the abundance of fish upon the spawning grounds during the spawning period four years previous, as the canners and fishermen claim, and as the records manifestly demonstrate, and as I believe, the run in 1905 will be

Fish trap at Sooke, ca *1900.*

large and the run in 1906 small. Certainly, propagation was at its maximum in 1901 and at its minimum in 1902."[17] How true this proved: the Fraser River canneries packed 877,136 cases in 1905, and only 240,486 cases the following year.

Salmon were taken by every means possible, legal and illegal. It was the fish trap that was the most efficient—as well as legal and cheap. Initially they were pile-driven weirs set along the shore where the salmon were known to migrate yearly. "For many years the investment of capital paralleled the rate of trap installations. Salmon traps have constituted a strategic factor in enlarging and stabilizing supply, although their efficiency has necessitated regulation in the interest of conservation."[18] These traps were last used in BC along the shores of Vancouver Island near Sooke in the early 1950s.

Vancouver Island's role in this industry is difficult to trace. Its part was small for in 1902 there were 42 canneries on the Fraser River, ten on the Skeena, two on the Nass, and 11 at

Cannery at Kildonan, Alberni Inlet.

various locations on the mainland coast, and the total pack of these canneries was 609,572 cases. The combined pack of the three island canneries was a mere 16,410 cases. By 1909–10 the island pack, from canneries at Victoria, Clayoquot, Alert Bay, and Quathiaski Cove totalled slightly over 94,000 cases and was valued at $612,040. Still, this was less than one-sixth of the Fraser River pack for 1909. A later study of the industry in 1911–14 does not even mention Vancouver Island by name in its lists of statistics. Another chart listing the major BC canneries up to 1960 accounts for 137 canneries on the mainland coast and the Queen Charlotte Islands, but lists nothing for the island, though in 1929, more than a dozen canneries were established on the island at various places, particularly on the west coast. A main reason for overlooking the island's pack was its small size.

As some of the best halibut banks in the North Pacific are off the west coast of Vancouver Island, it could be expected that Victoria and the island would benefit from the resulting halibut industry. Several factors explain why it failed to develop to any extent on the island. Again, competition in various forms was behind the island's problems. In 1915, for instance, Canadian fishermen took 18,609,000 pounds of halibut in BC waters, while Americans fishing the same areas took 13,160,000 pounds. As halibut is sold fresh, and as the large markets were to the south and east, it must be kept in ice or refrigerated. The transcontinental railways made the international marketing of halibut feasible, but only if there was a railway terminus close by. Vancouver and Tacoma and, after 1914, Prince Rupert were such places; not Victoria and not Vancouver Island. Thus while the total BC catch of halibut amounted to 21,706,000 pounds during 1909–10, only 709,500 pounds were landed on the island, and this was valued at slightly less than $40,000. While the island halibut industry continued to grow, even during the worst years of the Depression, so that by the year of 1938–39, halibut landings at Vancouver Island points totalled 586,600 pounds (the highest figure since 1930), this cannot compare with the landings at Prince Rupert totalling in excess of 14,000,000 pounds, or the 4,593,100 pounds landed elsewhere on the mainland.

As old as any of the coast fisheries, and far more romantic for those who see glory in man pitting himself against the sea, whaling was for many years the one island fishery unique to the BC coast. Legend has it that a man known only as "Peter the Whaler" hunted whales in the Burrard Inlet area early in the 1860s, although his activities, like those of the Nootka whalers, may be considered a backdrop to the industry. The business of whaling on a large scale did not begin until 1868. That year James Dawson, a Scot, and several Californians, including Captain Abel Douglass, formed Dawson and Douglass Company and began hunting whales from the Saanich Peninsula. The eight whales they killed and processed that year produced 2,400 gallons of oil. In 1869, the company moved its headquarters to Cortes Island and from the site now known as Whaletown, the partners successfully hunted whales for the next two or three years. By 1872 the whales had begun to disappear and the company, now known as the British Columbia Whaling Company and based on Hornby Island, sold its equipment, its boat, the *Kate,* and the land and buildings it owned on Hornby.

A scheme was proposed in 1890, by Captain T. P. H. Whitelaw, to begin whaling in the Strait of Georgia. Even though there were whales again (as no one had hunted them for 17 years), this proposal went nowhere. In 1899, the whale catch off the coast was one of the largest on record, but the catch was made by foreign vessels. Six years later the Balcom brothers, Reuben and Sprott, and Captain William Grant joined forces and started the Victoria Whaling Company. The company owned the *Orion* and *St. Lawrence,* and their first whaling station was built at Sechart, 13 miles due north of Cape Beale, Barkley Sound. Two years later the company built a second station on Union Island at the mouth of Kyuquot Sound. For about 20 years this company, which changed its name with confusing frequency, operated off the island's west coast, while

Eighty-foot-long sulphur-bottom whale.

also expanding to the Queen Charlotte Islands.

The west-coast catch in 1910 came to 600 whales. At this time a sulphur-bottom whale was considered to be worth $572, a finback $338, and a humpback $140, but the real money-maker was the right whale. Although seldom brought into the whaling stations, when one was caught it was time for a celebration for they were valued at $10,000 apiece. Prior to 1914, the best year for the whalers was 1911, when 812 whales were brought in; the company's income that year was published as $760,000. After the war the kill steadily decreased. No stations operated in 1921, and about this time the two Vancouver Island stations were closed permanently, the company concentrating its efforts in the Queen Charlotte Islands. This was the end of Vancouver Island's direct link with the whaling industry until after World War II.

Romantic as whaling may be to some, no aspect of the fishing industry caught the attention of writers to the extent that trolling did. Novelists and poets, biographers and historians, have all written of trolling, past and present, but mostly of the past. Trolling was the poor man's salvation during the Depression years. All the hand-troller required was a licence (2,943 were issued in 1928 and 3,385 in 1938), a skiff of some sort, oars, a length of line, and a lure. It has been estimated that during the late 1930s, between 500 and 700 hand-trollers, women as well as men, were fishing the area between Cape Mudge (near Campbell River) and Victoria-Vancouver. It was hard work, and no one ever got rich hand-trolling but, with luck, they graduated up the ladder to the point where they could afford an engine for their skiff. Profits increased proportionately with the fisherman's growing abilities, the variety of gear, and the size and power of the boat. Many men continued to buy larger boats until they owned trollers much like those seen in any Vancouver Island harbour today.

Anyone could go hand-trolling. Once out on the water and trolling his lure behind his skiff, the hard work of rowing at a certain speed hour after hour no longer mattered—the fisherman was his own boss. If he could not sell his catch, and this happened often in the 1930s due to a depressed world market, the fisherman could eat it. Any number of men carried this independence to extremes: after a summer of fishing, during which time they lived in beach camps, a group of fishermen would band together in some likely cove, build log cabins, and spend the winter prospecting and trapping.

This is just what happened at the head of Zeballos Inlet on the island's west coast during the winter of 1931–32. From their cabins near the mouth of the Zeballos River the men began prospecting and trapping. One of these men, Andrew Donaldson, whose family is said to have arrived with the first Cape Scott settlers, staked what was later known as the White Star Mine Ltd. Before leasing this property, the Donaldsons had shipped 47 tons of ore, all of which was mined by hand, that produced over 40 pounds of gold and 11 pounds of silver.

During the mid-1930s several other mines began working in the area. In 1938 the Privateer Mine, Ltd., the Mount Zeballos Gold Mines, Ltd., the White Star Mine, Ltd., Spud Valley Gold Mines, Ltd., and the Central Zeballos Gold Mines, Ltd. were all active in the Zeballos area. The Privateer was the largest, employing 130 men regularly, and between 1936 and 1939, this mine shipped 9,100 tons of ore to the closest smelter, which was then at Tacoma, Washington. However, such figures hardly suggest the activity in the area.

According to one unofficial list, there were 28 mining companies active in the area in 1938. The first gold bullion was produced at Zeballos on August 29, 1938. In October plans were drawn up for a hospital, and in December men started clearing the land for a townsite; already the hospital was under construction, as was a church, and a school was soon to be built. By 1939, there were over 700 men in the new town of Zeballos (no one bothered to count the women and children); there was an office for Canadian Airlines Ltd., and another for Ginger Coote Airlines Ltd., a sawmill, two hotels, a cafe, a lending library and, for those who did not care to read, the estab-

Main street of Zeballos, 1938.

lishment fondly known as "the Goat Ranch" was located about a mile from town. The miners could unwind here with the ladies, but the "Ranch" also served a second and more important purpose—it kept the miners and their money in town.

It was predicted that Zeballos was no boom town: she would last for decades as the ore deposits were huge. It was true that the deposits were large—the Privateer Mine shipped $6,500,000 of gold and silver between 1938 and 1948—but all of the mines closed down during the war years only to reopen to rising operating costs and diminishing returns. In 1948 the mines shut down for good, and Zeballos's future became another west-coast dream.

Zeballos was Vancouver Island's last link with her frontier-pioneer past. Between 1941 and 1944 the population of British Columbia rose by over 100,000. The province's total production in 1942 was valued at $863,796,680—the highest production rate in Canada after Ontario and Quebec. In 1945 the hourly wage rates in BC were generally the highest in Canada, and by 1947, when Canada's hourly rate reached 76¢, construction workers on Vancouver Island were paid as much as $1.40 an hour. The more than one million veterans returning from overseas found their homeland not only a world power but also one of the world's industrial leaders. "Progress" was the word on everyone's lips and nowhere in western Canada did "progress" change so much so quickly as on Vancouver Island. For the first time in its history, the island was an active participant in the present, and the future had no boundaries.

FOOTNOTES

Ellipses (. . .) have not been used to indicate the omission of a word or phrase, line or paragraph, from a quotation when the omission(s) did not alter the author's meaning. *Sic* has not been used in quotes to confirm the accuracy of idiosyncratic or obsolete spelling.

Chapter One: The West-Coast People

1. Sproat, p. 12.
2. Densmore, p. 47.
3. Brown, pp. 95—6.
4. Brown, p. 99.
5. Anderson, G. W., p.1158.
6. Sproat, p. 103.
7. Sproat, pp. 117—18
8. Sproat, p. 112.
9. Brown, p. 216.
10. Lillard, *Mission to Nootka*, p. 66.
11. Arima, p. 159.

Chapter Two: Closing the Pacific

1. Cutter, p. 154.
2. Cook, p. 58.
3. Wagner, *Apocryphal Voyages*, p. 9.
4. See Peter Caley's "Canada's Chinese Columbus," *The Beaver*, Spring, 1984.
5. Bancroft, *Northwest Coast*, Vol. 1, p. 166.
6. Beaglehole, pp. 293—4.
7. Beaglehole, p. 294.
8. Beaglehole, pp. 295—6.
9. Perez's *"la Rada de San Lorenzo"* became *"San Lorenzo,"* which in turn became *"'San Lorenzo de Nuca"*. A Spanish map of 1792 has Nootka Sound as *"Puerto de Nutca"*. During the same period Cook's "Friendly Harbour," became "Friendly Cove" and *"Santa Cruz de Nuca"*.
10. Beaglehole, p. 306.
11. Walbran, "Cruise of the Imperial Eagle," pp. 5—6.
12. *ibid.*, p. 11.
13. *ibid.*, p. 12.
14. Walbran, *British Columbia Coast Names*, p. 333.
15. Howay, *Voyages of the Columbia*, p. 55.

16. Scholefield, p. 155.

Chapter Three: Years of Expansion

1. Wagner, *Spanish Explorations in the Strait of Juan de Fuca*, p. 210.
2. Lamb, *A Voyage of Discovery*, p. 283.
3. Scholefield, p. 158.
4. Meany, p. 302.
5. Cook, pp. 339–40.
6. Sage, p. 120.
7. *ibid.*
8. Scholefield, p. 456.

Chapter Four: Fort Victoria

1. Lamb, "The Founding of Fort Victoria," p. 86.
2. Landerholm, p. 193.
3. Of the many accounts of "the Mystic Spring," the best remains Higgins's *The Mystic Spring and Other Tales of Western Life*.
4. Duff, "The Fort Victoria Treaties," pp. 10–11.
5. Finlayson, "History of Vancouver Island," p. 17.
6. Lamb, *op. cit.*, p. 89.
7. Rich, p. 402.
8. *ibid.*, p. 389.
9. Finlayson, "Biography," p. 11.
10. *ibid.*
11. Scholefield, p. 480.
12. Lillard, *Warriors of the North Pacific*, p. 88.
13. Finlayson, *op. cit.*, p. 14.
14. *ibid.*, p. 15.
15. *ibid.*, p. 16.
16. Bancroft, *History of British Columbia*, p. 124.
17. Scholefield, p. 483.
18. Kane, p. 145.
19. Museum of the American Indian, p. 6.
20. Kane, p. 149.
21. Finlayson, *op. cit.*, pp. 20–1.

Chapter Five: Company Men

1. Sage, 143.
2. Pemberton, p. 59.
3. *ibid.*, p. 59.

4. Scholefield, p. 503.
5. Bowsfield, p. 83.
6. Lamb, "The Governorship of Richard Blanshard," p. 11.
7. *ibid.*, p. 24.
8. *Dictionary of Canadian Biography,* 1871–1880.
9. Smith, James Douglas, p. 15.
10. One writer says "four magistrates," another "three" and names E. E. Langford, Kenneth McKenzie, and Thomas Skinner. Apparently they were appointed to the bench on March 29, 1853, on the basis of their social position in the colony; even though they were educated men, Douglas found their ignorance shocking.
11. Bancroft, *History of British Columbia,* p. 338.
12. Hendrickson, p. 17.
13. Smith, *op. cit.,* p. 57.
14. Sage, p. 192.
15. Scholefield, p. 542.
16. *ibid.*, p. 555.

Chapter Six: Hardrock and Soft

1. Bancroft, *op. cit.,* p. 187.
2. *ibid.*, p. 189.
3. Pemberton, p. 144.
4. *ibid.*, p. 146.
5. McKelvie, "The Founding of Nanaimo," p. 175.
6. Mayne, p. 35.
7. Waddington, p. 15.
8. Sage, p. 214.
9. Ireland, pp. 238–40.
10. *ibid.*, pp. 241–242.
11. Macfie, pp. 77–79.
12. Lillard, *West Coast Wild,* (see Sources)
13. *ibid.*

Chapter Seven: Breaking the Land

1. Bancroft, *History of British Columbia,* p. 228.
2. Finlayson, "History of Vancouver Island," p. 38.
3. Slater, p. 191.
4. Finlayson, *op. cit.,* p. 41.
5. Smith, *The Reminiscences of Doctor John Sebastian Helmcken,* p. 120.
6. Slater, p. 216.

7. Macfie, p. 185.
8. Hughes, p. 11.
9. Duncan, p. 4.
10. Mayne, p. 173.
11. Duncan, p. 13.
12. Ireland, p. 237.
13. Duncan, pp. 27–30.

Chapter Eight: Manifest Destiny

1. Fish, A., p. 186.
2. Murray, p. 37.
3. Unidentified; see Norcross, p. 4 and Maud, pp. 158–60.
4. Duff, "Fort Victoria Treaties," p. 40.
5. Higgins, pp. 15–16.
6. *ibid.*, p. 10.
7. Sage, p. 178.
8. *ibid.*, p. 179.
9. *ibid.*, p. 179.
10. Lillard, *Mission to Nootka,* p. 113.
11. Lillard, *Warriors of the North Pacific,* p. 70.
12. Lillard, *op. cit.,* pp. 109–10.
13. Lillard, *op. cit.,* p. 110.
14. Howay, "Introduction of Intoxicating Liquors," p. 167.
15. McKelvie, *Tales of Conflict,* p. 64.
16. *ibid.*, p. 97.
17. Lillard, *West Coast Wild,* (see Sources).
18. Lillard, *Warriors,* p. 76.
19. Lillard, *West Coast Wild,* (see Sources)
20. Sproat, p. 278.
21. *Dictionary of Canadian Biography,* 1861–1870.
22. Ormsby, p. 219.
23. Shelton, p. 79.
24. *ibid.*, p. 78.
25. Ormsby, p. 228.

Chapter Nine: Rogues, Red Lights and Rum

1. Jones, p. 255.
2. Dufferin, p. 252.
3. *ibid.*, p. 253.
4. Roper, p. 234.
5. Smyth, p. 71.

6. Unidentified; this type of writing was *de rigueur* at this time.
7. Kipling, p. 178.
8. Grant, p. 340.
9. Unidentified newspaper clipping, in scrapbook, collection of the author.
10. Unidentified newspaper clipping, in scrapbook, collection of the author.
11. Kilian, p. 50.
12. *ibid.*, p. 50.
13. Caine, p. 131.
14. Bell, p. 20.
15. Jones, p. 255.
16. McKelvie, *Magic, Murder and Mystery*, p. 59.
17. Unidentified newspaper clipping, in scrapbook, collection of the author.
18. Newell, pp. 104–5.
19. MacInnes, pp. 152–3.
20. Evans, "Victoria's Military Heritage," p. 17.
21. *ibid.*, p. 17.

Chapter Ten: Selling the Island

1. MacNab, pp. 172–73.
2. Shortt and Doughty, p. 184.
3. *ibid.*, p. 185.
4. *ibid.*, p. 206.
5. *ibid.*, p. 210.
6. Ruzicka, p. 100.
7. Roberts, p. 167.
8. Victoria & Island Publicity Bureau pamphlet.
9. Unidentified newspaper article, in scrapbook, collection of the author.
10. Unidentified newspaper article, in scrapbook, collection of the author.
11. Unidentified newspaper article, in scrapbook, collection of the author.
12. *Wrigley's British Columbia Directory,* 1919.
13. Farson, p. 64.

Chapter Eleven: Industrial Convolutions

1. Gallacher, p. 12.
2. Department of Agriculture, 1891, p. 731.

3. *ibid.,* p. 801.
4. *ibid.,* p. 801.
5. *ibid.,* p. 796.
6. Unidentified newspaper article, in scrapbook, collection of the author.
7. Gosnell, 1911, pp. 337–54.
8. Ormsby, p. 367.
9. *Dictionary of Canadian Biography,* 1881–1890.
10. *ibid.*
11. Mayne, p. 228.
12. Lamb, "Early Lumbering on Vancouver Island," p. 107.
13. *Report of the Forest Branch,* (1938), p. 5.
14. McKelvie, *Tales of Fort Langley,* p. 52.
15. Wright, p. 427.
16. Howay, *British Columbia and the United States,* p. 312.
17. Gosnell, 1903, p. 217.
18. Howay, *op. cit.,* p. 314.

SOURCES

More than 400 articles, books, brochures, manuscripts and pamphlets were consulted before and during the writing of this book. Below are listed the sources that are directly related to the preceding text.

Published Sources

Anderson, A. C. A *Brief Description of the Province of British Columbia* (1872)
Anderson, G. W. *A New, Authentic and Comprehensive Collection of Voyages Round the World* (1784)
Anonymous. *Esquimalt 1912–1962* (n.d.)
Arima, E. Y. *The West Coast (Nootka) People* (1983)
Baird, Ian. A *Historical Guide to the E & N Railway* (1985)
Bancroft, Hubert Howe. *History of British Columbia* (1887)
    History of the Northwest Coast, 2 vols. (1884)
Beaglehole, J. C. *The Voyage of the Resolution and Discovery* (1967)
Bell, Archie. *Sunset Canada* (1918)
Bolton, Herbert Eugene. *Fray Juan Crespi* (1927)

Bowsfield, Hartwell. *Fort Victoria Letters 1846–1851* (1979)

British Columbia, Province of. *First Report of the Department of Agriculture* (1891)

  Report of the Department of Agriculture (1900–42)

  Report of the Forest Branch (1919–39)

  Annual Report of the Minister of Mines (1896–1940)

Brown, Robert. *The Adventures of John Jewitt* (1896)

Caine, W. S. *Trip Round the World* (1888)

Canada, Dominion of. *Annual Report of the Department of Fisheries* (1890)

  Annual Report of the Fisheries Branch (1909–39)

Cook, Warren L. *Floodtide of Empire* (1973)

Cutter, Donald C. *California Coast* (1969)

Dennis, J. S. *Vancouver Island* (1905)

Densmore, Francis. *Nootka and Quileute Music* (1939)

District 69, Historical Society. *Parksville Then and Now* (n.d.)

Drucker, Philip. *The Northern and Central Nootkan Tribes* (1951)

Duff, Wilson. "The Fort Victoria Treaties," *BC Studies*, No. 3 (1969)

Dufferin & Ava, Marchioness of. *My Canadian Journal* (1891)

Duncan, Eric. *Fifty-Seven Years in the Comox Valley* (1934)

Farson, Negley. *Going Fishing* (1943)

Fish, Andrew. "The Last Phase of the Oregon Boundary Question," *Quarterly of the Oregon Historical Society*, Vol. XXII, No. 3.

Fish, Gordon. *Dreams of Freedom*, Sound Heritage Series No. 36 (1982)

Gallacher, Daniel T. "Exhibit as Overviews: The Case of British Columbia Modern History," National Museum of Man, Mercury Series (1979)

Gosnell, R. E. *The Year Book of British Columbia* (1903)

  The Year Book of British Columbia (1911)

Gough, Barry M. *Gunboat Frontier* (1984)

Government Printer. *Lists of Voters in the Second Electoral District* (1874)

Grant, George E. *Ocean to Ocean* (1873)

Gregson, Harry. *A History of Victoria* (1970)

Hendrickson, James E. *Journals of the Colonial Legislature of Vancouver Island and British Columbia*, 5 vols. (1980)

Higgins, D. W. *The Passing of a Race* (1905)

Howay, F. W., Sage, W. N., and Angus, H. F. *British Columbia and the United States* (1942)

Howay, F. W. "The Introduction of Intoxicating Liquors Among the

Indians of the Northwest Coast," *British Columbia Historical Quarterly*, Vol. 1, No. 3.

Voyages of the "Columbia" to the Northwest Coast (1941)

Hughes, Ben. *History of the Comox Valley* (n.d.)

Ireland, Willard E. "Captain Walter Coloquhoun Grant: Vancouver Island's First Independent Settler," *British Columbia Historical Quarterly*, Vol. XVII, Nos. 1 and 2.

"Gold Rush Days in Victoria," *British Columbia Historical Quarterly*, Vol. XII, No. 3.

Jones, E. G. "Our British Neighbours," *The West Shore* (August 1885)

Kane, Paul. *Wanderings of an Artist* (n.d.)

Kilian, Crawford. *Go Do Some Great Thing* (1978)

Kipling, Rudyard. *A Diversity of Creatures/Letters of Travel, 1892–1913* (1927)

Lamb, W. Kaye. *A Voyage of Discovery to the North Pacific Ocean and Round the World*, 4 vols. (1984)

"Early Lumbering on Vancouver Island", *British Columbia Historical Quarterly*, Vol. II, 1938.

"The Founding of Fort Victoria," *British Columbia Historical Quarterly*, Vol. VII, No. 2.

"The Governorship of Richard Blanshard," *British Columbia Historical Quarterly*, Vol. XIV, Nos 1 and 2.

The Letters and Journals of Simon Fraser, 1806–1808 (1960)

Landerholm, Carl. *Notices & Voyages of the Famed Quebec Mission to the Pacific Northwest* (MCMLVI)

Large, R. G. *The Journals of William Fraser Tolmie Physician and Fur Trader* (1963)

Lillard, Charles. *Mission to Nootka* (1977)

Warriors of the North Pacific (1984)

West Coast Wild (to be published 1987)

Macfie, Matthew. *Vancouver Island and British Columbia* (1865)

MacInnes, Tom. *Chinook Days* (1926)

MacNab, Frances. *British Columbia for Settlers* (1898)

McKelvie, B. A. "The Founding of Nanaimo," *British Columbia Historical Quarterly*, Vol. VIII, No. 3.

Magic, Murder and Mystery (1966)

Fort Langley (1947)

Tales of Conflict (1949)

Maud, Ralph. *The Salish People*, 4 vols. (1978)

Mayne, Commander R. C. *Four Years in British Columbia and Van-*

couver Island (1863)

Meany, Edmond S. *Vancouver's Discovery of Puget Sound* (1957)

Mozino, Jose Mariano. *Noticias de Nutka* (1970)

Murray, Keith. *The Pig War* (1968)

Museum of the American Indian. *A Rare Salish Blanket* (1926)

Newell, Gordon. *Sea Rogues' Gallery* (1971)

Newbitt, James W. "The Diary of Martha Cheney Ella," *British Columbia Historical Quarterly,* Vol. VIII, No. 2.

Norcross, E. B. *The Warm Land* (1959)

Olsen, W. H. *Water Over the Wheel* (1963)

Ormsby, Margaret A. *British Columbia: A History* (1964)

Pemberton, J. Despard. *Facts and Figures Relating to Vancouver Island and British Columbia* (1860)

Pethick, Derek. *Victoria: The Fort* (1968)

Pettit, Sydney G. "The Trials and Tribulations of Edward Edwards Langford," *British Columbia Historical Quarterly,* Vol. XVII, Nos. 1 and 2.

Rattray, Alexander. *Vancouver Island and British Columbia* (1862)

Rich, E. E. *The Letters of John McLoughlin* (1943)

Roberts, Morley. *The Prey of the Strongest* (1906)

Roper, Edward. *By Track and Trail* (1891)

Sage, Walter N. *Sir James Douglas and British Columbia* (1930)

Scholefield, E. O. S. *A History of British Columbia,* Vol. 1 (1914)

Shelton, W. George. *British Columbia and Confederation* (1967)

Shortt, Adam and Doughty, Arthur G. *Canada and Its Provinces,* Vol. XXI (1914)

Slater, G. Hollis. "Rev. Robert John Staines: Pioneer Priest, Pedagogue, and Political Agitator," *British Columbia Historical Quarterly,* Vol. XIV, No. 4.

Smith, Dorothy Blakey. *The Reminiscences of Doctor John Sebastian Helmcken* (1975)

James Douglas (1971)

Smyth, Eleanor Caroline. *An Octogenarian's Reminiscences* (n.d.)

Sproat, Gilbert Malcolm. *Scenes and Studies of Savage Life* (1868)

Thurman, Michael E. *The Naval Department of San Blas* (1967)

Victoria & Island Publicity Bureau. *Victoria Sightseeing Drive* (1935)

Virgin, Victor E. *History of North and South Saanich* (1978)

Wagner, H. R. *Apocryphal Voyages to the Northwest Coast of America* (1932)

Spanish Explorations in the Strait of Juan de Fuca (1971)

Waites, K. A. "Responsible Government and Confederation," *British*

Columbia Historical Quarterly, Vol. VI, No. 2.

Walbran, Captain John T. *British Columbia Coast Names* (1971)

Whitford, H. N. and Craig, Roland D. *Forests of British Columbia* (1918)

Wright, E. W. *Lewis & Dryden's Marine History of the Pacific Northwest* (1967)

Unpublished and Miscellaneous Sources

Cairns, H. L. "Notes on the Road History of British Columbia," unpublished Ms.

Evans, Gregory. "Victoria's Military Heritage," unpublished Ms.

Evans, John Newell. "The Diary of John Newell Evans, Cowichan Pioneer," unpublished Ms, held by the Special Collections, McPherson Library, University of Victoria.

Finlayson, Roderick. "Biography of Roderick Finlayson," unpublished Ms., held by the Provincial Archives of British Columbia.

"History of Vancouver Island and the Northwest Coast," unpublished Ms., held by the Provincial Archives of British Columbia.

Lillard, Charles. Scrapbooks, a collection of seven, containing clippings and letters, *circa* 1890–1918.

Rogerson, Mary Doreen. Scrapbooks, a collection of 221, containing clippings, brochures, and pamphlets, *circa* 1848–1980, held by Charles Lillard.

Ruzicka, S. E. "The Decline of Victoria as a Metropolitan Centre of British Columbia, 1885–1901". MA thesis, University of Victoria.

Walbran, Captain (John T.) "Cruise of the Imperial Eagle," held by the Provincial Archives of British Columbia.

INDEX

Alberni Mills, 112; prostitution at, 153; 182; history of, 217–18.
Alberni Valley, 201; 202; 210.
Anderson, R., 125.
Astoria, 51–53; 57.
Banfield, William, 217.
Baranof, Alexander, 43; compared to James Douglas, 89.
Barkley, Charles William, 34–36.
Barkley, Frances, see Barkley, Charles William.
Bell, James, on Victoria, 109; on farming, 134.
Bering, Vitus, 24–25.
Blanshard, Richard, background, 85; named governor of VI, 85; reaches VI, 85–86; first dispatch, 86; second dispatch, 86–87; complaints, 86–87; Fort Rupert murders, 87–88; tenders resignation, 88; appoints Legislative Council, 88; on the PSAC, 119; 121; bachelor, 122.
Blenkinsop, George, 87; 99.
Blinkhorn, Thomas, 121; 125.
Bolduc, J. B. Z., 62.
Brabant, Augustin, 19; 148.
British Columbia, creation of, 108; Queen Victoria names, 108; Douglas made governor of, 108–09; land proclamations, 127; VI joins, 156; joins Confederation, 158–59; politics, 185; railroads and Confederation, 185–88; Depression premiers, 204; and mining, 211–12; 220–23.
Broughton, William, 47.
Brown, Robert, 101; and the VIEE, 112–14; on Indian situation, 152–54.
Bull, John, 126.
Busch, Henrich, 24.
Buttle, John, 113.
Cadboro Bay, 62.
Cameron, David, first chief justice, 92–93; opposition to, 124.
Campbell River, 151; 210.
Cape Scott settlements, 190–92; 202.
Captain Jack, 143–44.
Castley, H. T., 207–08.
Catherine the Great, 24.
Chee-ah-thluk, 141–42.
Chemainus, 127; 210; 219; 221.
Chief Jefferson, 151–52.

Chinese, 162; 163; 164–67; in the coal mines, 189–90; 212.
Chirikov, Alexei, 24–25.
Coal, first mined, 73; "discovered" by W. F. Tolmie, 97–98; need for, 102; coal production, 209, 212, 215.
"Coal Tyee," 102.
Coles, John, 126.
Colnett, James, 40; 44.
Columbia River, 2; 6; 51–53.
Colwood or Esquimalt Farm, 125.
Comox Valley, 127; 130; colonization of, 131–36; roads, 132–33; population of, 202, 210.
Constance Cove, 125.
Cook, James, 6; on houses, 14; on religion, 18; on coast, 30–32; 207.
Cooper, James 88–89; 92; background, 121; on VI, 121–22; 125; 132.
Courtenay, George William, 73.
Cowichan Valley, colonization of, 127–130; census, 129; roads, 132–33; tourism, 201; see Farson, Negley, 210.
Craigflower, 125; 126.
Crosby, Harry, 197.
Crosby, Thomas, on deforming heads, 70–71; 148–49; on slavery, 153.
Cumberland, 210; strike at, 213.
Curtis Point, see The Gorge.
Cuthbert, Herbert, 195.
Cutler, Lyman, 138.
Deans, James, 125.
De Cosmos, Amor, 155–56.
Deeks, George, 126.
Demers, Modeste, Bishop of VI, 78.
Deshnev, Semyon Ivanovich, 24.
Dixon, George, 36.
Donaldson, Andrew, 231.
Douglas, James, at Fort Vancouver, 56; to VI, 58–60; establishes Fort Victoria's location, 61–62; replaces McLoughlin, 72; report of 1848, 76–78; in 1849, 84; considered for governor of VI, 84–85; appointed to Legislative Council, 88; as governor, 95; and Nanaimo, 102–05; description of in 1858, 106–07; proclamation of in 1857, 108; governor of BC, 108–09; and retirement, 116; farming on VI, 118–19; Douglas

Pemberton, J. Despard, writer and colonizer, 83–84; introduces "castration" bill, 95; names Nanaimo, 103; on Nanaimo, 105; crosses VI, 112.

Pena, Tomás de la, 22.

Pérez, Juan, discovers Nootka Sound, 21; age and background, 22–23; sails north, 23; on the coast, 25–26; names VI discoveries, 25; trading, 25–26; sails south, 26; 29.

Pérouse, Comte de La, 45–46.

Peter the Great, 24; 27.

Pickett, George E., 139.

"Pig War," 137–39.

Port Alice, 223.

Port Hardy, 2; 210.

Portlock, Nathanial, 36.

Prohibition, 194–95.

Prospectors and gold, first at Fort Victoria, 76; California gold rush, 80; rush to the Fraser River, 95–96; and Victoria, 107–12; Leech River, 114–16; at Zeballos, 231–233.

Puget, Peter, 35–36; 45.

Puget Sound Agricultural Society, 87; moves to VI, 118–19; four farms, 119; history of farms, 125–26; San Juan Island, 136; 207.

Pulp mills, 223.

Quadra, Bodega y, 29; meets with Revilla Gigedo, 43; and Vancouver, 48–49.

Quail, "Poker" Jack, 176.

Qualicum Beach, 2.

Quantrill, William Clarke, 168–170.

Quimper, Manuel, 44.

Reid, James M., 125.

Restricted Area, 170–72.

Roberts, Morley, 190.

Robson, Charles R., 151–52.

Ross, Charles, 65; activities, 67; dies, 67; family, 67–68; 122.

Russian American Company, *see* also Baranof, Alexander; 76; 78; 98.

Saanich Peninsula, 64; farming, 126; 127; 182–83.

Salmon, canneries, 225–28; production, 226–28; trolling, 230–31.

Saltspring Island, 129; Haida attack Beggsville, 151.

San Blas, 22.

Sangster, James, 125.

San Juan Island, 74; ranching and fishing, 78; Garrison Bay, 137; British-American occupation, *see* "Pig War".

Sayward, William, 219.

Scott, R., 125.

Sealing, 224–25.

Seeman, Berthold, 74.

Seymour, Frederick, replaces Douglas as governor of BC, 156; difficulties of position, 156–59.

Sharp, William, *see* Quantrill, W. C.

Shepard, Henry S., 219.

Ships
Active, 48.
Alice, 121.
America, 71–72.
Ancon, 134.
Antofogasta, 179.
Argonaut, 40, 44.
Atrevida, 45.
Beaver, 55, 59, 61, 65, 98, 134, 144, 146–47.
Boston, 150.
Cadboro, 57, 59, 62, 103–04.
Captain Cook, 34, 35.
Chatham, 47.
City of Victoria, 197.
Columbia, 38, 121, 150.
Concepción, 44.
HMS Constance, 73.
Constantine, 98.
Cormorant, 73, 85.
HMS Daedalus, 87, 144.
HMS Daphnae, 144.
Descubierta, 45.
Discovery, 30, 32.
HMS Discovery, 35.
Driver, 85.
Duchess of San Lorenzo, 124.
Emma, 134.
England, 87, 144.
Enterprise, 114.
Experiment, 34.
Felice Adventurer, 36.
Fisgard, 78.
Golden Hinde, 28.
Gustavus II, 43.
HMS Grappler, 131.
Harmon, 32.
Harpooner, 99, 119.
Harvester King, 197.
HMS Herald, 74, 78.
Imperial Eagle, 34–35.
Iphigenia Nubiana, 36.
Iquique, 179.
King George, 36.

936 7029